The Words Between the Spaces

Using language – speaking and understanding it – is a defining ability of human beings, woven into all human activity. It is therefore inevitable that it should be deeply implicated in the design, production and use of buildings. Building legislation, design guides, competition and other briefs, architectural criticism, teaching and scholarly material, and the media all produce their characteristic texts. When these prescribe what is to be built then, in a sense, they can be said to 'design' the eventual building. When they describe what is already built they are formative of our judgement and responses.

The authors of this book, one a linguist, the other an architect and historian, examine how such texts relate to issues of national identity, power structures, the creation of heritage, and the evaluation of projects by professional and lay critics. The role of images in these texts is crucial and is discussed in detail. The authors use texts about such projects as Berlin's new Reichstag, Scotland's new Parliament, and the Auschwitz concentration camp museum to clarify the interaction between texts, design, critical debate and response.

Texts such as Prince Charles's *A Vision of Britain* and the 1919 Tudor Walters Report on 'Housing for the Working Classes' had a wide influence on thinking, debate and, ultimately, on what was built and what was left unbuilt. Through a close reading of these and other texts, the authors examine how the underlying ideological forces worked through language. Finally, they discuss how questions about language and texts might influence both the teaching and the practice of architecture.

Thomas A. Markus is Emeritus Professor of the University of Strathclyde and Jubilee Professor of Chalmers University of Technology, Göteborg and **Deborah Cameron** is Professor of Languages at the Institute of Education, London University.

THE ARCHI*TEXT* SERIES

Edited by Thomas A. Markus and Anthony D. King

Architectural discourse has traditionally represented buildings as art objects or technical objects. Yet buildings are also social objects in that they are invested with social meaning and shape social relations. Recognizing these assumptions, the Archi*text* series aims to bring together recent debates in social and cultural theory and the study and practice of architecture and urban design. Critical, comparative and interdisciplinary, the books in the series will, by theorizing architecture, bring the space of the built environment centrally into the social sciences and humanities, as well as bringing the theoretical insights of the latter into the discourses of architecture and urban design. Particular attention will be paid to issues of gender, race, sexuality and the body, to questions of identity and place, to the cultural politics of representation and language, and to the global and postcolonial contexts in which these are addressed.

Already published:

Framing Places
Mediating power in built form
Kim Dovey

Gender Space Architecture
An interdisciplinary introduction
Edited by Jane Rendell, Barbara Penner and Iain Borden

Behind the Postcolonial
Architecture, urban space and political cultures in Indonesia
Abidin Kusno

The Architecture of Oppression
The SS, forced labor and the Nazi monumental building economy
Paul Jaskot

Embodied Utopias
Gender, social change and the modern metropolis
Edited by Amy Bingaman, Lise Sanders and Rebecca Zorach

Forthcoming titles:

Colonial Constructions
Architecture, cities and Italian colonialism
Mia Fuller

Spaces of Global Cultures
Anthony D. King

Writing Spaces
Greig Crysler

**Thomas A. Markus and
Deborah Cameron**

The Words Between the
Spaces

Buildings and Language

London and New York

First published 2002
by Routledge
11 New Fetter Lane, London EC4P 4EE

Simultaneously published in the USA and Canada
by Routledge
29 West 35th Street, New York, NY 10001

Routledge is an imprint of the Taylor & Francis Group

Typeset in Frutiger by Florence Production Ltd, Stoodleigh, Devon
Printed and bound in Great Britain by St Edmundsbury Press,
Bury St. Edmunds, Suffolk.

British Library Cataloguing in Publication Data
A catalogue record for this book is available from the British Library

Library of Congress Cataloging in Publication Data
A catalog record for this book has been requested

ISBN 0–415–14345–4 (hbk)
ISBN 0–415–14346–2 (pbk)

Contents

Foreword

The book you are about to read brings together two fields of study that are rarely combined in a systematic way and may be rather unlike other books you have read. The two fields in question are architecture, the study of buildings and the built environment, and discourse analysis, a branch of linguistics which studies language as it is actually used in real-world contexts. In this book, we explore how language is used, and what it does, in the particular context of writing and talking about buildings. Our title, *The Words Between the Spaces*, is meant to draw attention to the significance of language for our understanding of the built environment.

Writing a book on this subject requires expert knowledge about both buildings and language. Few individuals are equally knowledgeable about both, and we are no exception to that generalization. One of us (Thomas Markus) is an architect, the other (Deborah Cameron) a linguist. In writing this book, we have each brought our own specialized knowledge to bear on our chosen topic. Our discussions over a long period have produced a set of ideas and arguments which 'belong' to both of us equally, and for that reason we use the pronoun 'we' throughout the book. At the same time, however, our respective contributions to the book do reflect our differing areas of expertise. It takes many years to learn the special way of looking at buildings, or language, which distinguishes the trained architect, or linguist, from the layperson. Inevitably, then, the two of us – respectively an architect and a linguist – approach questions of architecture and language from different directions, and use different analytic tools to examine those questions. The linguist does not have the architect's command of architectural theory and history, nor can she interpret a plan, say, with the same ease and insight he can. The architect, conversely, is less practised than the linguist in noticing the intricate patterns made by grammar in a text or discerning its generic structure. The two have different stores of background knowledge, and different technical terminologies. Our skills, in short, are complementary rather than identical, and that is also reflected in the way the book is written. We have not tried to produce a seamless text that reads like the product of a single mind; readers will probably be able to guess which of us was primarily responsible for which parts of the text.[1]

Another thing that will be evident to the reader of this book is its authors' cultural location. The texts and buildings we use as examples in the chapters that follow are, overall, a fairly diverse collection: our discussion deals with built structures in, for instance, China, England, France, Germany, Indonesia, Japan, Poland, Scotland, Sweden and the USA. However, a rather significant proportion of our case studies come from England and Scotland, the countries where we ourselves are located. Sometimes, too, the texts we analyse were actually produced in the UK, even though they are about buildings located elsewhere. Since we are writing for an international audience, constructing arguments which, we hope and believe, are applicable to discourse about architecture in many societies rather than just the UK, the seeming insularity of our choices requires some explanation.

To begin with, we should point out one obvious constraint on our choice of texts: language itself. Discourse analysis is not only concerned with the *content* of texts, *what* they say, but also and importantly with *how* they say it: the details of their organization, grammar and vocabulary. Since these details are often lost in translation, this kind of analysis can only be carried out on texts in a language the analyst understands well. Between them, the authors of this book are able to read several languages, but since we cannot assume all our readers share any single language other than English, we have generally avoided presenting any detailed analyses of texts that are not in English. (In Chapter 7, which is concerned with the relationship of language and images, we do discuss one French text. We also refer in Chapter 2 to various historical texts originally written in languages other than English, such as Latin and French, but we do not analyse the language of these texts closely.)

English is, of course, an international language: not all our English-language texts come from countries where English is the first language of the majority of the population, nor were they all produced specifically for an audience of native speakers of English. For example, one of the buildings we discuss in Chapter 3 is the headquarters of the Scandinavian airline company SAS, which is located outside Stockholm in Sweden. The literature we analyse relating to this building was also produced in Sweden – but in English, which is widely spoken and routinely used for a range of purposes in Scandinavia. In Chapter 6 we examine texts relating to the Auschwitz museum which now exists on the site of the former Nazi concentration camp in Poland. Again, these texts were produced in English, addressed to an international audience of visitors to the museum and/or its website. So, confining ourselves to texts in the English language does not have to mean, and in this book does not mean, confining ourselves to the textual products of a single nation or culture. On the other hand, it does prevent us from choosing examples from those parts of the world where languages other than English are dominant – China and Latin America, for example, where the relevant texts would be likely to be written in (respectively) Chinese and Spanish or Portuguese.[2]

A bias towards English-language texts is one thing, but what about our decision to make such extensive use of *British* examples, rather than, say, examples from Australia, Canada, India, Singapore and the USA? This is, in part, a question of cultural knowledge – the analysis of discourse calls for an extensive knowledge of the context in which it is produced and read – and also it is a question of *access* to textual data. Among the textual genres we have found it particularly illuminating to analyse are kinds of writing that do not usually circulate in the public domain (for instance, briefing documents relating to privately commissioned buildings, such as the call centre which we discuss in Chapter 4). To obtain relevant texts, we sometimes had to use professional contacts with particular institutions or architectural practices, and these on the whole were 'local' (i.e. British) contacts – though in some cases they reflected the involvement of the author who is an architect in European networks. In addition, it is often helpful to analyse a selection of different texts relating to a single building (e.g. the competition brief, the jury's report, press coverage of the competition and its outcome, popular and scholarly assessments of the merits of the finished building, etc.). Again, it is far easier to collect this material systematically when the analyst is 'on the spot'.

In fact, our choice of material for this book was quite strongly influenced by circumstances specific to the time and place of its composition. When we began work on it, we both lived and worked in the city of Glasgow in the west of Scotland: at that time and for several years afterwards, it happened that public discussion in both Scotland and Britain more generally was intensely preoccupied with architectural issues. Our home city of Glasgow was preparing for a year-long festival of architecture and design, Glasgow 1999; Scotland's new Parliament building was the subject of a major architectural competition; in the capital of the United Kingdom, London, plans were underway to mark the year 2000 with a series of new and striking built structures along the River Thames. For us, these initiatives were particularly useful, because they generated a steady stream of discourse – both expert and popular, in a range of styles and genres – about buildings and the built environment. For certain buildings, such as the Scottish Parliament and London's Millennium Dome, it was possible to compile over time a massive archive of writing about them, spanning every phase of planning and design (sometimes construction too), and representing every conceivable point of view on their merits. We were well placed to accumulate this material, and we make use of it in several chapters of this book.

There is a bias towards *written* language in the materials we have chosen to analyse, and the reader may wonder why. Was relevant spoken data not, in principle, equally available to us, and equally of interest? Certainly we can think of spoken discourse genres that would have made interesting examples for analysis, such as the deliberations of competition juries or the discussions that take place between architects and clients. But this kind of discourse is most often produced behind closed doors, in private rather than in public, and is therefore difficult for researchers to access. It is true, as we have already noted, that some of the written texts we analyse were not produced for public circulation either; but persuading people to let you see a copy of a 'private' document – so long as it is not highly confidential – is usually easier than persuading them to let you record their private spoken interactions. Apart from being difficult to negotiate, the recording and subsequent transcription of non-public speech is also very time consuming, and in the event we decided not to attempt it: our few spoken examples come from 'public' sources, mainly the broadcast media. That should not be taken to imply, however, that we consider talk about buildings unimportant. Rather, investigating it in detail has proved to be beyond the scope of this particular project.

In addition to material from our own time and place, we have made some use of historical examples, such as the brief for an early nineteenth century lunatic asylum and an official report on housing produced in the early twentieth century. The value of these examples obviously does not lie in their practical significance for architects working today. We have chosen them, rather, because they provide very clear examples of our general thesis concerning the relationship between language, social and spatial structures (in the examples just given, for instance, those associated with gender and social class). We also explore this relationship in our analyses of contemporary cases such as the European workspaces and the Japanese housing development we discuss in Chapters 3 and 4, and some of the heritage monuments we examine in Chapter 6 (where issues of race/ethnicity and nationality are relevant as well). But it can sometimes be easier to 'see' the kinds of structures we are concerned with when the social and spatial categories they are built around (e.g. different kinds of 'lunatics', domestic spaces like 'parlour' and 'scullery') are *not* part of your own, taken-for-granted reality. Historical examples are useful, in other words, because our distance from the past they belong to makes them seem more abstract, and so helps us to grasp general principles which we can then apply to contemporary cases. Often in this book we follow this logic by starting with a historical example and moving on to analyse present-day examples in more detail.

We recognize, of course, that even our present-day examples will not be equally familiar or 'relevant' to everyone. Something like the Scottish Parliament building is unlikely to be a major topic of discussion among readers located in Seattle or in Seoul. But the aim of this book is *not* to inform readers about the details of particular buildings, nor indeed do we claim that all the buildings we discuss are especially interesting or significant, socially or architecturally. Our examples are exactly that – examples. We use them to exemplify the point that buildings, and our experiences or perceptions of buildings, are shaped in important ways by the language that is used *about* buildings. It is an argument which we believe to be generally applicable, across languages, cultures and contexts. We have illustrated it with examples reflecting our own knowledge and interests, which are inevitably 'partial' in both senses of the word. However, we hope that our readers, wherever they are located, will be inspired to apply the same approach to examples reflecting their own experiences and concerns – to the textual conventions of their own languages and the architectural traditions of their own cultures. If *The Words Between the Spaces* enables readers to go beyond our specific examples and make meaningful connections between language and architecture in a range of social and cultural contexts, then we will have achieved our main purpose in writing this book.

Acknowledgements

Permissions to use and copyright acknowledgements for all figures are made in the appropriate places. In addition we have received valuable help from a number of individuals and organizations.

Tony King, co-editor with one of the present authors of this Archi*text* series, gave valuable help, from the time when the earliest proposal was made to the very end when his deep and careful reading of the final manuscript not only alerted us to errors and possible causes of misreadings, but also to more basic issues about our own position.

Before we started writing we were given the opportunity by two people to collaborate on two projects – both of which convinced us that we actually *could* work together. The first was a joint presentation we made in the Glasgow Film Theatre to staff and students of the Glasgow School of Art on the Burrell Gallery. This was the result of an invitation from Roger Palmer of the School of Art. The second was a joint article commissioned by Pat Kane of *The* (Glasgow) *Herald*, on the competition for the Scottish Parliament building. To both of these we remain grateful.

We wish to thank those who helped us with documentation and information on the brief and briefing process for several of our case studies: Richard Hywel Evans on the Cellular Operations call centre in Swindon; Dr David Reilly, Director of the new Glasgow Homoeopathic Hospital, and MacClachlan Monaghan, its architects; and Ian Standing of Associated Architects on the new School of Jewellery, Birmingham.

Jaroslaw Mensfelt, of the Auschwitz-Birkenau State Museum, Oświęcim, Poland, helped us with considerable background material on the museum.

John Paterson of the Parliament Building Project Team of the (then) Scottish Office, Edinburgh, helped us with briefing and competition documents.

Of course the views about these buildings, designs or briefs are entirely our own, and cannot be attributed to any of the people we have named. But their ready help is gratefully acknowledged.

Chapter 1: Why Language Matters

Language is a neglected subject in discussions of architecture, which is conventionally regarded as a visual rather than verbal activity. 'Architects', observes theorist and practitioner Ellen Dunham-Jones, 'tend to refer to themselves as visual people' (1997: 16). This professional self-image is faithfully reflected in popular representations of architects, which typically show them poring over plans, making drawings and models, or manipulating images on computer screens. But in reality, architects' work is both visual *and* verbal: language plays some part in almost everything they do.

This point is underlined by Dana Cuff's detailed study of architectural practice (Cuff 1992), for which she observed and interviewed numerous professionals and students. In training, she notes, students are encouraged to spend long hours in the studio, where they do not only draw, but also talk with instructors and each other; at regular intervals they face 'crits' delivered by architect-teachers in the medium of spoken language. In practice, the talking continues. Cuff cites findings showing that the average architect has only about half an hour a day when his or her work is uninterrupted by some kind of interaction (the architects she spoke to herself thought this an overestimate). Even the most 'creative', schematic design phase of a project rarely matches the idealized picture in which a solitary designer spends long silent hours at the drawing board. Making a building is a collaborative process which involves continual dialogue – with clients, with colleagues, with other professionals like engineers and landscapers, with building contractors. Cuff aptly describes what goes on in these interactions as 'constructing a word-and-sketch building' (1992: 97). She also makes clear how much *written* language is produced in any architectural project. Meetings are recorded in memos and minutes; letters may have to be written to various authorities and community representatives; agreements and contracts must be drawn up. Other texts to which architects may refer include building and planning regulations, briefs or building programmes, design guides and handbooks. Many of these texts are linguistically dense and complex, with a high proportion of verbal to visual material.

The observation that language pervades architectural practice is in one sense very obvious and banal. Everyone knows that architects must talk to clients, hold meetings with contractors, write memos, read planning regulations, and so on. But although architects may spend a lot of time actually engaged in these activities, few would spend much time reflecting on them. Whereas architects are expected to reflect on issues of design in a way that might be called 'abstract', 'theoretical' or 'analytic', they are not expected or encouraged to reflect in the same way on issues of language and its relationship to design. Language may be all around them, but it remains very much a background phenomenon, a part of what the ethnomethodologist Harold Garfinkel called the 'seen but unnoticed' of everyday life.

In this book, our aim is to place language in the foreground: to 'notice' as well as 'see' what role it plays in the making of buildings. We argue that the language used to speak and write about the built environment plays a significant role in shaping that environment, and our responses to it. We try to show that reflecting systematically on language can yield insight into the buildings we have now, and the ones we may create in future.

The significance we claim for language in relation to the built environment is a function of its significance in human affairs more generally. Natural languages[1] are the richest symbolic systems to which human beings have access, and the main purposes for which we use language are fundamental to the kind of creatures we are. One of those purposes is, of course, communication with other people. Humans are not telepathic, and it is mainly by way of language that we are able to get more than a rudimentary sense of what is going on in another person's mind. But we also use language as an aid to our own thinking, whether or not we communicate our thoughts to others.[2]

Both these functions of language are relevant to the activities of designing and making buildings. True, language is not the only symbolic system involved: architects need to make mathematical calculations, and to represent form and space in drawings and models of various kinds. But they also need to use language to conceptualize what they are doing and convey it to others (given that making a building is typically a collaborative process). We say, 'a picture is worth a thousand words', but people rarely communicate, or think, in pictures alone; if called upon to elaborate the meaning of a picture or a mathematical formula – or, as we shall see, a building – they will use language.

Architects, like many other professionals, make use of linguistic resources developed over time for the purpose of reflecting, in speech and writing, on the phenomena which are their distinctive concerns. Architecture has its own linguistic *register* (the term used by linguists to denote a set of conventions for language-use tailored to some particular situation or institution – other examples include 'legalese' and 'journalese'). One obvious feature of the register of architecture is the extensive technical vocabulary architects must learn in the course of their training. Learning what words to use is every bit as necessary as learning how to draw plans, calculate loads or use computer software for modelling; for the technical vocabulary of architecture is not merely a convenient shorthand, it is a system for thinking with. It provides the classificatory schemes which enable architects to 'see' as they do – and, importantly, as other architects do. Professional registers are often criticized as mystifying jargon whose main purpose is to exclude outsiders; but while that may indeed be one of their functions, they also allow a professional community's accumulated knowledge to be codified and transmitted in precise detail. In architecture as in medicine or law, 'learning the language' is inseparable from mastering the craft as a whole.

But when we claim that language plays a significant part in the theory and practice of architecture, we are not thinking only about technical terminology. Architects do not interact only with other architects, nor are the buildings they create expressions of some unique inner vision which need not be discussed with anyone else. As most introductory texts point out early on, architecture is a 'social art'. Any practice which is social must have a verbal component too, given that language provides humans with their primary means of social interaction.

Language-using is itself a form of social practice: as such it is implicated in the reproduction of the beliefs, relationships, attitudes and values that exist in a given society – and also, of course, in attempts to challenge the status quo. In other words, language is not simply a neutral vehicle for conveying factual information. All natural languages provide their users with multiple ways to represent the same object, state, event or process; the expression of differing perspectives on reality, just as much as the communication of facts about the world, appears to be among the purposes that language evolved to serve. The linguistic choices speakers and writers make can cue hearers and readers to make certain inferences about the meaning of an utterance or text, and these go beyond its purely informational content. Often, as we will see later on, they are ideologically significant, implicitly presupposing certain values and social relations. While they remain implicit and unnoticed, these presuppositions are difficult to resist or challenge. Noticed and made explicit, however, they can become objects of critical scrutiny.

Encouraging readers to take a critical position, both on language and on buildings, is an important goal of this book. Following Markus (1993), we regard buildings as primarily social objects (i.e. not just aesthetic or technical ones) which can and should be subjected to social critique. There are a number of issues this kind of critique may focus on. For instance, it may focus on the way a building's design reproduces particular kinds of social and power relations among its various categories of users (e.g. managers and workers in a factory building or staff and visitors in a museum). It may focus on the kinds of activities and social encounters a building design facilitates, and what other activities and encounters it makes difficult or impossible. It may also focus on the capacity of a design to endorse

– overtly or covertly – certain social values (e.g. 'privacy' or 'community') at the expense of alternatives.

Various tools have been developed for thinking critically about the social workings of buildings, many involving direct analysis of their form and the way they organize space. We want to suggest that the analysis of language is also a useful tool for understanding buildings as social objects. Texts[3] about buildings often turn out to be a source for the social, political and ideological values which other critical techniques reveal by analysing buildings directly. In this book, we will treat the analysis of buildings and the analysis of texts about them as complementary approaches to the same project. By focusing on the texts, we hope to alert readers to their non-obvious or 'hidden' meanings. Where appropriate, we will also show how these meanings emerge in actual buildings.

Because we want readers to be able to replicate the kinds of analyses we offer, we are not going to use a highly formal and technical linguistic apparatus. But some linguistic apparatus will be necessary, because the linguistic patterns which produce certain effects are not necessarily evident from a surface reading. Identifying them requires a deeper analysis, one which is attentive to linguistic form as well as content, and to regularities which manifest themselves across whole texts and sets of texts. At this point, therefore, we must spend a little time clarifying, for the benefit of readers with no specialist knowledge about language and linguistics, what we do and do not mean by those terms.

'LANGUAGE' AND 'LINGUISTICS': BEYOND STRUCTURALISM AND SEMIOTICS

At the beginning of this chapter we said that language is a neglected topic in discussions of architecture. Some readers may have found this claim puzzling, for it is certainly not true that the subject of language goes unmentioned in architectural writing. On the contrary, it has long been commonplace for writers and theorists to make comparisons and analogies between architecture and language. In his book *Words and Buildings,* the architectural historian Adrian Forty devotes a whole chapter to language metaphors in architectural discourse, which he sub-categorizes under six main headings (Forty 2000, Ch. 4).[4] He mentions, for example, the idea that works of architecture are 'texts' that can be 'read', tracing it back as far as Quatremère de Quincy's 1803 essay *De l'Architecture Egyptienne.* This analogy, essentially between buildings and literary works, has been reinflected over time, but is still a familiar one. Another productive metaphor compares architecture to grammar rather than literature, suggesting that buildings, like sentences, are constructed by combining a set of formal elements according to a set of formal rules. Forty traces this idea back to 1802, when Durand published his influential teaching text, *Précis des Leçons d'Architecture*; he comments that the analogy had obvious attractions for educators charged with producing competent professionals in a relatively short time. However, the 'grammar' analogy has also attracted historians and critics. It is developed systematically in such works as John Summerson's *The Classical Language of Architecture* (1963), and Charles Jencks's *The Language of Postmodern Architecture* (1977), which includes chapters actually entitled 'Words', 'Syntax' and 'Semantics'.[5]

The 'architecture as grammar' metaphor prefigures, and in more recent works such as Jencks's, overlaps with, what is probably the most important linguistic analogy of recent times: the application to architecture of ideas developed in the early twentieth century by Ferdinand de Saussure in Europe and C.S. Peirce in the USA under the headings of 'structuralism' (Saussure) and 'semiotics' (Peirce).[6] As Adrian Forty notes (2000: 80), 'Strictly speaking, semiotics and structuralism propose language not as a metaphor for architecture, but rather that architecture *is* a language.' We want to make clear straight away that this is not our own position. But we are aware that the structuralist equation of architecture and language has been influential (as well as controversial): we recognize that many readers will find it 'natural' to approach a book which announces its subject as 'buildings and language' with the assumptions of structuralism in mind. To make our position clear, therefore, we must explain how and why it differs from the structuralist position. That entails giving some preliminary attention to what structuralism says about language, and how the principles of structuralist linguistics have been applied to the domain of architecture.

The pioneer of structuralism, Ferdinand de Saussure, was a Swiss linguist who had been trained in the comparative-historical methods of nineteenth century philology; his major achievement, however, was to develop an alternative to those methods, which subsequently became the basis for the modern discipline of linguistics. The great work which bears his name, the *Cours de Linguistique Générale* (*Course in General Linguistics*), was not written by Saussure, but reconstructed from his students' lecture notes after his death and published in 1916. The *Cours* elaborated a method for studying the structure of a single language at a single historical moment: 'synchronic' analysis, as opposed to the 'diachronic' (historical) approach that had previously prevailed. He proposed that a language could be regarded as a self-contained system of signs (it is easiest, though something of an oversimplification, to equate 'signs' with 'words' for the purpose of following Saussure's reasoning here). Signs are entities composed of a signifier (a form, like the sound sequence /kæt/, 'cat') and a signified (a concept, e.g. 'feline domestic animal'). The link between signifier and signified is not natural but arbitrary (in French the same signified is paired with the signifier *chat*, in Hungarian with *macska*, and so on). Arbitrary signs work not by corresponding directly to things in the world, but by contrasting with one another. A sign-system in other words is a system of differences, in which the individual signs acquire meaning by contrast with other signs.

The most immediately graspable illustrations of this principle are not, iron-ically, linguistic at all. In introductory textbooks a popular example is the sign system used for traffic signals: red means stop, green means go. Although they have become so familiar that they may seem 'natural', the meanings of red and green in this system are in fact arbitrary – designers could have reversed them, or used blue and yellow instead.[7] The point is not their substance but the differ-ence between them. Another simple example of a sign system might be the coins in a system of currency. On its own, a nickel (say) is entirely meaningless and valueless; its value can only be determined with reference to the whole system and by contrast with other terms in that system (a nickel is worth half as much as a dime, a fifth as much as a quarter, a twentieth of a dollar . . .). These contrasts only operate within the relevant 'code', in this case the US monetary system.

Saussure understood that the principles he was outlining applied to systems other than languages, and he suggested that linguistics would in time come to be regarded as part of a more general 'science of signs' which he called 'semi-ology', though nowadays a more common term in English is 'semiotics', which was the label used by Peirce. This insight was taken up by theorists in various disciplines outside linguistics, who pointed out that many cultural phenomena can plausibly be regarded as sign systems, in which formal contrasts are produc-tive of meaning. The anthropologist Claude Lévi-Strauss applied the structuralist approach to kinship systems; the critic Roland Barthes applied it to literary texts and to the 'fashion system'. And it has also been applied to architecture and its products (buildings, cities).

As a number of writers have pointed out, architecture is a challenging case for this approach, because, in the words of the semiotician Umberto Eco (1986: 57): 'apparently most architectural objects do not *communicate* (and are not designed to communicate), but *function*'. It might seem then that the meaning these objects convey is confined to a rather simple denotation of their primary use: a roof denotes covering, a stair the possibility of movement up and down. However, Eco argues that architectural objects also have, in common with other primarily functional human artefacts (e.g. clothing, whose primary function is to cover the body), a series of secondary 'connotative' or symbolic meanings. He gives the example of Gothic architectural styles connoting 'religiosity', a mean-ing which depends on associations between the vertical emphasis of a Gothic structure and the elevation of the soul towards God, and between strong contrasts of light/shadow and mysticism. These associations are part of a partic-ular 'language' or code, which is not the only one in existence: Eco suggests that the Greek temple, though formally quite distinct from a Gothic cathedral, was intended to communicate quite similar religious meanings. The temple, however, is built in a different idiom from the cathedral: the meaning 'religiosity' is tied to different formal signifiers in the Gothic and Classical architectural codes, just as the meaning 'feline domestic animal' is tied to different sequences of sounds in the English, French and Hungarian languages.

Semiotic and structuralist approaches, Adrian Forty suggests (2000: 81), are 'concerned not with what things mean, but with how meaning occurs'. One basic principle, as noted already, is that meaning works by contrast: the meaning of form A is grasped through its difference from form B in a given communication system, as with the contrast between red and green lights in the traffic signal system. Eco alludes to two significant formal contrasts in relation to the Gothic cathedral: vertical versus horizontal and light versus dark. Another scholar who has used structuralist techniques, Donald Preziosi (1979), systematically analyses plans of Minoan palaces in order to identify the formal properties of what he calls their 'architectonic code': the basic elements that are found in these buildings, and the rules that govern the combination of those elements into larger spatial structures. At the level of *formal* analysis, that is to say identifying the formal contrasts which make up the code, it appears that the structuralist approach is readily applicable to architectural phenomena. But complications arise with the other element of the Saussurean sign, its signified, or in plainer language, the *meaning* which is conveyed by the use of form A as opposed to form B. At this point we confront the issue of whether what Preziosi calls the 'architectonic code' is capable of communicating meaning *independently*, in its own right and on its own terms. Natural languages like English and Hungarian clearly do function in this way: if someone speaks Hungarian, utterances delivered in that language do not have to be translated into any other language before they can be understood. But can the same be said about architecture? Do buildings communicate directly, in their own semiotic codes?

In his discussion of the Gothic cathedral, Umberto Eco mentions a number of historical interpretations of its connotative or symbolic meaning, dwelling in particular on the interpretation of the light/dark contrast which is offered in Suger's *De rebus in administratione sua gestis*, a twelfth century text. 'There [Suger] lets it be understood, in prose and in verse, that the light that penetrates in streams from the windows into the dark naves ... must represent the very effusiveness of the divine creative energy' (Eco 1986: 67). Noting that this meaning of light is referred to in various neoplatonist texts of the middle ages, Eco concludes that 'for men of the twelfth century the Gothic windows and glazing ... connoted participation [in the divine essence]' (1986: 67). The point of interest here is *not* whether this is the single 'correct' interpretation – as Eco points out, meaning is subject to change, and clearly, succeeding ages imposed other meanings on Gothic cathedrals (the Romantics, for example, suggested that they represented the vaults of Celtic forests). Rather, the point of interest is the kind of evidence Eco considers relevant to the question of what Gothic cathedrals meant at any given time: *textual* evidence. The meaning of the cathedral is explained by Suger 'in prose and in verse' – not in stone and in glass.

Other texts reveal to the historian that Suger's interpretation is not idiosyncratic but part of a wider discourse, neoplatonism. Later commentators would offer different interpretations, but once again, the medium for these would be language. Buildings, it seems, do not explain themselves. While something like the contrast between light and dark in a Gothic cathedral may be apprehended directly, the *significance* of that contrast is not apprehended directly. Rather it is apprehended with the assistance of language, in the primary and literal sense of that term.

Eco reaches the conclusion that architecture is not a fully autonomous communication system: 'while the elements of architecture constitute themselves as a system, they become a code only when coupled with systems that lie outside architecture' (1986: 79).[8] We take a similar view; but we would go further than Eco does in claiming that in the matter of communication or semeiosis – the making of meaning – architecture is not just different from language, it is heavily dependent on the resources of language. Treating architecture *as* a language has the unfortunate effect of obscuring the role played by actual language, speech and writing, in shaping our understanding of the built environment. It is that relationship between buildings and language – an interactive rather than analogical one – which is our central concern in this book.

In the last few paragraphs we have argued against one of the claims which is implicit (and is sometimes made explicit) in structuralist/semiotic approaches to architecture – that the formal codes of architecture are autonomous systems capable of communicating directly. But the question also arises whether similar claims of autonomy are warranted in relation to language itself. As we have already said, natural languages are 'autonomous' communication systems in the sense that utterances in a natural language can be understood without recourse to some other language. But from this observation it does not necessarily follow that languages mean in just the way Saussurean structuralism suggests. Indeed, there are reasons to doubt this. While Saussure's work remains influential outside the study of language, it has little currency among linguists today, for in the course of the last century it has become clear that Saussure's principles can describe only a small part of the workings of natural language systems. It is one of the ironies of intellectual history that Saussure's methods have turned out to be more illuminating about certain non-linguistic sign-systems than they are about the linguistic systems he originally developed them for.

A particular and much-discussed problem with the Saussurean approach to language is its idealism. As Gottdiener and Lagapoulos say in their introduction to *The City and the Sign* (a collection of semiotic work which includes Umberto Eco's essay): 'structural linguistics, structuralism and semiotics approach the study of structures and systems of communication by neglecting the relation between systems of signification and the non-semiotic, material processes of the social world' (1986: 16). This neglect of historical, social and political considerations in the Saussurean tradition is systematic and deliberate. Saussure's aim was to abstract linguistic systems away from their users, uses and historical/ social contexts: he set out to define a 'pure' object for linguistic study, and this was precisely why his work was so revolutionary. It is a cardinal principle of Saussurean structuralism that sign-systems are treated as self-contained: meaning is produced by contrasts which are internal to the system. This makes it difficult to raise questions about the sign as a social and historical construct, subject to influences from outside the system.

In linguistics today, the study of meaning is usually divided into two sub-disciplines, called 'semantics' and 'pragmatics'.[9] Semantics deals with those elements of meaning which are internal to the linguistic code. It describes, for instance, the meaning relationships among words (e.g. 'light' is the antonym of 'dark'; the proposition 'Pongo is a dog' entails that 'Pongo is an animal') and the logic of grammatico-semantic operations like negation (e.g. 'Elvis is dead' and 'Elvis is not dead' cannot both be true simultaneously). Pragmatics, on the other hand, is concerned with the interface between the linguistic code and the real-world situations in which that code is used. It studies the way utterances are interpreted in context – which is not, as it turns out, a simple matter of decoding the meanings of words and grammatical forms. Rather it is a question of making *inferences* about what speaker A in context C, and given facts X, Y and Z about the world more generally, might intend to convey by uttering sentence S. Decoding the meaning of the sentence is just the tip of the interpretive iceberg. (As artificial intelligence researchers have found to their chagrin, computers may be able to parse complex grammatical strings perfectly, but unless they are programmed with massive amounts of additional information and with the capacity to process it so that pieces of existing knowledge, when put together, yield new knowledge that was not in the original database, machines cannot generate an appropriate response to the simplest remark.) A purely formalist analysis of meaning fails to capture important aspects of the making of meaning in real-world social situations.

Some commentators have made similar criticisms of formalist approaches to the meaning of the built environment. Talking about certain contemporary tendencies in architectural theory and practice, Ellen Dunham-Jones suggests (1997: 18):

> By focusing on form as the vehicle for meaning, Venturi and Scott Brown's decorated sheds, Rossi's typological transformations and Eisenman's deconstructions all maintain critical distance from the social and economic conditions of society itself. Issues of production and use are seen as largely irrelevant to the meaning of the building. They are dismissed as circumstantial, as outside the essence of architecture . . . social hierarchies and the modes of production are accepted as givens, outside the concern (or control) of the architect.

Focusing on form as the main determinant of what a building 'means' leaves out things which, in the real world, are fundamental to its meaning. For example, formalism abstracts buildings from their environment in a completely artificial way – as if the other structures with which they are juxtaposed (and which can change over time) contributed nothing to our understanding of them. Formalism glosses over meanings which derive from the social uses of buildings, and the social conditions which gave rise to those uses. It is difficult to think of any building (be it a tenement house, a shopping mall, a cathedral or a concentration camp) whose 'meaning' could be discussed in any illuminating way without foregrounding questions like 'who built it?', 'why?', 'with what historical events and social institutions is it associated?', 'how has its use changed over time?', and so on. Formalism, at best, pushes such questions into the background. This is not to say that the choice of architectural forms is either meaningless or analytically irrelevant, rather that form in any specific instance becomes meaningful and relevant only in relation to the whole context: social, temporal and spatial.

Our position in this book will be that *both* buildings *and* language are irreducibly social phenomena, so that any illuminating analysis of them must locate them in the larger social world. In accordance with that position, the main approaches to language that we have chosen to draw on in this book are *pragmatic* and *sociolinguistic*: they relate linguistic phenomena to the social context in which they arise. These approaches represent a reaction within linguistics itself against the formalist tradition inherited from Saussure. The subfield of linguistics we will be drawing on most extensively is *discourse analysis*, which specifically sets out to describe the characteristics of texts and to relate them to the social contexts in which they are produced and interpreted. At this point let us look more closely at what discourse analysis is, and what it does.

'DISCOURSE' AND 'DISCOURSE ANALYSIS'

The terms 'discourse' and 'discourse analysis' are used in a number of academic disciplines, and this generates its own problems, as the linguist Norman Fairclough has noted (1995: 18):

> The term discourse is widely and sometimes confusingly used in various disciplines . . .
> It is helpful to distinguish two main senses. One is predominant in language studies:
> discourse as social action and interaction, people interacting together in real social
> situations. The other is predominant in post-structuralist social theory (e.g. in the work
> of Foucault[10]): a discourse as a social construction of reality, a form of knowledge.

Fairclough adds that one aim of his own work is to bring these two senses of 'discourse' together. Our aim is not dissimilar; but before we can pursue it, we need to unpack what 'discourse' means to linguists.

In linguistics it is common to conceptualize a language as a 'system of systems'. No one sets out to analyse 'English', say, in an undifferentiated way; instead linguists focus on particular 'levels' of linguistic organization, such as phonology (the level of sounds), morphology (roughly, the level of words), syntax (the level of sentences). As the linguistic units being analysed increase in size (e.g. words are bigger than sounds and sentences are bigger than words), linguists may imagine themselves moving 'up' a level in space.[11] Obviously, this is an imaginary space: language is not really organized like geological strata or the storeys of a building, but the image is helpful for some purposes. It is helpful in this discussion because 'discourse' in linguistics is often defined as the level of organization 'above the sentence'. Whereas a syntactician looks for the principles that govern the formation of grammatical sentences, a discourse analyst looks for pattern and structure in stretches of language longer than one sentence. S/he is interested in what makes some sequence of sentences function as a text, an organized whole as opposed to a random collection of unrelated parts.

Another way linguists define 'discourse' is as 'language in use'. This is the definition underlying Norman Fairclough's assertion, quoted above, that discourse is language produced by 'people interacting together in real social situations'. Again, there is an implied contrast here with the approach taken by syntacticians, who typically analyse decontextualized, made-up sentences ('the cat sat on the mat' or 'colourless green ideas sleep furiously'). The rules which underlie the production of grammatically well-formed sentences can be specified without reference to the context or the purpose of their utterance; but the principles which underlie the production of intelligible discourse cannot. 'Discourse' is language used in some context, for some purpose. And although Fairclough's formulation ('people interacting together') most readily suggests spoken language, it is also appropriate to apply the term 'discourse' to writing. Writers too are using language in a context for a purpose; and it can be argued that writing involves interaction just as speech does, albeit under different spatiotemporal conditions,[12] since written language is made meaningful only when a reader engages with a text.

If discourse is what we create when we use language in social contexts, it becomes possible to see how the linguist's definition of discourse as 'language in use' might relate to the social theorist's definition of discourse as 'a social construction of reality, a form of knowledge'. If you take the position that 'reality' and 'knowledge' are ongoingly constructed by social actors through the various practices they engage in, it is evident that speaking and writing are among those practices – indeed they are part and parcel of virtually any social practice one cares to name. Language-using is a key tool for the 'social construction of reality': at any given moment, language itself may be regarded both as the product or sediment of a speech community's previous constructions of reality, and as the starting point for developing new constructs. Studying language in use, therefore, using an approach which does not remove it from the rest of social reality (and history), is a source of insight into the way in which reality has been and continues to be constructed.

We hope that the remarks just made on the social construction of reality and the role language plays in that process clarify our position on a particularly vexed theoretical issue. Scholars who make use of the ideas of Foucault and other post-structuralist theorists are sometimes accused by their critics of believing, absurdly, that nothing exists except language. We do not take that position, and in fact nor do most of the thinkers to whom the claim is attributed. A less tendentious formulation of what they are claiming might be that meaning cannot be created outside symbolic systems, and therefore that language, as our primary symbolic system, is a potentially relevant consideration in the analysis of any and all phenomena which 'mean' something.

An example that has nothing to do with buildings may help to make this argument clearer. When one person kills another, that is obviously not just a matter of language – in material reality someone ends up dead no matter what is or is not said and written about it – but it is through language that communities (and indeed killers) define the act, its meaning and its consequences. The same material act, depriving a person of their life, does not always 'mean' the same thing: depending on the circumstances and the assumptions the community holds, it could be classified as a crime, 'murder', or as 'self-defence' or as an 'act of war' or as a 'judicial execution'. Killing is not dependent on language, but the meaning we accord it is. In a somewhat similar way, we will argue that buildings are not linguistic objects, but the meaning we accord to them is heavily dependent on texts about them, texts whose medium is written or spoken language.

DISCOURSE ANALYSIS AS A CRITICAL TOOL

Some linguists who practise discourse analysis are interested primarily or exclusively in *describing* the workings of language in use. Others, however, adopt a self-consciously critical perspective. As well as asking the descriptivist's question 'how does this text work?', critical discourse analysts pose the question, 'what or whose interests does it serve for this text to work in this way?'

Here the linguist's sense of 'discourse' starts to converge very closely with the social theorist's sense, and especially with Foucault's concept of 'power/knowledge' (*pouvoir/savoir*). In modern societies, one very significant kind of power is the power to represent reality in a particular way, and to have your representation accepted not merely as one choice among others (for as we observed earlier in this chapter, there are always choices about how to represent a state of affairs in words) but as 'the truth': the 'natural', 'obvious' or 'neutral' version of reality. Critical discourse analysis looks for patterns of linguistic choice which contribute to a particular construction of the reality being represented. It also tries to relate these patterns to the power relations which are operative in the relevant context, and to the interests which are at stake.

Some concrete examples will help to make this clearer. Not surprisingly, many critical discourse analysts have chosen to examine the representation of reality in the mass media, from which many people now obtain most of their information about current events and politics. Analysts have looked at the way lexical and grammatical choices in newspapers and TV news reports can create varying impressions of the same real-life events. Such variations are often ideologically significant.

For example, one early study carried out in the 1970s by the Glasgow Media Group examined the reporting of industrial disputes in television news broadcasts, and found that the actions of employers and unionized workers were consistently described using different words (Eldridge 1995). Managements made 'offers', whereas unions made 'demands'; workers were described as 'threatening' to strike whereas managers were described as 'pleading' with them not to. The pattern here is that words used to describe the union side's actions have the semantic feature 'aggressive' whereas those used to describe the actions of employers have the feature 'co-operative'. The Glasgow Media Group argue this conveys an overall sense that industrial conflict is caused by worker aggression (and not, for example, by capitalist exploitation or by bad management). You could in principle describe a workplace dispute by reversing the two sets of terms (e.g. 'workers today offered to work for 5% more pay, but management demanded they work for no increase'). This alternative account strikes most people as clearly 'biased', but the other is not more neutral, only more familiar.

On television the 'unions = aggressive, employers = co-operative' pattern was extremely consistent, and this is especially interesting given that British television companies, by contrast with newspapers, have a statutory duty not to take any political stance. Critical discourse analysts who uncover the sort of pattern just mentioned would not, however, accuse the TV companies of a conscious, anti-union conspiracy. Rather they would argue that certain ways of representing industrial disputes have become 'naturalized', so that people no longer recognize them as incorporating any political or ideological stance. The linguistic pattern is a clue to what is taken as simple common sense on this issue, and the repetition of the pattern means that, other things being equal, it will continue to be common sense.

The patterns of lexical choice identified by the Glasgow researchers created a kind of 'schema' for processing a certain class of events, namely industrial disputes. Another linguistic device which can have similar effects is the conventional use of certain metaphors in relation to particular topics. Thus for instance the critical discourse analyst Teun van Dijk has drawn attention to the prevalence of 'invasion', 'swamping' and 'flooding' metaphors in discourse on the subject of immigration in Europe (van Dijk 1987). As he points out, these metaphors represent immigration as a threat to the host community, suggesting that fear and resistance are 'natural' responses.

Grammatical patterns are also of interest to critical discourse analysts. Reality is not only constructed by the words you choose, but also by which words occupy which slots in sentence structure. Consider, for instance, the admission by a US presidential spokesperson that 'mistakes were made'. This formulation makes use of the fact that transitive verbs can be either active or passive. If you make them passive, as in this case, you have the option not to mention the agent of the action: the spokesperson chose a grammatical construction which would not require an explicit indication of who 'made mistakes'. It is an error to think that all uses of the passive are intended to conceal agency or responsibility (or that they actually succeed: arguably, 'mistakes were made' fools no one, it just makes the guilty party look evasive into the bargain), but passives can be used to do that, and it is useful to be on the look out for it.

Some critical discourse analysis has focused on the way professionals exercise power through particular uses of language. For example, in many contexts where professionals interact with laypeople (e.g. social workers or counsellors and their clients, magistrates and defendants, doctors and patients) there is an obvious asymmetry in who may ask questions and who is required to answer them. One study of questions asked in an English magistrates' court (Harris 1984) found not only that defendants were effectively prohibited from asking questions, but that the questions magistrates asked were often so 'conducive' in form (i.e. the form restricts the range of possible answers) that defendants had little or no choice about what to reply. Another 'powerful' move professionals often have the non-reciprocal right to make is to reformulate the gist of what other parties have just said ('so, what you're telling me is . . .'). In doing this, they may well be redefining another person's reality; and because the discourse conventions of asymmetrical encounters make challenging professionals' formulations a 'deviant' and difficult move, the redefinition will usually stand as the 'official version'.

These examples concern spoken interaction, but professional or institutional power may also be exercised through written texts. An example discussed by Norman Fairclough (1992) is the way in which, during the period following the election of Margaret Thatcher's Conservative government in Britain in 1979, public institutions (schools and universities, hospitals, government departments) began increasingly to address the public as consumers. What had been previously represented as a 'social contract' between citizens and the state was now persistently reformulated to look more like the kind of contract a buyer has with a seller. This process, which some social theorists have labelled 'marketization', involved borrowing certain linguistic genres and ways of using language from the spheres of business and commerce. Public institutions adopted 'mission statements' and sent out glossy 'charters' to every household; they adopted the terminology of 'total quality management' (including in some instances the term 'customer' for, say, parents of children at state schools, or university students); and their writing style shifted, from the traditional bureaucratic language of official communications to the more 'conversational' norms of promotional discourse (e.g. advertising and PR material).

Although it was not only a linguistic change (there were also, for example, changes in the funding of many public services), the institutional adoption of new ways of writing and speaking to/about the public was a crucial part of the marketizing strategy. It illustrates Foucault's observation that power in modern democratic states is not usually a matter of brute force and terror, but of authority based on institutional claims to knowledge and truth (the psychiatrist knows who is insane and should be locked away; the social worker is empowered to judge whether people are adequate parents or functional families; the psychologist or educationalist can measure people's intelligence and determine what kind of education they should receive or what job they should do, and so on). This sort of authority requires consent if it is to function effectively; and it can be argued that discourse in the linguist's sense – both talk and written text – plays an important role in constructing consent. In democracies, powerful institutions do not just do things, they typically try to communicate their goals in ways which are favourable to the creation of public consensus, and to educate people in any new roles (e.g. 'consumer of state-funded services') or new beliefs (e.g. 'business is the best model for all public institutions') that they wish them to take up. Producing discourse in new genres and styles, which addresses people in new ways, is one strategy for educating them and winning their consent. Conversely, it should be acknowledged that producing discourse is also one strategy for generating and organizing resistance to the powers that be.

All this may seem a long way from the subject of this book, which is discourse about buildings. But many of the insights of critical discourse analysis are applicable in that context too. In the following section we will explain how the critical perspective might be applied to discourse about buildings, and introduce the main themes which we will take up in later chapters.

BUILDINGS AND DISCOURSE

Buildings themselves are not representations. They are material objects which enclose and organize space. However, it is one of our arguments in this book that buildings often do this (or more exactly, their designers do it) on the basis of texts which *are* representations. Just like the kinds of representations mentioned above – newspaper reports of strikes, professionals' reformulations of laypeople's stories, or government agencies' representations of the citizen as a consumer – the textual representations which architects and designers work with are not just neutral descriptions of a prior reality. They are products of linguistic choices which construct reality in particular ways. And the constructions of reality which are made apparent in discourse will very often also be apparent in the way a building organizes space. A building's users may never see any of the documents which preceded its construction, but because those documents condition the architect's decisions, their contents profoundly affect how the building will be experienced and used.

In the chapter which follows this introduction, we will give an account of the development over time of various textual types and genres which are relevant to the processes of creating and using buildings. After that, we will take up a series of themes which those texts suggest.

The first theme is *classification*. One of the functions of language is to classify, categorize and subcategorize aspects of reality; while one important task in designing buildings is to subdivide and categorize spaces, their uses and their users. In Chapter 3 we consider the relationship between the linguistic classifications of reality found in texts like briefs, and the way space in the resulting buildings is divided, organized and labelled.

The second theme is *power*. In Chapter 4 we observe that many texts about buildings are examples of institutional discourse: a certain kind of power and status is needed to produce them, and power is also enacted by them. We will look, in addition, at the non-architectural discourses of power/knowledge on which texts about buildings often draw. Designing buildings for particular uses (e.g. confining 'lunatics' in the nineteenth century or providing workspace for corporate employees today) typically involves reproducing the power relations which are associated with the relevant field of activity (e.g. psychiatry or business). Implicitly, architects are instructed in those relations by texts such as briefs, which very often borrow from the expert discourse of other fields to present certain relations of power as natural and inevitable.[13]

The third theme is *value*. One very obvious feature of a lot of discourse about architecture, both expert and popular, is that it makes aesthetic, functional and indeed moral judgements on buildings. Within the profession, the making of such judgements on designs for particular buildings is institutionalized in the architectural competition. In popular discourse it is a striking feature of newspaper journalism and style magazine writing. In Chapter 5 we will look at the language of value, and at the rhetorical techniques of persuasion which are used in efforts to construct consent on the question what should count as a 'good' or a 'bad' building. We will also consider what is *not* on the agenda of most evaluative discourse about buildings.

In Chapter 6, we will move from general themes to two more specific topics in discourse on buildings: *heritage* and *national identity*. We will explore the ways in which buildings, and texts about buildings, are used (as, in fact, they are very frequently) in creating representations of the past and of the nation.

In Chapter 7, we will consider an important issue in all attempts to analyse discourse about buildings, namely the relationship between linguistic and non-linguistic representation of buildings in texts, i.e. *images*. Most architectural texts incorporate non-verbal elements such as drawings, photographs, maps, and so on. What contribution do these make to the overall meaning/understanding of a text?

Finally, in the Afterword, we will discuss the implications and possible practical *applications* of the arguments and analyses we have presented.

Chapter 2: Buildings and their Texts

A Brief History

INTRODUCTION

In this book we discuss the role of language in the process of producing build-ings, and in shaping our responses to what is produced. Our approach to the subject is thematic (we outlined the main themes at the end of Chapter 1), and the texts we will analyse are taken from different places and periods of history: the discussion will therefore move backwards and forwards in time rather than presenting a continuous narrative. Before embarking on that discus-sion, however, it is useful to orient the reader by locating the major textual categories from which we will draw our examples in historical context.[1]

This is not a question of writing the *history* of architectural texts, for those texts are in reality a heterogeneous collection: they cannot plausibly be repre-sented as a single unified genre or tradition, evolving steadily from its beginnings in antiquity to the present multimedia age. At most, one might hope to inter-weave their various *histories*, revealing a complex mixture of continuity and change in the purposes and preoccupations of those writers who took up the subject in their different ways. Even then, a comprehensive treatment would require more space than we can spare.

In this chapter, then, we provide a somewhat selective overview, surveying European texts by type or genre, and placing these in a roughly chronological order. We begin with the major treatise, continuing with modern manifestos, competition and other briefs, design guides, professional texts, non-professional texts with an architectural content, and legislative texts. We are interested not only in content but also in *context*: in the purposes and audiences for which texts are written, in their relationship to knowledge in other areas of inquiry, in the social and historical circumstances which influence their production and circula-tion, and – not least – in the ideological interests at stake in them. We are also interested in what might seem a naïve or trivial question: why do people write about architecture at all?

TREATISES: VITRUVIUS IS ALIVE AND WELL

Vitruvius was a not particularly successful Roman architect of the first century BC. His treatise *De Architectura,* the first and most influential architectural text in the West, is over two thousand years old (Vitruvius: Morgan 1960). In it there is a mixture of *description* of buildings of the past, that is their arrangement for convenience of use, and their proportions and ornamentation, and *prescription* which lays down the appropriate forms for new buildings. A key form is that of the 'orders', the system of columns, capitals and associated mouldings, of which Vitruvius knew three: Doric, Ionic and Corinthian. Strict rules of proportion, symmetry and detail were laid down for each order. He was backward looking in the architecture which he found inspirational and which he used as a precedent to validate his recommendations – it was Hellenistic. In contrast there is surprisingly little reference to either the design or the constructional innovations of the Romans. There is praise for, and criticism of, other architects' work – both Greek and Roman.

Vitruvius's book also contains material about climate, siting and planning of buildings, building types, musical harmony, building materials, surveying instruments, hoists, sundials, water pumps, and siege machines. So in addition to beauty and utility Vitruvius was also concerned with technology. His trilogy of '*firmitas, utilitas, venustas*' in Sir Henry Wotton's famous translation became 'firmness, commodity [and] delight'. Sound construction, utility and beauty were hallmarks of good architecture. *Firmitas* and *utilitas* are developed in recommendations about building technology, siting and planning. But in considering *venustas* he sensed an inherent conflict between beauty and utility. One way to resolve this was to use something that both worked outstandingly well and was startlingly beautiful as a model: the human body. 'Therefore if nature has designed the human body so that its members are duly proportioned to the frame as a whole, it appears that the ancients had good reason for their rule, that in perfect buildings the different members must be in exact symmetrical relations to the whole general scheme' (73). The body's proportions are, he says, consonant with mathematical proportions, 'the perfect number' and they, in turn, with musical harmony, all in line with Pythagorean and Platonic principles. The body image is also present in the gender-specificity of three orders: Doric is equated with manliness, Ionic with matronliness and Corinthian with girlishness.

The legacy of Vitruvius's treatise is still visible in present-day writing about architecture, a point we illustrate with reference to a recent text by Colin St John Wilson, architect of the new British Library in London. St John Wilson is not only an eminent practitioner but, as one-time Professor and Head of one of the most prestigious schools of architecture, in Cambridge University, a teacher. Just before the library opened he published *Architectural Reflections: Studies in the Philosophy and Practice of Architecture* (1992), thus laying claim also to scholarship and theory. Why, at this stage in his career, did he undertake to write? What drove him to leave a legacy not only of buildings and educated architects, but also of a text?

It appears that St John Wilson was struggling both in his teaching and in his practice with the 'contradiction that lies at the heart of architecture . . . a condition of metaphysical distress', the contradiction between the art and the function of buildings. 'No other discipline claiming to be an art is so deeply divided within itself . . . [since] architecture is a public and practical art based upon a spoken pact with society. We are required to engage in a dialogue with those for whom we build in order to discover what to build' (viii). He sets himself the task of retrieving, from Aristotle and Aquinas, the distinction between a Fine and a Practical Art and intends to show that architecture is the latter, always serving an end other than itself. That end is 'purposefulness', or 'function' (x). Though neither the ancient Greeks nor the medieval schoolmen needed, he says, to make this distinction (but, strangely, they did), the 'themes of purposefulness and use are the generating principles in the nature of architecture understood as a Practical Art' (xiv).

There are several things to interest us in these prefatory remarks. First, he unequivocally defines architecture as art, albeit a 'practical' one embedded in function, purpose and use. Second, he refers to a 'spoken pact', without describing what it is, or who speaks. Third, he appeals to ancient philosophy. Perhaps writing is a way of attempting to seal the 'spoken pact'. Also it may be a way of dealing with the 'distress' he refers to, which is not only architecture's but also the individual architect's: '. . . writing has been (for me) the best way to explore the issues at stake both in the broadest philosophical terms and also in response to the particular need that we each have to formulate a credo' (viii). In using writing as a kind of therapy, we shall see that St John Wilson is following an old tradition. He might have added to his comment about the discipline of architecture being more deeply divided within itself than any other, that it also seems to demand, more than any other practical discourse (compare, say, engineering or medicine) a continuous historical and theoretical justification for what it is doing and teaching.

St John Wilson's reflections range as widely as Vitruvius's, and in many ways his text is similar: it contains a general architectural theory; philosophy, with a particular focus on language coupled to approval of Wittgenstein, and of architects such as Loos, who tried to put Wittgenstein's ideas about language into architectural form; history; his own heroes of twentieth century architecture (Scharoun, Aalto, Lewerentz and Asplund); and the corruption of Classical form by Speer in the service of Nazism. Amongst his historical references are both Vitruvius, and Alberti who in the fifteenth century wrote *De Re Aedificatoria* ('About matters to do with building'), in many senses the second treatise, in which he repeated Vitruvius's formula of 'Ten Books' (of architecture) but used it for new purposes; as van Eck (1998, 1999) argues, rather than being a treatise on a practical art, he modelled his argument much more on the productive arts, especially Classical and Renaissance rhetoric.

Certain themes dominate St John Wilson's text: art versus use, or form versus function; appeal to ancient precedent; critique, both positive and negative, of other architects' writing and design; and introspection about the act of writing itself. Picking up Vitruvius's references to the human body as a model for perfect proportions in buildings, he emphasizes how continuous the idealization of the human body has been from Classical antiquity to Le Corbusier's *Modulor*. Invoking Adrian Stokes's psychoanalytic interpretations of artistic experience, he also proposes that 'architecture and the human figure (are) linked as the supreme metaphors in a code through which all that is most urgent in human conflict and its resolution could be represented – the "body-figure", Michelangelo's sole metaphor not only in sculpture and painting but also in architecture' (12). St John Wilson uses the architecture-as-grammar metaphor which we have already dealt with in Chapter 1. It is one which is as current as it is ancient; it enabled, for instance, Richard McCormac, a Past President of the Royal Institute of British Architects, to speak of architecture as 'narrative', with 'architectural sub-clauses', having its own 'rhetoric', and the movement through its spaces as a 'dramatic . . . and richly expressive episodic text' (McCormac 1995: 9).

References to Vitruvius and Alberti show St John Wilson's awareness that he is working in a two thousand year old tradition, which was always given structure by such themes as language and the human body. Moreover it was one in which theory-construction and writing caused as much *angst* to his predecessors as they do to him.

THE PAIN OF WRITING

Vitruvius in his very first paragraph apologizes to the Emperor, to whom the work is dedicated, in case his writings incur displeasure 'by an unseasonable interruption'. But it is not until he arrives at the opening of his Book V, already half way through his work, that he suddenly appears to wake up to the possibility that his readers may find that his book '. . . give(s) rise to obscurity of ideas'. 'Books of unusually large size' may be an advantage in writing about history or poetry, but in architecture 'such fullness and amplitude of treatment will only be a hindrance, and will give the reader nothing but indefinite notions'. So, for readers who are hard pressed for time and will suffer frequent interruptions, he tries to write concisely and 'in a few pellucid sentences . . . briefly', creating short Books 'on unusual subjects which many persons will find obscure' (129–30).

Alberti (Alberti c 1450 and 1485: Rykwert *et al*. 1988), 1,500 years later, is more reticent about *why* he wants to write. Realizing the focal role of buildings in society, he decided '. . . for many reasons too lengthy to enter into here,

to collect and commit them [the principles of architecture] to these ten books'
(5). But he too is aware that his subject is complex and difficult for most readers,
and writing about it fraught with difficulty. 'But since it is our desire to be as
limpid, clear, and expeditious as possible in dealing with a subject otherwise
knotty, awkward and for the most part thoroughly obscure, we shall explain, as
is our custom, the precise nature of our undertaking' (7). Considering whether
to write about architecture at all, he finally undertook the 'difficult' and risky
enterprise because, if he had not, what was at stake was nothing less than 'the
total extinction [of] a discipline' (154). He sees a serious risk of promiscuous use
of the orders, the appearance of disorderly, undisciplined forms and the disappearance of the architect's authority unless the theoretical framework can be
stabilized and validated by being written down.

'I have worn myself out in composing this work', complains Filarete, slightly
later,[2] dedicating to Piero de' Medici his treatise on architecture – a subject that
is 'arduous and difficult to understand' (Filarete c 1460: Spencer 1965: 5).

For all these authors contradiction, indefinite notions, obscurity, boredom,
complexity, difficulty, awkwardness and finally, for St John Wilson, distress, are
ever-present dangers in writing about architecture. One would think that these
would be good reasons for avoiding the task like the plague. Yet after Alberti,
dozens of other eminent designers and teachers continued to produce texts. Why?

One answer is that treatises were public relations projects to show the
author's knowledge and skill, and to ensure a flow of commissions from the
patrons they were addressing. In the case of Vitruvius the addressee was no less
than the emperor Augustus who had built '. . . and [was] now building extensively'. In the case of Alberti it was Pope Nicholas V and, in the first printed
edition some years later, Lorenzo de' Medici. Filarete was writing both for the
Sforzas, his Milanese patrons, and for the Medicis in Florence. St John Wilson
does not overtly address his text to potential patrons, but his motivation is com-
parable to his predecessors' insofar as he writes in defence of his position at a
time when he feels himself obstructed and misunderstood. Thus he characterizes
his essays as 'campaign dispatches to peg out and define my position during
lulls in the fighting of the Thirty Years [sic] War to build the British Library at
St. Pancras' (1992: xvi).

A second answer might be found in the apparent anxiety about being seen
to be both innovatory (as a designer) and orthodox (as a scholar); drawings and
actual buildings can only imply this marriage, but language is needed to make it
explicit and confirm that the author was both original and rooted in tradition.

Third, as is argued by art historian John Onians (1988: 5–6), writing was
the instrument by which theoretical ideas came to be more powerful than
direct experience. It is the opposite of action, which 'presents us with the material
results . . . unaccompanied by verbal reasons for them', while 'texts present
us with elaborate sets of verbal reasons and no physical actions'. Increased

education caused theory, and hence the text, to become more important than experience – that is, the experience of actual buildings. Often theoretical texts 'persuade people that their spontaneous reaction is incorrect and that the real reason for what is happening to them is something other than that which they might naturally suppose' (1988: 5). Onians cites parents and governments as agents who promote literacy and education the better to be able to exercise power through words; and he implies that Renaissance architectural theory plays a similar role. So 'meanings inherent in forms' (whatever they may be) were replaced 'with meanings attached by [sic] words' (6).

Onians argues that the tradition of treatise-writing develops largely independently of either architectural practice or the way buildings were experienced; the texts relate more closely to philosophy, rhetoric and literature than to actual buildings. He attributes to Serlio, in the sixteenth century, the first bringing together of a sensibility derived from texts and the instinctive responses springing from experience.

The division between theory and experience to which Onians draws attention has a political significance. Theoretical knowledge is the province of the educated, and access to education has always been sharply differentiated by social class. When it was only an élite who were educated enough to read, textual production helped architects to gain their livelihood: the same élites who were literate also had surplus capital to invest in buildings, and might well be predisposed to commission the authors whose texts graced their libraries. In many contemporary societies, literacy itself is near-universal, but theoretical texts continue to be instruments of power through their influence on élites, since élite readers are in a position to apply what they read to policy and practice in various social domains. As the power of texts increased, it was through these means rather than simply through the distribution of commissions that class distinctions came to reproduce power structures in architecture. Treatises functioned as propaganda, staking out positions in theoretical and ideological debates whose consequences, ultimately, are material. This was a function of writing for Alberti, and it remains a function of writing today for authors like St John Wilson or Prince Charles (the Prince, indeed, having wealth as well as influence, is able to combine the roles of propagandist and patron).

Another answer to the question of why the Vitruvian tradition survives might be that the conflict between beauty and utility, or form and function, is deep, and, in design practice, never fully resolved. Each attempt looks like a new failure. So writing about it absolves the conscience, or (as for St John Wilson) is an attempt to heal the wound. Yet as authors often acknowledge, more or less explicitly, the act of writing is fraught with the same possibility of failure; language is not a perfect medium of expression, and in using it to address the unresolved conflicts of architecture there is a danger that the writer will only reopen painful wounds.

The conflict with which the authors are grappling is deeper even than that between beauty and utility, or form and function. If all building involves order-making, articulation, division (between functions, between outside and inside, between the space of strangers and that of inhabitants, between nature and human creation), then all of it is, or risks being, an instrument of alienation or even imprisonment. The more agonizingly beautiful the created object, the more acute the conflict. It is the underlying message of Piranesi's eighteenth century *Carceri* drawings of a dark, fantastic, impossible and paradoxical underground world which, we believe, has nothing to do with prisons. Here spaces and surfaces are without spatial logic or architectural coherence. Statues are indistinguishable from human figures; instruments of torture from implements of construction. In several of the drawings there is a glimpse of a 'normal', Classical upper world, with orderly buildings built to rule. He seems to be saying that it is this upper, rule-bound world of architecture which sits upon a lost, free, creative and mysterious subterranean space and is the real prison. What has been lost is a mythical, albeit rather frightening, non-alienating order. Writer after architectural writer tries to recover this in texts, as Piranesi tries to in graphic images.

THE LOSS OF INNOCENCE, AND FORM AS THE HEALER

In many post-Vitruvian (or in reality, post-Albertian) texts the invention of architecture, of 'Adam's house in Paradise' (Rykwert 1972), is represented as an archetypal harmony between nature, human beings and their buildings. This harmony is lost by a kind of 'Fall'. Since then all architecture aims to recover it. The persistence of this dream is evident in the structure which was intended to commemorate the year 2000 in Paris: a 200 metre high wooden tower near the *Bibliothèque Nationale*, which, according to *Architecture Today* (6 March 1998: 8), is a symbol of 'the harmony between man, nature and the city' (for 'city' read 'architecture'). In the first, Vitruvius's, version of this dream, the loss is embedded in a very powerful myth, which harmonizes nature not only with architecture but also with language. He says that in a great storm the trees, bending towards each other rubbed together and caught fire through friction. Human beings, till then like wild beasts, not only sought solace in the warmth of the fire, but gave up using signs and began to speak. Language was invented. And, at the same moment, they conceived the possibility of constructing shelters, first of branches and twigs, then of shaped timber and finally in stone. Architecture, in the form of the (Classical) column, was born.

Alberti saw the shelter offered by the roof and the wall as what originally 'drew and kept men together', rather than fire and water (the storm). He frequently returns to the beauty-utility issue, and sees nature as the arbiter: '. . . when we gaze at the wondrous works of the heavenly gods, we admire the beauty we see, rather than the utility we recognise' (155). 'Delight and splendour' must go alongside 'utility and strength'; these qualities are 'so closely related that if one is found wanting in anything, the rest will not meet with approval' (189). But his priorities are unambiguous: 'To have satisfied necessity is trite and insignificant' (156). His description of, and prescription for, the orders is far more detailed than Vitruvius's. Mathematical proportion and musical harmony are again invoked, and he too looks to the human body as a model of grace and perfection (Book 9). Alberti recognizes explicitly architecture's social objectives, though his description of the social order might not be to our taste today: 'some buildings are appropriate for society as a whole, others for the foremost citizens, and yet others for the common people' (94). This view of social function causes him to attend in great detail to the planning of a small range of building types. Rather than the backward looking historicism of Vitruvius, he sees in Roman precedent the roots of stylistic innovation for his own time. As in Vitruvius there is a wealth of detail about materials, construction, climate, water and drainage, tools and machinery.

The body image we have noted in Vitruvius, Alberti, Le Corbusier and St John Wilson became a standard feature of architectural theory. To Filarete the building 'is derived from man, that is, his form, members and measures' (13). Even its entrances and exits are modelled on the 'passages' of the body; this calls to mind Mary Douglas's discussion (Douglas 1966) of body orifices, where sexual, nourishing or waste substances cross the liminal boundary between inside and outside. Hence the need for elaborate ritual and taboo, just as at doors and city gates there are rituals and architectural elaboration. And in a number of the post-Vitruvian texts, the anthropomorphism of architecture is illustrated with a human figure inscribed into a circle or square, or, as in Francesco di Giorgio's fifteenth century treatise, where human figures are actually inscribed into the plan and onto the elevation.

But the central idea which gives shape to Alberti's treatise is expressed in the very first Book: 'the whole matter of building is composed of lineaments and structure' (7). There is debate about the exact meanings of the two words, but they approximate to *design* and *construction*: to an imaginative, conceptual process, followed by a concrete one which brings together materials, manual skill and machines. Another way this dual process could be described is as art and as craft. The purpose of 'lineaments' is to 'find[ing] the correct, infallible way of joining and fitting together those lines and angles which define and enclose surfaces of the building [and to] prescribe an appropriate place, exact numbers, a proper scale, and a graceful order for whole buildings and for each of their constituent parts, so that the whole form and appearance of the building may depend on lineaments alone . . . Nor do lineaments have anything to do with material . . . we may recognise the same lineaments in several different buildings that share one and the same form.' 'It is quite possible to project whole forms

25 □

in the mind, without any recourse to the material ... [using] lineaments conceived in the mind' (7).

The separation of conception – a mental, imaginative process, which for architects usually requires drawings – from realization, which requires materials and manual or mechanical skills to make the drawings concrete, now seems obvious. But not only is this separation at the heart of the form-function conflict, its first formulation came to influence deeply both later theory and the whole organization of building production in society. Eventually one group of people was educated and trained in abstract ideas about form and abstract knowledge about physics and materials (later to become engineering), and drawing. Another group was educated and trained to 'read' drawings, make new ones representing processes rather than products, and use hands, tools and machinery to form materials into their pre-ordained forms located exactly, with surveying instruments and so on, into their pre-ordained positions. For us, in considering texts, not only did two different professions, or branches of the building industry, develop, with correspondingly different educational and professional institutions, publications and texts, but two different forms of representation: writing and drawing. The latter will be discussed in Chapter 7. Eventually, of course, equations, bar charts, schedules, critical path diagrams and computer simulations take their place alongside drawings. But in the fifteenth century drawings for both processes are in the same treatise; the division gradually becomes sharper and, with it, the texts too become more differentiated.

Post-Vitruvian texts integrated humanistic philosophy, design description and prescription, planning guidance and constructional detail. Vitruvius's text was illustrated by later translators and editors, as was Alberti's a century after it was written. The genre developed for three hundred years, with major contributions by Serlio (1540), Vignola (1563), Palladio (1570) and Scamozzi (1615), all, in their many editions and translations, profusely illustrated.

The influence of treatises in the Vitruvian tradition cannot be overstated. For instance, in the late seventeenth century one of the first meetings of the French Royal Academy of Architecture agreed 'to consider [Vitruvius] to be the first and the most learned of all architects and that he must exercise the principal authority amongst them. His doctrine is admirable as a whole and should be adopted without deviation and also be followed in the greater part of its detail.'[3] However the tradition of focusing exclusively on form, through the orders, was coming to an end, and new texts were appearing. Amongst the first was Desgodet's *Cours d'Architecture* (dictated in about 1725 but not recorded in manuscript form until 1745). What is novel here is that besides the customary treatment and illustrations of the five orders, the author develops the idea of functional building types, far more elaborately than in the rudimentary post-Vitruvian texts. The systematic collection of the types known at the time, each fully worked out in detail, included a hospital, a town hall, a law court, palaces and some private houses.

The influence of Classical texts was broad and deep: they circulated throughout Europe, in the Spanish colonies of South America, in North America – from Jefferson's Washington, University of Virginia and Monticello to the ubiquitous 'colonial', in the European academies of architecture, and in the libraries of popes, princes and kings. The diffusion of the Classical style continued to the present century, and the major means of its diffusion was not imitation of what had been built previously, but observation of the precepts in theoretical texts. These established Classical architecture as the proper representation for almost any kind of political power: the Roman Empire; Byzantium and medieval Christendom; the new humanism of the Renaissance; French monarchy; the new Republics of America and France after their revolutions; in a stripped-down form, 1930s Fascism and Communism both in Europe and further afield, as in Mussolini's African colonies; and, as 'attachments' to postmodern buildings, where transglobal capitalism is validated by drawing on ancient culture.

FUNCTION AND TECHNOLOGY FOREGROUNDED

In the eighteenth century something began to happen to architectural texts. Limitations of space prevent us from analysing the underlying theoretical developments in detail: we concern ourselves rather with the new kinds of textual production to which those developments gave rise.

First, there was a significant increase in the production of the 'functional' genres dealing with building types. Architects were seen to need not only instruction on ideal forms, but also guidance on meeting the everyday demands of the real, socially more complex world. Second, under the influence of Enlightenment reason and respect for science, the ancient and mystical rules for form and style were no longer considered adequate. Probably the most influential text reflecting these developments was J. F. Blondel's *Cours d'Architecture* (1771–1777) based on his course at the Academy, which he had taken twenty years to write, with the last parts published posthumously. His collection of building types is truly encyclopaedic, covering not only the major traditional ones like town halls and basilicas, but also baths, arsenals, prisons and slaughterhouses. Blondel's discussion of form marked a break with the idealist standpoint, that beauty resided in the object itself – a view he held to be shrouded in obscurantist mist. Instead it arose directly from the sensations of the experiencing subject. For buildings, evoking the appropriate sensations entailed creating an appropriate affective *character* which expressed the building's purpose. Character could be 'light, elegant, delicate, rustic, naïve, feminine, mysterious, grandiose, audacious, terrible, dwarfish, frivolous, licentious, unpretentious, uncertain, vague, barbaric, cold, poor, sterile or futile'; and each of these was appropriate to a type. For example, 'naïve' was the character for pheasantries, zoos and dairies. One essential element both for the illustration of 'character' and for the study of types is an orderly classification (see Chapter 3 below). Classification systems became a key feature of Blondel's and subsequent texts.

The late eighteenth century saw the birth of the principle of *architecture parlante* – the idea of 'speaking' forms which would arouse in the viewer not just appropriate feelings but a direct understanding of a building's function. Though Blondel dismissed what he regarded as the extravagances of neo-Classical architects like Ledoux, a revolution in taste and thinking flowered in their work. Late eighteenth and early nineteenth century treatises, notably those by Boullée (1780s; 1976) and Ledoux (1804; 1981) no longer have any of the Vitruvian features. Forms now rule the day by *speaking* of function. Consider, for instance, Boullée's description of what he was trying to achieve in his design for a Palace of Justice consisting of a vast, colonnaded, light super-structure of courts, raised above a lower storey prison of unrelieved gloom and solidity.

> I decided that I could incorporate the Poetry of architecture by placing the entrance to
> the prisons underneath the Palace. It seemed to me that if I placed this august Palace
> above the shadowy lair of Crime, I should not only show to advantage the nobility of
> the architecture on account of the resulting contrast, but I should also have an
> impressive metaphorical image of Vice overwhelmed by the weight of Justice . . .
> [The Palace] appears to be part of the Heavens, [surrounded] by brilliant light,
> [and] the prisons at ground level, as if they were the precarious tombs of criminals.
> (1976: 98–9)

This kind of figurative language had to be matched in the text by sumptuous engravings of buildings in the landscape, under dramatic skies, with strong shadows cast by mysterious light sources. Such poetic and dramatically illustrated texts constitute a new genre of writing about architecture, indicating that the old, post-Vitruvian textual format and structure was no longer seen as adequate to capture new theoretical ideas. (Here we might comment, however – and see also Chapter 1 – that the perceived need for such elaborate texts to explain it is at odds with the claims made for 'speaking architecture' as a direct and unmediated form of communication.)

Despite the neo-Classical architects' claims to a concern for social function and technology, theirs was a theory and practice committed to imagery and form, and still, though now in a somewhat bizarre way, drawing on the resources of the Classical orders. A reaction (both theoretical and textual) was inevitable, and it was personified in the first Professor of Architecture at the new *École Polytechnique* (polytechnic school) founded in 1795 – J.N.L. Durand. We will briefly sketch the institutional changes which brought Durand to prominence, because these changes had profound consequences for the development of architectural discourse, as well as for the practice of designing and making buildings.

The *École* grew out of a strong mathematical and engineering tradition, which had been harnessed to military purposes. Even in the Academy of Architecture, the second Director (Philippe de La Hire 1686) was a mathematician. And since the early days, eminent architectural teachers of the Academy also taught in the engineering schools; for instance, both engineering and architecture were taught in the early eighteenth century to members of the *Corps des Ponts et Chaussées* (Corps of Bridges and Roads). In 1791, under Revolutionary reorganization, this became the *École Nationale des Ponts et Chaussées* and its pupils, in 1793, came under the control of the War Ministry; in the same year the *École Centrale des Travaux Publics* (Central School of Public Works) was set up and, in 1795, became the *École Polytechnique*. Durand, a pupil of Boullée, became its Professor of Architecture, continuing in that position until 1830.

In 1795 an alternative stream for architectural education, founded on the old Royal Academy, started in the *Institut Nationale des Sciences et des Arts*, as the *École Spéciale de l'Architecture* which, in 1803, became the *Académie des Beaux Arts* (Academy of Fine Arts). Architects were taught alongside students of painting, sculpture, music, declamation, and engraving. Finally this became the *École des Beaux-Arts* (EBA) in 1819.

After all the upheavals and institutional changes of the Enlightenment, the French and the industrial Revolutions, and the drive of reason and military power, the *Polytechnique* and the *Beaux-Arts* traditions – architecture-as-technology and architecture-as-art – were firmly established. These two discourses have survived worldwide, in various mixtures, to this day, and they are reproduced through textbooks, scholarly papers, promotional texts of educational institutions and the popular media.

Durand and his engineering colleagues were in a hurry to turn out the graduates that would be needed in the huge military and civil construction programme of post-Revolutionary and Imperial France. Unlike the concurrent, five-year traditional academy-based course, his course was two years long. Students were told not to worry about the orders, but simply to locate columns as dots at the intersection of the gridded graph paper on which they drew their plans. To the academicians Durand's drawings of capitals – each a simple trapezium with no indication of detail or order – were a scandal. His lectures focused on economy, utility, efficiency, and standardization of both detailed elements and entire buildings. Form and beauty inhered in materials and construction, so the old autonomous discourse of form, proportion, the human body, abstract beauty and the ornamental details of the orders was a waste of time.

Clearly new texts were needed for this kind of thinking and teaching. Durand produced two very influential ones. In one, his *Parallèle*, etc. (1801) he drew to the same scale, plate after magnificent plate, the plans and elevations of every kind of building, from every period and every part of the world. They came from China, Egypt, the Islamic world and Europe. They included temples, mausoleums, bridges (including the latest engineering marvels, such as the first all-iron bridge in the world, at Coalbrookdale on the Severn in England), prisons, hospitals, arsenals, gates, amphitheatres and *bourses* (exchanges), amongst dozens of other types. The very drawing technique, which treated Gothic, Classical, Baroque and modern details in an identical way, spoke volumes about the significance of the plan, function and structure. This was a typological source-book for his students. His second main work, the *Précis*, etc., first published from 1802 to 1809, consisted of his design teaching material. It was hierarchical in structure, starting with small elements like columns, combined into larger units on plan and elevation like porches or arcades, then into entire rooms or spaces, and eventually into entire buildings. Two hundred years later Durand would doubtless have been a leader in computer aided building design. For every type of building a quarter or half plan was shown on the graph paper grid (since it was symmetrical about one or both axes, showing more was a waste of paper). This agglomerative, modular and metrically repetitive architecture was far more splendid and monumental than such a description might lead one to believe. Durand's graduates not only became important practitioners and teachers, but some even returned to join the old guard academicians at the EBA.

Throughout the nineteenth century major theoretical and pedagogic battles, which needed the constant production of texts, raged in and around the EBA. One giant in these debates was Quatremère de Quincy who developed the idea of 'type' as an organizing principle, as a 'sort of kernel' based on func-tion, around which imaginative variations were made possible. This required a taxonomy of classified elements, and a kind of syntax of combinatorial rules. It also required two major works: his *De l'Imitation* (1823) and his three-volume *Encylopaedie Méthodique: Architecture* (1788–1825, 2nd ed. as *Dictionnaire Historique d'Architecture*, 1832).

A later giant was Viollet-le-Duc who rehabilitated the Platonic idea of a relationship between the essence of a thing and its form. But the essences were now not the archaic, Classical properties in the sense of 'divine origins', the human body and secret mystical harmonies, but nature itself, and specifically the act of making. Making in fact is nature. Once the 'structure . . . the plan . . . and the means of construction [are] established . . . the building is dressed in its own spirit' (*Entretiens*, etc., 1863, Vol. I: 286). Though the real engineering discourse on structures, materials and services had, by now, shifted to its specialized texts, schools, and professional institutions, construction and the nature of materials still played a crucial role for Viollet-le-Duc. Middleton (1978: 2) calls Viollet-le-Duc's two major works 'the great text books of nineteenth-century architectural theory; . . . the truths they embody might be disputed, but they remain unrivalled. Indeed, they are as yet unassailed. The so-called theory of architecture that has been used to support the modern movement in architecture is no more than a potpourri of notions and isolated slogans, taken up, unacknowledged for the most part, from Viollet-le-Duc.'

THE MANIFESTO REPLACES THE WEIGHTY TOME

Professional education became divided, patronage changed, and what remained of the hitherto shared culture of patrons, authors and designers and the academies was finally fractured by the First World War. So the text, which had been the chief instrument for maintaining the power of a dominant élite over architecture, took on a new role.

Whether or not we accept Middleton's critique of the *content* of the modern movement's early twentieth century texts as just rehashing old ideas, the modern texts represent in their *form* at least a radical break with the tradition of embodying theoretical ideas about architecture in vast, encyclopaedic volumes. Modern texts were more in the nature of polemical manifestos, addressed to a relatively narrow readership of architects, artists and designers. Influential examples of the manifesto genre include the productions of the Futurists (1914), Tony Garnier (1917), Gropius's Bauhaus (1919), CIAM and the Athens Charter (1931), the MARS Group (1932) and Archigram (1960s).[4] Although the western European tradition to which the genre belongs has increasingly been challenged by the rise of theoretical approaches formed in differing cultural and historical conditions (for instance, Venturi's anti-utopian Contextualism in North America and Kurowkawa's Metabolism in Japan), key European manifestos continued to be studied in architecture schools worldwide until well into the late twentieth century, and they still remain influential.

As we noted above, the manifestos differ from previous texts in making no attempt to be encyclopaedic in their scope and coverage. Even lengthier examples, such as Le Corbusier's *Vers une Architecture* ('Towards an architecture', 1923) and *La Ville Radieuse* ('The radiant city', 1935) are slim in comparison to the earlier volumes, and quite decontextualized. Little energy is spent in making reference to other texts, let alone entering into critical dialogue with other authors. *Vers une Architecture* mentions Le Corbusier's erstwhile master, Perret, and Blondel as authors, but not their work; the only other authors named are a certain Dieulafoy on medieval proportions, and himself. These texts were unashamedly propaganda, often explicitly linked to politics. The volumes were usually small, often typographically radical, and usually illustrated by the authors' own sketches and drawings.

As the massive, comprehensive historical, descriptive and prescriptive treatise has declined, new genres have arisen. They include monographs on individual architects, 'schools', places, periods and building types, usually so sumptuously illustrated that many students as well as lay readers will see, buy and treat them as primarily picture books; speculative, theoretical work, especially in feminist

31 □

approaches to architecture and on the borders between architecture and cultural studies; and of course the tradition of historical scholarship continues. But the development of 'theory' today, as far as the student or practising architect is concerned, is less dependent on these texts than on the polemical manifesto, such as Derrida and Tschumi's in defence of Deconstruction (1986). For the schools it is no longer possible – nor perhaps even desirable – since Guadet (1902–1904) to give students a corpus of canonical texts, in which theory is combined with design precepts. Intellectual discourse about architecture is no longer concentrated in texts belonging to a single discipline: it may be found in, for instance, philosophy (Lefebvre 1974), new spatial theories (Hillier *et al*. 1984, 1996), politics (Harvey 1973; Castells 1977), or in the recent explosion of litera-ture in environmental science, ecology, computing and engineering technology. This fragmentation began, as we have noted, as far back as the eighteenth century, and it did not diminish or impoverish architectural discourse; it merely dispersed it. We will return later on to the proliferation of 'architectural texts without architects' (or schools and departments of architecture), but first we turn to some important intra-professional text-types.

TEXT PRESCRIPTIONS: COMPETITIONS, BRIEFS AND DESIGN GUIDES

Written texts often prescribe what a particular building should be like. In the case of a specific project such texts can form the basis of a public competition, or be the brief whereby the client communicates his or her ideas to the chosen designer. Another kind of text is not for a specific building but for a *type*; there is a long history of such design guides, written by, or at least for, architects.

In the case of the specific project open to competition, there are complex psychological steps in the chain between first concept and final realization. The person or group writing the brief has a set of intentions – objectives, values, purposes and perspectives relating to the building to be produced. Initially these intentions are often quite vague and their transformation into a text is itself a difficult linguistic task. Once written down and published the competition entrants have to transform the text into their own concepts of what is being sought, in part using a kind of guesswork as to what might have been in the minds of the sponsors when they wrote. This transformation is not necessarily explicitly verbalized; many designers will work directly from the written text and at once start to transform it into space and form. In fact architects often claim that it is not possible to understand the sponsor's intentions fully from a text until this second transformation starts. They see this early image-forming stage not necessarily as a way of providing a solution but as a way of exploring the problem. But, equally, it could be seen as a way of closing the text; as a way of shaping open intentions so as to point to a preferred solution.

The sponsor's jury examines the design representations of the finished building in the form of drawings, though other material might also be provided (e.g. a written report, three-dimensional models and computer-based visualizations or data) and then evaluates them. In that process there may be much discussion, but usually little is recorded. The evaluations are comparative and lead to the creation of a rank order and the choice of a winner. Once this is done the jury writes and publishes a report which justifies to competitors and the public the decision reached.

The idea of the competition dates back to the institutionalization of architectural education, where it was a teaching tool rather than a way of obtaining a design for a real project. Egbert (1980) traces its beginnings to the academies of fifteenth century Florence. By the time the *Accademia di San Luca* was founded in Rome in 1593, the practice of awarding prizes to the best students was established; but it was not until 1708 that formal architectural competitions were held. The seventeenth century French Royal Academy of Architecture held its first competition in 1702, but it was 1720 before the regular *Grand Prix (de Rome)* competition started as an annual event. Winners were sent to Rome for extended study and were assured of pre-eminent professional and teaching positions on their return.

Briefs for the *Grand Prix* competition, written by professors at the Academy, were at first dictated to the entrants; it was not until the early nineteenth century that they were printed. But it seems they were quite elaborate, even when the subjects were merely 'a church porch' (1702), 'a Doric entrance to a palace' (1720), 'a main altar' (1724), 'a town hall facade' (1742), 'a triumphal arch' (1747) or 'a concert hall' (1761). Certainly they became so as they focused on complex functions, such as 'public baths' (1774), 'a school of medicine' (1775) and 'a lazaretto' (1784). After the Revolution the scale and complexity required that the briefs contain much more functional prescription: for an urban market for a 'very large town' (1792), 'a cavalry barracks' (1793), and 'an industrial fair situated on the banks of a large river . . . [and] having a specific place for an exhibition of national industry' (1802).

Such academic prize competitions became diffused internationally in the nineteenth century, and still exist today. But since the writers of the briefs were teachers and architects rather than actual clients, there was little in the way of realism, especially concerning social needs, political agendas and economic constraints. The designs were self-fulfilling outcomes of the limited principles being taught, and language played a dominant role in achieving the outcome. This navel-contemplating way of teaching design, where the brief was written, even if only by implication, so that the solutions would inevitably reproduce the teachers' preconceptions, is still commonplace even in the routine 'studio design' project where there is no competition for prizes. And the idea of competition, though not necessarily formalized, is deeply embedded in academic institutional structures. However, deviations from the usual conventions are becoming more common, where clients from the outside world have a role, where co-operation in teams rather than individualistic competitiveness is encouraged, and where students write their own briefs.

The competition, then, was institutionalized in pedagogic practice before public and private clients began to use it for real projects – a practice which has itself become increasingly institutionalized and is now common. Significant examples to the middle of the last century of projects involving national or international competition (our list is partly based on de Haan and Haagsma: 1988) include Washington's White House (1792), the Westminster Houses of Parliament (1835), the Crystal Palace (1850), the Berlin Reichstag (1882), the Eiffel Tower (1886), Stockholm Town Hall (1903), Helsinki Station (1903), the Chicago Tribune Tower (1922), and Sydney Opera House (1956). The movement of the competition brief out of the schools and into the 'real world' inevitably affected its characteristics as a text. Writing a brief for a real client with a specific site, a timetable and a budget is a different thing from writing a brief as a purely theoretical exercise. The text became more elaborate, covering legal issues, requirements as to the site, details and areas of the required accommodation, specifications for technical issues such as lighting, heating, acoustics, structural loading and energy consumption, possibly some limits concerning building materials (the 1997 brief for the new Scottish Parliament building excluded brick), and occasionally stylistic restrictions (the 1835 competition for the new Houses of Parliament in Westminster required designs to be Gothic or Tudor).

The writing of competition briefs, their publication, the judging of entries, the subsequent justification for the juries' decisions, and the building of the winning design, have often been fraught processes, generating yet more texts as commentators argue about the merits of competing entries and the wisdom (or disinterestedness – charges of nepotism and corruption have not been uncommon) of the judges' decision. Violent debates surrounded the 1835 Westminster Parliament designs by Barry and Pugin; Paxton's 1850 design for the Crystal Palace; and the 1863 Bradford Wool Exchange design by Lockwood and Mawson in which Ruskin became deeply embroiled. Harper's list of Victorian architectural competitions from 1843 to 1900 (1983) details all designs published in *The Builder* magazine over this period; the critiques and commentaries which accompanied these give insight into contemporary values and architectural polemics. Tostrup (1996, 1999) has given a detailed account of the rhetoric surrounding competitions for public buildings in Oslo from 1939 to 1990.

When a client writes a brief without opening the design up for competition, the text becomes even more specific. Even if the architect is not involved in the writing of the brief, he or she may already be appointed so the brief becomes the opening statement in a kind of dialogue, which may well continue throughout the design and even during building.

Before the end of the eighteenth century there were few detailed briefs of any kind. It was sufficient for clients – kings, princes, popes, town councils or aristocratic individuals – to write a short letter to their chosen architect.[5] Among the interested parties there existed a solid consensus about matters of style, form and space, and this obviated the need for extensive textual specifications. Architects and their clients came from the same social class, had similar educational backgrounds, used the same speech forms and read (or wrote) similar theoretical texts. So the mere fact of *naming* a building type – specifying, say, a country house, church or casino – ensured that a whole cluster of requirements regarding style, siting, ornament and spatial structure were transmitted to the designer, and achieved by him, without needing to be spelt out in detail (though of course debates and discussions could take place before or during construction).

But by the end of the eighteenth century, this consensus was beginning to break down, partly as a consequence of Enlightenment reason, but also and more importantly because of the breakdown in the old social and physical (urban) structures which resulted from the industrial revolution. All kinds of new clients sprang up: industrial entrepreneurs, new urban authorities, charitable and educational organizations, and the state itself. All kinds of new building users came into being, especially among the urban poor and the new *bourgeoisie*: factory workers and managers, mass-consumers in urban markets, urban school children and their teachers, visitors to popular exhibitions and to museums, literate users of public libraries, users of public baths and wash-houses, and the vastly increased and heterogeneous institutional population of hospitals, prisons, workhouses and asylums (Markus 1993). New designers also appeared. Some were professional architects, but their social background was much more varied than hitherto, and hence their use of language too. Others were engineers, speculative builders or philanthropists. So the whole process of commissioning and producing buildings became much less predictable.

Public and private building sponsors and clients, by the very fact of having surplus capital to invest in major projects, belonged to those classes with the political power that accompanies economic power. They sought to achieve not only a set of overt objectives – for instance, industrial production, public health or instruction, sanitary mass food retailing, or attractive and secure display of rare collections – but also the covert objective of reproducing in form and space the political structures to which they owed their position or their allegiance. In a less homogeneous and consensual social context it could no longer be taken for granted that the designer would share and so reproduce automatically the social and political commitments of the client. Consequently an implicit division of labour appeared. Designers would be given jurisdiction over formal and stylistic issues, which they were free to debate as polemically as they wished in the academies and schools, in journals, textbooks and through mass media. They could also, within the cost limits of the budget, exploit the most ingenious technical, engineering solutions to a design problem. Clients or their representatives, however, would take charge of defining the non-formal and non-technical aspects of the problem, by writing a detailed briefing text. In this text everything would be done to give the underlying assumptions an appearance of objectivity, technicality and neutrality, so as to put them beyond debate. The 'covert brief' would be achieved partly by silence on issues where design outcomes could safely be assumed, such as the spatial structure of plans, and partly by a use of suitably camouflaging language. We discuss these linguistic strategies in more detail in Chapter 4.

Finally we need to mention another kind of prescriptive text written by, or for, architects: the design guide. Here there is no specific project. The guide depends on the identification of a building type. Although there are rare pre-nineteenth century examples, such as the 1770s and 1780s papers and books on new types of hospitals, connected one way or another with the French Academy of Sciences (Markus 1993) the genre flourished after 1800. Often these were written by architects who had already established a reputation in designing a certain type (marked * below). For instance, for libraries della Santa brought out his important pioneering work in 1816; for libraries, museums and art galleries there is Papworth and Papworth's 1853* guide; for baths and wash-houses Baly's 1852* massive book of models; and for schools, apart from the models based on pedagogy (see below), Barnard's 1848* and Robson's 1874* texts. Sometimes the models are partly historical exemplars to be followed, partly abstract. This was the case in the early collections of a general kind, such as Furttenbach's (1628), Sturm's (1720, on hospitals) and Goldman's (1720) early eighteenth century texts, and the typological material in, for instance, Blondel and Durand which we have already noted, as well as the massive nineteenth century German collections, such as Durm (1880 *et seq.*).

In Britain model designs became part of the stock-in-trade of Parliamentary and legislative texts. The *Minutes of the Committee of Council on Education* from 1840 onwards included type plans for schools; the *Report of the Committee on the State of Madhouses* (1819) for asylums; the *Report of the Committee on Gaols* (1819) for prisons, and the *Annual Report of the Poor Law Commissioners* (from 1834 onwards) for workhouses. These plans, usually drawn up by named architects, became important instruments for the execution of legislation. The tradition of official design guides has continued, almost to the present day, encompassing, for example, health centres (HMSO 1973) and schools (Ministry of Education 1949–1963). Ideological assumptions about medicine, professionals, patients, education, children, etc., are subtly present not only in the text but in the illustrations too, as we will show in later chapters.

ARCHITECTURAL TEXTS WITHOUT ARCHITECTS

Bernard Rudofsky's now famous phrase 'architecture without architects' (Rudofsky 1965) referred to buildings. Our adaptation of it refers to texts, but it carries the same implication: that the creation of important architectural texts is not confined to the academy or to the professional institution. In the last two centuries model designs were used as materializations of abstract political and philosophical ideas, and buildings and space as enriching facets of poetry and fiction. Their authors, by themselves or sometimes with the help of architect advisers or professional draughtsmen, regarded buildings as important metaphors for ideas.

Acts of Parliament or laws sponsored by particular local councils often combined social and political objectives with building objectives. For instance, the 1779 Penitentiary Act laid down legal, financial, staffing and management systems for the transportation, imprisonment and other punishment of offenders. But it also contained specifications for this newly named type (the penitentiary), with its moral overtones of 'penance'. There were detailed specifications for classification, the site, the accommodation required for 600 male and 300 female prisoners, the daily regime of work, surveillance, exercise and food, the design of the infirmary and exercise yards, the weekly communal worship and its space, medical care, the size and furnishing of individual cells, and even clothing designed to be both clearly indicative in case of escape and also to 'humiliate'. The political and punitive objectives were seamlessly woven into a web that contained all the building and material minutiae.

Two texts, also from the field of criminology, demonstrate the link between abstract political principle, philosophy and human sentiment on the one hand, and buildings on the other. The first is John Howard's famous series of 1770s and 1780s texts on *The State of the Prisons of England and Wales* (Howard 1777, 1784). Primarily this embodies a philanthropist's view of punishment, health, sexual morality, discipline, work, hygiene, and war. Having outlined the evils of the system he saw in operation, he says that 'the first thing to be taken into consideration is the *prison itself*' (1784: 20, emphasis in original). He proceeds to illustrate 'the outlines' of a model county gaol, later to be developed to 'perfection' by a 'more skilful hand', through which morality, decency, work-habits and religion will be restored to its inmates. The second, even more striking text, is that by Jeremy Bentham – jurist, political philosopher and social reformer. When he invented his circular Panopticon prison (1787–1791) he prefaced his book (Bentham 1791a, 1791b) with a determinist declaration about the power of buildings which has probably never been equalled:

> Morals reformed – health preserved – industry invigorated – instruction diffused –
> public burthens lightened – Economy seated as it were upon a rock – the Gordian
> knot of the Poor-Laws not cut but untied – all by a simple idea in Architecture!

Unfortunately for our purposes the strength of so many politicians' and reformers' faith in architecture as a tool of social engineering is more evident in their building programmes than in their writings. So the Palladianism that Jefferson introduced to North America, or the neo-Classicism of Stalin, Hitler, Mussolini and Ceauşescu in Europe, have been written about by others, but not by them. Prince Charles's aversion to modernism, and his taste for the vernacular, on the other hand, has impelled him to write his own texts, an important example of which we discuss in Chapter 7.

DESIGN BY LAW

A special category of text written by non-architects, but having the most profound architectural and planning outcomes, is the legal text. The language of building or planning law and regulation, like all legal language, is hierarchical in structure, built on (what are allegedly) firm categories and precise definitions, and often deals with *pro*scription of what cannot be done, rather than *pre*scription of what can or should be done. Law-making bodies, by definition, have great power. In legislation they can, beneath a cloak of evidently desirable practical aims such as public safety, public health, sanitation, hygiene or fire prevention, achieve a wide range of ideological objectives. Building and town plans are the mediating instruments. Thus, for instance, the mid-nineteenth century Parisian legislation (itself rooted in the 1793 Revolutionary plans of the Commission of Artists) had its *raison d'être* in the need for massive sanitary reforms for waste disposal and water supply. This was urgently required as a result of a doubling of the city's population in the previous half century. But the transformation of Paris was not only underground. Napoleon III, working with the new Prefect, Baron Haussman, in the 1850s, achieved a total visible transformation, in the form of *ronde points* from which wide, straight boulevards radiated in star shapes. These, besides marking the underground sewerage network, allowed cavalry to ride in wide *enfilades*, cannons to fire in straight lines, and the medieval chicanes and labyrinths to be isolated and controlled. The memory of 1848 was vivid.

The regulation and ordering of civic life through planning law goes back to antiquity. The Roman *agrimensores*, land surveyors, whose methods and instruments were known to Vitruvius, were responsible for the division of agricultural land, and the gridded military camp and town plans. Zoning by social class and function, the segregation of public from private spheres, trading, and defence were all signified by these plans. The rules they used became codified in town planning law and the results are evident throughout Europe, North Africa and other former colonial territories to this day.

The pre-industrial mercantile town, from the sixteenth century onwards, needed strict building and planning controls for its growth and safe functioning.

One obvious set of laws governed the actual conditions of exchange; since one way of regarding the pre-industrial city is as a huge market, laws of exchange were enforced. Some governed only economic activity – for instance, limits on types of goods, opening and closing times, control of weight and measures, prices and trading practices. Others, relating to market places, design and location of stalls, and street selling, had formal and spatial implications for the city.

But other laws were designed to safeguard the entire mercantile functioning of the city. For instance, Amsterdam's 1533 laws about drains and sewers was followed by the sweeping 1565 Building Ordnance which laid down standards not only for piling of foundations, sewers and privies but street and canal widths, building heights and construction. These effectively provided a suitable and profitable environment for merchants, traders, financiers and investors. The working class population which was essential for this enterprise lived in uncontrolled and squalid interstitial space which Mumford (1961: 444) says was characterized by 'overcrowding, skimping, niggardly provisions even for light and air, [and] a general worsening of the whole environment'. He says this was the 'worst manifestation of [pre-industrial] capitalism . . . in its brute nakedness'.

Cities were often impelled to legislate after catastrophes like floods, plagues, earthquakes or fires. After London's Great Fire of 1666 a series of Building Acts were passed which controlled street widths, proscribed gables onto streets, specified standards of wooden construction in window and other details, and of party walls, eaves and so on. The whole space and form of London was changed. In Paris after a series of accidents with houses slipping into the Seine, balconies and cornices falling off buildings, and streets collapsing into cellars tunnelled beneath streets, building regulations, with elaborate texts, were designed to prevent such occurrences.

The scope of legislation for the governance of industrial cities expanded vastly to cover huge new retail markets, lighting, paving, slum clearance, and sanitary provision. As Mumford points out with regard to Amsterdam, the laws, and the legal texts which were its instruments, were class-biased. Only when threats or nuisances knew no class boundaries was regulation universal – for instance, in provisions to prevent the spread of cholera. In other respects throughout the nineteenth century, as shown by Chadwick's 1842 'The Sanitary Condition of the Labouring Population of Great Britain' (Chadwick 1842) and Engels' 1845 study of Manchester (Engels 1845, 1969), the industrial proletariat were beyond the reach of regulation in overcrowded slums, cellars, garrets and the streets. Everywhere commissions on towns and housing found the same conditions, and everywhere legislation in public health, housing and planning was devised to mitigate the effects of industrial urbanization. It can be shown that this effort did improve matters, sometimes for everyone, but more often selectively by further marginalizing those suffering the worst economic deprivation. The same thing is observed today in the third world, where the phenomenon of urban squatters in *favelas* and marginal settlements is universal. Marginalized sectors of society occupy marginal space, in marginal shelters, and represent a form of resistance.

In the twenty-first century the legal system permeates the design of cities and buildings. Besides the older form of regulation, there is now permissive legislation which allows individuals and corporations a good deal of freedom to establish their own control and regulatory instruments for the use and policing of space, surveillance, and the positioning and design of advertising. The enforcement of general regulations is extended to specific cases by legal contracts, leases and agreements. Whole branches of law are devoted to it. The long history of this kind of regulation and the related legal processes demonstrate the way in which space and form, the basis of architecture and urban design, are law-governed, which also means they are text-governed. Another way of putting it is that legal texts actually design cities and buildings and they, in turn, 'design' society.

CONCLUSION

Here we have attempted to place in historical context some of the most important textual genres in which architects and others have reflected on aspects of architecture, and sought to regulate it: treatises and manifestos, texts intended for teaching, competition and other briefs, design guides, and legal documents of various sorts. We have focused most closely on those genres whose purposes are overtly prescriptive. In recommending what architects should or should not do (or in the case of legal texts, more bluntly, telling them what they may or may not do), writers of treatises and textbooks, briefs and design guides, etc., intend to constrain current and future building design. Since the materialization of textually embedded propositions in actual buildings is one of our main concerns in this book, we will be returning frequently to these textual genres, especially in Chapters 3 and 4.

There are also, of course, textual genres whose effects are less directly constraining, since they are produced after rather than before the building designs they discuss. In this category we might place, for instance, historical scholarship; the kind of architectural criticism that appears in the print and broadcast media; guidebooks, exhibition and museum catalogues; and estate agents' or developers' promotional literature. Such texts may purport simply to describe existing buildings, but on closer examination this is almost never their sole function. Some of them have an explicit evaluative purpose; others are implicitly or covertly evaluative (a point we pursue in Chapter 5). Consequently, it would be misleading to suggest that they are not prescriptive, even if their effect on building design is less obvious and specific than the effect of, say, a brief on the building it contains specifications for. Praise or blame for an existing building, whether it was constructed yesterday or centuries ago, conveys – and is often intended to convey – a message about what is (un)desirable in future buildings. As we noted above, writers from Vitruvius to St John Wilson and Prince Charles often refer to existing structures for this purpose. In addition, while texts that cannot affect the design of a building (because it has already been completed) they can still shape our experiences, interpretations and judgements of that building (recall here Onians's remark, quoted above, on the way theoretical knowledge can overshadow experiential knowledge, to the point of persuading people that their spontaneous reactions are 'incorrect').

With these points in mind, we will take it that all kinds of texts about buildings contain some 'prescriptive' element, and that all have an ideological dimension. We hope it will be clear, even from this brief and partial outline of the historical development of some important text-types, that writing about architecture was an ideological enterprise from the first, and that changes over time in the available or preferred forms for doing it can be related to broader social changes. In the chapters that follow we will explore this general point in more detail by focusing on specific examples drawn from a range of genres and periods. We begin by examining some texts relating to one of the enduring concerns of architectural discourse: classification.

Chapter 3: Classification

INTRODUCTION

One function of language is to enable its users to label, differentiate and classify aspects of their experience. In relation to the built environment, this function manifests itself in the production and reproduction of expert and lay taxonomies, i.e. labelled categories which stand in particular relationships with each other. Architects learn to think in taxonomies of building types, architectural styles, functions and users. Lay people may have a less rich metalanguage, but their experience is also affected by the labels that are given to buildings, spaces within buildings, and activities. In this chapter we will look at the ways in which classifications which appear first in text are then materialized in space, and at the consequences of this.

In the following account we have chosen examples from a wide historical time-span, stretching from the early nineteenth to the late twentieth centuries, to demonstrate not only the relevance of our argument about classification under various historical and cultural conditions, but also to underline the social and cultural specificity *of* those conditions.

In some cases, the taxonomies which are most salient in a brief are not classifications of space *per se*, but of something else. For instance, as we show in Chapter 4, the brief for William Stark's Lunatic Asylum in Glasgow (1807) is essentially a socio-medical taxonomy of the inmates the building was designed to house, categorized by gender, social class and diagnosis; this taxonomy of persons is faithfully reflected in the organization of space in the building. The brief for the Burrell Gallery in Glasgow (1970), which we discuss later in this chapter, draws on an art-historical or curatorial taxonomy of the collection's contents, which again finds expression in the design of the building itself. Such classifications are not 'innocent': they reflect and reify hierarchies of value.

Hidden behind commonplace labels for buildings, and for spaces within buildings, is a history of debates about social relations and values which it is worthwhile to excavate and examine critically. The connotations that attach to different terms, and pervade whole bodies of discourse, are likely to affect people's attitudes to and experiences of certain kinds of buildings (e.g. 'tower block' versus 'skyscraper') or certain kinds of spaces (e.g. the range of labels, having different social status connotations, used for public eating places, such as 'canteen', 'restaurant', 'mess', 'café', 'deli', 'drug store' or 'snack bar'). Labels embody a hierarchy of value which need have nothing to do with the merits of specific buildings.

Examining the labels used for spaces within a building can alert us to the way spatial divisions become naturalized, though in fact they are the product of specific cultural/historical developments, and may subsequently be used to enforce those developments more widely. As an example of the way architectural classification may operate as a form of social engineering we will examine a report on public housing from 1918 in which what are presented as norms for the efficient organization of domestic space effectively impose on working class people a middle class norm of what 'respectable' family life for *them* should be.

Using categories and then arranging the categories into a systematic order is classification. Things, people, objects or ideas are distinguished from each other and then grouped according to differences and similarities. David Reason (Ellen and Reason 1979: 222) distinguishes between categorization, where this ordering is informal, not necessarily stable, possibly *ad hoc*, nor bound by formal rules, and classification, where there are rule-bound, articulatable systems of categories which '. . . figure as privileged and sanctioned (and sanctionable) arrangements of the ("social" and "natural") world'. We use the latter term, classification, here, without bothering too much about this distinction.

Many people are involved in the creation of categories and their ordering into a classification system. The most highly developed are those of botanists and zoologists, whose systems go back to antiquity, who have used them as a way of understanding the natural world and its evolution. Others of course have done this too – for instance, anthropologists, philosophers, doctors and librarians who do it as a way of understanding culture, knowledge and disease, and a way of ordering books. And the variety of classifying strategies have been studied by linguists. Of course not all classification systems are consciously constructed by professionals; many are folk taxonomies of, for instance, food or plants, which evolve gradually as part of cultural evolution in general and of language development in particular.

The theoretical debates around the whole business of classification are very much alive. First, they revolve around the rules for determining similarity and dissimilarity, and second, around the question whether a classification, although rooted in the mind and hence conceptual, nevertheless somehow reflects the 'real' world. Or is it *only* a social construct, achieved through language, which orders things according to the cultural habits, power, social relations and perceptions of the classifier? This question is of great importance in many areas of science, as well as in studying folk classifications. For us, dealing with the design of buildings, and texts about them, it would be difficult to argue that the categorization of people, objects, activities and space, which is so varied and changes so rapidly, is a stable system reflecting some 'real' world. It is quite clearly a social construct, achieved through language. A recent example illustrates this. The new Rover/BMW engine factory near Birmingham was designed around a concept of productive labour in which an attempt was made to eradicate the distinction between workers and management, or blue collar and white collar workers, by the linguistic device of labelling all employees as 'associates'. Accordingly the spaces previously labelled and occupied by the two groups either became integrated, as in the company restaurants, or the distinctions were re-established by function or activity – for example, tool maintenance or accounting. The use of language in this case was in part a rhetorical device (critics might say 'management-speak') which was supposed to embody a democratic demolition of class barriers and hierarchy. At the same time this linguistic device made it easier to establish new working practices of teamwork, widened responsibility, and flexibility.

The classification systems used in connection with building design and use are but one (important) aspect of linguistic practice, itself a facet of social prac- tice. They are often embedded in, or go alongside, general descriptions, discursive text about what a building ought to do or does, critical texts and promotional or sales literature. Moreover all these, if they are written before a building is designed – such as briefs – are prescriptive texts, intended to influence what is later designed. Both the prescriptive texts and the resulting building itself, once the latter is in use, are intended in some way to shape use and perceptions: the behaviour of the occupants and visitors, the way the functional programme is fulfilled, the way critics will comment, or the market value of the building.

There at least five steps from language to the actual experience of the concrete building.

Step 1 is the writing of a general discursive text about a building to be designed, which embodies aspirations, intentions, visions, objectives, and expressions of purpose. Such texts range from the highly rhetorical and generalized visions of a 'world class' production facility, *agitprop* drama or 'open learning', to more concrete intentions such as the plan to carry out all machine repairs in-house, to break down barriers between the audience and the professional actors, or to create a flexible curriculum and timetable.

Step 2 is to establish the categories of people, ideas, activities, processes, or objects which will be instrumental in achieving the aims spelled out in Step 1. When these categories are grouped and put into a hierarchical order we have a classification. Usually this categorization and classification is not explicitly spelled out, but embedded within the discursive text of Step 1. For instance, for a factory, repair work and repair workers may be identified amongst other processes and workers, and in a theatre, production, staging, listening and looking, or ticket sales may be identified amongst other activities, or producers, actors, audiences, and front-of-house staff amongst other participants. Or in a university the teaching and learning activities will be identified by subject, and teachers and students will be categorized accordingly.

Step 3 consists of constructing a set of labels for spaces to accommodate the categories established in Step 2, such as a repair workshop, an auditorium or a seminar room. Usually briefs contain a schedule of accommodation, in which labels for functionally or organizationally related spaces are grouped together, and then arranged in a hierarchical system of, say, main departments, with subgroups, sections and individual spaces within each.

Step 4, the transformation from language to space and form, consists of designing and producing the building in accordance with Step 3. The drawings will usually carry the labels from Step 3, and in the finished building one will often find the same labels inscribed onto walls or doors at floor levels, wings, blocks, lift directories and individual spaces.

Step 5 is the management of the building's programme, by explicit or implicit rules, and the use pattern and behaviour of the occupants. So repair is carried in the repair workshop, audiences sit in the auditorium, and students and teachers meet in a seminar room at a prescribed time, for a prescribed activity.

The intention of all building sponsors is to move seamlessly from Step 1 to Step 5, from language to behaviour and experience, so as to achieve their objectives. Usually the link between one step and the next, moving either forward or backward, is highly predictable, especially where, within a given culture, the institutions and their regimes are well established. Here the linguistic processes of categorization and classification are both formative and confirmatory of established social practice, spelling out with precision exact roles and relationships – who does what, where, when, and with whom, or what objects or processes are grouped with what others, and located where in relation to other groups. The 'inhabitants' of the building, such as its owners or controllers – those with an economic or social investment – not only have the power to write these texts and choose their language, but also ultimately to enforce concordance between the texts and use.

But there are instances where this concordance is not so smooth, complete or predictable, with fractures and slippages in the interfaces between any of the five steps.

There may be a gap between Step 1 and Step 2 in that the intentions of the former, general, discourse, are not borne out by the categories of the latter. For instance, many 'mission statements' in industry, academia, and public institutions include the aims of a non-hierarchic structure and decision making, transparency, flat-pyramid organization and public accountability. In the event, however, the categories established in Step 2 often show a deep, hierarchical structure; this can be observed in industry, for instance, with divisions, departments, sections, and groups within sections, or in universities, with faculties, departments, sections, and research groups, in each case with clear lines of responsibility and control. We will see in one example below, the new Glasgow Homoeopathic Hospital, that despite the general rhetoric of breaking down the rigid boundaries of conventional medicine, the actual division of the organization into staff and patients, and then its further subdivision, is achieved through quite orthodox categories of institutional medicine. This is all the more surprising when one considers its small size, which might suggest greater opportunities for de-institutionalization.

Gaps between Steps 2 and 3, and 3 and 4, are quite rare; indeed it is often the task of a designer not only to design and label the actual building (Step 4) but first to define the labels in the brief (Step 3) using the categories created by the sponsor in Step 2.

On the other hand, the gap between Step 5, use, and all the previous Steps, is often large; people and the organization simply do not behave in the intended or predicted way. In extreme cases such 'misbehaviour' is subject to disciplinary action – such as being ejected from a library reading room for eating or drinking there instead of the café. In other cases it is more subtle and complex – such as the example we discuss below of the Scandinavian Airlines System (SAS) headquarters, where most encounters and interpersonal exchanges do not take place in the spaces specifically labelled and designed for these.

This description of the five steps might suggest that they follow each other logically, and are clearly distinguishable. Nothing could be further from the truth, as we will show in our five cases. Quite often categories are implied, but not explicitly stated. Sometimes categories from one step are mixed up with those of another, especially those in Steps 2 and 3. And frequently a step may be missing altogether, the author having skipped it by a shorthand compression of the sequence.

One effect of the language of classification is that it tends to resist both social change and design innovation, since category labels are strong and slow to change. They are generally a conservative force; stability is precisely their role. Like many linguistic practices, category labels are so much part of everyday language that they naturalize features of the social and material worlds so that they are taken to be obvious and basic 'realities'. So, for instance, gender categories, and distinctions between public and private, adults and children, the built and the natural, professional and lay (say doctors and patients), and performers and audiences, with their subcategories – all of which appear in building texts and indeed in buildings – are the accepted norm. When the language categories and the associated labels and spaces *do* change, even quite radically, behaviour and actual relations may nevertheless remain much as they were before, modelled on older categories. This may be a form of resistance, or it may simply be a question of time and education before behaviour matches intentions.

When there is a desire to create new social relations which cross the boundaries between familiar categories there is not only the problem of finding appropriate language for these relations, but also of labelling the spaces which have to accommodate the new forms of behaviour based on these relations. Thus a redefinition of domestic gender roles and of the notion of privacy – to provide both equality of work and roles at the same time as finding a new balance between privacy, on the one hand, and the dangers of domestic violence behind closed doors on the other hand – involves a rethinking of both domestic life, and its spaces and spatial boundaries. New community-based educational methods, in which people of all ages study together, and in which there is mutual teaching and hence the roles of teacher and learner are less clearly demarcated, involve the rethinking of 'school' and its spaces in a way which makes this feasible. New, ecologically based, construction which incorporates natural elements like earth, turf roofs, and planting, have design ramifications beyond the merely technical; for instance, 'indoors' and outdoors' may no longer be meaningful categories. Shifts in Western medical practice towards those traditional in the East, in which doctors and patients together with patients' relatives and friends work together in both diagnosis and treatment, demand a rethinking of labels and functions for spaces; thus conventionally separate doctors' and patients' spaces such as entrances and eating places may no longer be relevant. Theatres in which audiences join actors in the performance demand quite different stage and auditorium arrangements – indeed such spatial categories may become redundant or, worse still, an actual hindrance.

It is not always possible, or necessary, for analytical purposes to collect material on all the steps from 1 to 5. In the examples below there are cases where evidence on one or other step is missing; but each illustrates some of the processes we have just discussed.

The five cases which follow are different in kind. The first, on housing, and the second, on an art gallery, show a straightforward process from language, to space and ultimately to use, in which there are strong ideological implications. The third, of a small hospital, is a case where there is an internal conflict in the discourse; where two or more voices speak and where the designer cannot fulfil more than one set of objectives. The fourth, of a modern office block, is a case where the language has certainly formed categories and shaped the design of the building, but where its users resist the overt and covert intentions of the brief and of the building itself, and do not behave in the 'planned' way. The fifth and final case, of a craft school, shows how the aims of a general, radical rhetoric in a text can to some extent be achieved, but in key aspects it is subverted and deep seated conventional power structures are reproduced.

CLASSIFICATION AND CLASS

For our first case we take a text which deals with housing. In 1918 the British Government produced the *Report of the Committee Appointed by the President of the Local Government Board and the Secretary of State for Scotland to Consider Questions of Building Construction in Connection with the Provision of Dwellings for the Working Classes in England and Wales and Scotland and Report upon Methods of Securing Economy and Despatch in the Provision of such Dwellings*. It is generally referred to as the Tudor Walters Report, after the MP chairman of the Committee. (Our references are to numbered paragraphs.)

This document was of great significance in determining government housing policy, and its influence was felt for the decades between the two World Wars, indeed even after 1945, and in countries other than Britain, which tried to construct national housing policies. Today, when in much of the world the market rather than central government governs housing policy, similarly coded messages about class and gender, and in some parts of the world about race, are embedded in the texts of developers and advertisers.

The immediate aim was to provide cheap, reasonable quality housing, mostly for rent, to the men returning from the war (many of them war-injured) and their families. Such provision was undoubtedly seen as one method to check the dissatisfaction with poor living conditions which, it was feared, would lead to popular unrest and political upheaval in Britain. The Report needed legislation for its implementation, and was quickly followed by the famous Addison Housing Act of 1919.

We have chosen this text because it represents one of the most comprehensive attempts to control housing and living conditions (and therefore to control lives) by a bureaucratization of the process, using welfare policies, medical and scientific argument, and modern technocratic policies about production. And the central plank on which these were based was a definition of social *class* (the 'working classes' of the title) – hence this chapter on *classification* is an appropriate place to consider it.

Tudor Walters engages in detailed discussion of, and recommendations for, design, layout, construction and costs of houses, with many model house plans.

The people for whom this housing is to be built are the 'working classes' – sometimes also referred to as the 'poorer classes'; he also distinguishes 'artisan classes', 'single workers', 'lodgers', 'well paid' and 'ill-paid' sections of the population (27), and the 'middle-class' (161).

The categories of accommodation named in the text and labelled on the plans are: living room, bedroom, scullery, parlour, WC, coals, bathroom, and wash-house. Two of these, and one category about which there is silence, are of particular interest to us, being specially significant in terms of class connotation.

The first is the 'parlour'. Tudor Walters says that the parlour is 'perhaps the most debatable point [in the whole Report]' (86). Apparently, from the witnesses his committee heard, 'the majority desire [it] . . . [for] older members of the family to hold social intercourse with their friends without interruption from the children'; in case of sickness; as a 'quiet room for convalescent members of the family'; for use during long illness or 'weakness'; for 'home lessons by the children'; it is 'needed for the youth of the family in order that they may meet their friends'; and for 'serious reading or writing [and] occasional visitors whom it may not be convenient to interview in the living-room in the presence of the whole family'. By eliminating dirty cooking, washing, washing-up etc. from the living room (to the scullery), it allows the living room to become a family room, a 'meal room' (87), a room for the 'cleaner activities of the family' (87). With gas for cooking (in the scullery) the living room fire can now have 'a little oven and a small hob with which minor cooking operations can be carried out', with, in addition, a back boiler for hot water. Nevertheless, despite such tidying up of the living room to make it much more fully used, the desire for a parlour is still retained by most working class people (87).

These gradual distinctions and segregations of functions, people and spaces mimic, in miniature, the ever finer distinctions, which reach a peak in the nineteenth century, in middle class and 'gentry' class houses. In these 'parlour' *never* appears (e.g. *The Gentleman's Country House and its Plan*, Jill Franklin 1981); instead there are drawing rooms, dining rooms, libraries, studies, morning rooms, billiard rooms, music rooms, business rooms, breakfast rooms, gentleman's (sic) rooms, smoking rooms, hall (not only as an entry space, but in its older, ceremonial, manorial tradition), and picture galleries. In addition there are in these houses huge servants' wings, with kitchens, and nurseries with school rooms. Throughout the house there is a fine discrimination and segregation between domestic, entertaining and service functions and persons. The Tudor Walters designs and labels similarly expand the range of specialized spaces for specialized functions; 'everything in its proper place'. There can be little doubt that this drive towards tidying up and segregating functions and domestic activities had its roots in the middle class houses in which members of the committee, as well as most of its witnesses, lived.

After World War Two 'parlour' disappears from the *Housing Manuals* (Ministry of Health 1944, and Ministry of Health and Ministry of Works 1949) and other official housing guides. In its place further specialization of space appears, with three distinctive new house plans – houses with dining rooms, dining-kitchens, or living-dining rooms. And, in each case 'working kitchens' (which we discuss below) are added.

The second label of significance for us is the 'scullery' – for cooking, the clothes copper and wringer (and hence clothes washing and drying), dish washing, and usually the bath. In many places the Report makes it clear that the scullery is the domain of the woman and that these tasks, even undertaken outside the house, are women's tasks: the 'housewife when working in the scullery' (118); in the communal wash-houses it is 'her' clothes, and 'herself' (169) which appear. But, unlike 'parlour', 'scullery' is a label shared by middle class and working class housing. In the former it is the place for 'wet and dirty work such as peeling vegetables, cleaning fish and the washing up' (Franklin: 64), and a special (low) class of servant, the 'scullery maid', appears in the list of servants and servants' sleeping apartments.

Significant too, are the silent labels of the Report, notably 'kitchen'. The concept of such a specialized space was not seen as appropriate or necessary for working class families. (It was, of course, long established in the middle and upper class home.) Cooking, in middle class houses, is clearly separated from 'dirty' work, and usually separate categories of staff are engaged for the two types of work, whereas for working class houses it was considered adequate not only to cook in the same space as food, dishes and clothes were washed, but also, in some types of house, where personal (body) washing took place.

By World War Two the 'scullery' disappears from working class housing, and it becomes a 'working kitchen'.

The comparison of space labels for working and middle class houses shows how class and gender distinctions operate in such classifications. Moreover these labels change over time in accordance with class and gender status.

THE ORDERING OF KNOWLEDGE

In the case we will shortly discuss, that of the School of Jewellery in Birmingham, the categories and their classification emerged as part of the general discourse about education and training, and are not the explicit focus of the brief. However, in the case of libraries, museums and art galleries, buildings dedicated to the collection, storage and use (in the case of libraries) or exhibition (in the case of museums and art galleries) of objects, classification in texts is an explicit concomitant of the classification of the objects themselves. These latter have to be classified in order that they can be easily retrieved, for new items to be located in the appropriate place and for security and cataloguing purposes. The classification systems for books, such as the Dewey Decimal, UDC and Library of Congress, are maps of knowledge which they divide into major fields and then, by continuous subdivision in a hierarchical structure, arrive at a precise subject field which, in some cases, is occupied by only a single book. Clearly such a system depends crucially on a particular epistemological position about the nature of knowledge itself. Books classified and catalogued according to such a system can then be physically located in a position which, by virtue of its relation to other positions, represents the epistemological slot of the book's subject matter. The spaces of the library, and its shelving, act as material classifying devices.[1]

In the case of museums similar principles apply. The objects have to be organized, catalogued and located in space according to some principle; this may be a theory of nature, such as evolution, or a theory of work, food, entertainment or whatever. In the case of art galleries, the theoretical/historical framework is usually constituted by authorship (i.e. the artist and his or her 'school'), the place of the object's origin, the date of its creation, its material, and possibly such details as purpose or sponsoring patron. These, in any combination, are theories of art.

Our second case is the Burrell Gallery in Glasgow. William Burrell was a wealthy Glasgow shipowner who spent a lifetime collecting paintings, ancient pottery, furniture, tapestries and carpets, stained glass and architectural remnants. When he died in 1958 he left this collection and a sum of money to build a suitable gallery for them, to the City of Glasgow. In 1970 an international competition for the design of the gallery was held. The winning entry, chosen from amongst 242 entries, was built in a country park at the edge of the city.

The competition brief to which all the designers worked was a substantial document, with four main sections at the second level. These dealt with general conditions, general information, schedule of accommodation and instructions. Each of these four were divided into subsections which in turn were further divided in a strictly hierarchical descending 'tree' of several levels. In the first main section there was one subsection in the fifth level – which dealt with how designs would be disqualified, and in the second section one dealt with the rights of the Trustees and others. The schedule of accommodation, at the fourth level, divided the collection by region (e.g. 'European' or 'Far Eastern'). At the fifth level, the European collection was divided by period (e.g. '1400–1600'). Each of these was further subdivided into type of object – painting, sculpture, tapestry, glass, silver, furniture and so forth. Finally every individual item in the collection was listed in a schedule, and related to its particular section. The non-European fourth level sections were not further subdivided.

If one draws a dendogram of the types shown in Figure 1, and represents each section, subsection etc. by a rectangle whose area is proportional to the length of its text, one can observe several phenomena which arise directly from

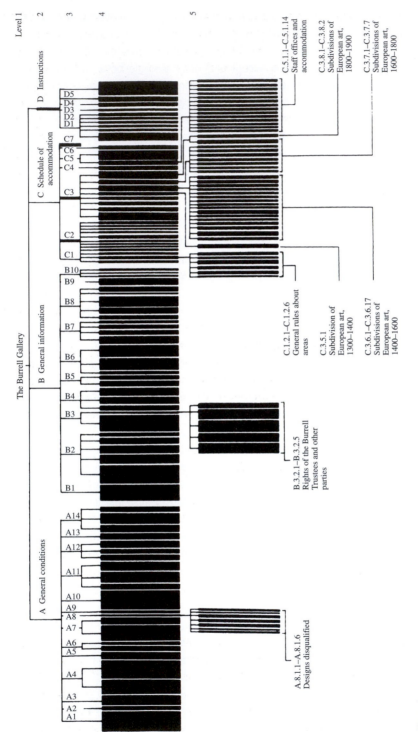

Figure 1

TEXT STRUCTURE OF THE BURRELL GALLERY BRIEF (1970).

At levels 4 and 5 the length of the bars is uniform and their width is proportional to the length of each bit of text. Therefore the area of each rectangular block is a scale representation of the volume of text in the corresponding section. At levels 2 and 3 the text is merely a series of headings and subheadings with the exception of the four marked in thicker lines, which represent a small amount of text accompanying the heading or subheading. Only European Art is classified down to level 5; all other parts of the collection remain classified at level 4. This is the author's diagram, but is based on, and gratefully acknowledges, work by one of his students, Salman Othman, who in his Special Study Project "A Case Study of the Burrell Collection", 1985 (Department of Architecture and Building Science, University of Strathclyde, Glasgow) made the first attempt to analyse the Burrell Gallery brief.

the classification adopted in the schedule of accommodation section. First, that the schedule is 'deep' – reaching down to level five (but in fact there are sixth and seventh level divisions, which are not shown here). Second that non-European art (of which there is, in fact, a vast amount) is less finely discriminated than European; the former only being labelled at level four, the latter at level five and deeper. Third that the drawing shows the relative articulation of the text – in that the larger the rectangles, and the deeper the tree, the greater is the articulation. One can assume that those matters which are most articulated were considered to be the most important, where nothing could be left to chance. These turn out to be disqualification, legal rights, and the schedule of (labelled) accommodation, and specifically that for the European part of the collection.

The consequences of the classification in the schedule of accommodation was the creating of separate spaces for each of the labelled sections, subsections etc. Within these spaces are located the group of objects judged to share essential characteristics. Moreover the adjacency of the spaces follows approximately the sequence in the schedule, although the visitor is not necessarily tied to following such a linear sequence since the gallery, overall, is spatially relatively shallow, with many rings – which give the opportunity for alternative routes, short cuts and complete omission.

Bringing conceptual, and then spatial, order to such a heterogeneous collection of objects is no easy task for a curator or cataloguer. Whatever strategy is adopted is merely one amongst a number of alternative systems, each of which represents a theory of art. And that which is adopted will not only determine the overall conceptual and spatial order, but will be evident in the labelling (mini-texts) of each individual item on the wall or in a glass case. This is therefore deeply formative of the visitor's experience and knowledge.

One obvious effect of the classification used here is the valorization of Western over non-Western art.

THE HUMAN BODY AS OBJECT

In both the cases so far discussed, one for housing people the other for housing art objects, the control of people's relations to each other and to objects and processes was of course a key objective of spatial ordering, even though this is not immediately obvious, with the focus being either the house or works of art. But there are other types of building where people, and in particular their bodies, are the central and evident focus. These buildings and their regimes are normally called 'institutions'. During the last two centuries, worldwide, institutions have absorbed a major portion of building investment. The huge hospitals, prisons, asylums and workhouses, children's orphanages and almshouses of Europe and North America became representative symbols of the nineteenth century and consumed no less resources in the twentieth.

In these institutions people suffering from moral, physical or psychological disorders – or merely from the 'disorder' of being unemployed, or too young or too old to look after themselves – were accommodated, treated or confined. The goal was to protect, 'cure', or punish them, in order that they should survive, become more compliant members of society, or to make them less dangerous to society or to themselves. Many of these institutions were set up and run by individuals and organizations which treated the inmates as subjects for various therapeutic experiments. Since Foucault's early writings (e.g. 1963, 1975) there has been an avalanche of studies of the scientific and social paradigms within which these institutions worked. It is clear that the ever-increasing refinement of categories of patient, prisoner or inmate, and their classification, formed an essential part of these institutions' regimes. In hospitals, for instance, the divisions, wards, consultants' teams and bases, labelled by varieties of disease and processes (e.g. orthopaedics, infectious diseases, coronary units, or surgery), was, and still is, the material manifestation of the conceptual divisions found in medical textbooks and curricula.

Much has been done in recent decades to make institutions smaller, less alienating, with more attention to individual needs and freedom of choice over aspects of lifestyle. The third case, which we now examine, falls within this trend and yet, even by modern standards, is unusual. It is the new Glasgow Homoeopathic Hospital. Its design was the subject of a competition which was one of Glasgow's 'City of Architecture and Design 1999' projects (*Glasgow: UK City of Architecture and Design 1999* 1999). Phase I was built and in use within a year.

Homoeopathy has a two-hundred-year-old tradition as an 'alternative' medical regime, relying on the administration, to a sick person, of small doses of drug which in a healthy person would produce symptoms like those of the disease being treated; often these drugs are based on natural rather than synthetic substances, and there is emphasis on the power of 'self-healing'. Glasgow Homoeopathic Hospital has been one of Europe's centres since the mid-nineteenth century, and now has a major clinical, research and teaching facility. It occupied a large converted mansion for much of the twentieth century. The new building was built on a site adjacent to, and forming part of the campus of, one of the city's major teaching hospitals.

Material for the general discourse (Step 1) is drawn from the competition *Outline Brief*, (West Glasgow Hospitals University NHS Trust 1999). This opens with a set of 'aspirations'. Some of these relate to therapeutic issues; 'self heal', 'traditional and complementary care', 'modern and traditional approaches', 'healing purposes', 'whole person care', 'an approach to healing separate to mainstream medicine', a combination of 'complementary and orthodox forms of care', 'self-caring patients', 'holistic interpretation with orthodox care', 'natural resources', 'patient comfort', 'understanding health and well-being'. The intention was also to include such complementary methods as acupuncture, neurotherapy, relaxation therapy and hypnosis. There is also emphasis on a multi-disciplinary approach, on allowing free movement, and on flexible use of space.

Other issues are more building, environment and site-related: the building should 'signal its healing purpose to viewers outside', its 'harmonious interior environment will help in the process of healing', the building will have an 'atmosphere of a therapeutic community', and it will reflect 'ancient roots but [will] look to the future', and it will be 'a positive agent for change [with a] distinctive character [which] will . . . emphasize its role in helping people to self-heal'. This requires a 'significant new' building of the 'highest quality . . . [with a] character and quality . . . [with a] special function'. It will use a 'palette of predominantly "natural" materials [and have] functional flexibility'. The role of nature is a major theme: there must be recognition of the 'possible importance of plants and trees to patients' feelings of comfort and security, [and of the] special properties of medical plants'. Related to this are issues of a naturally controlled environment, with emphasis on the quality, adequacy and ease of control of lighting (natural lighting being preferred), 'energy saving . . . low energy consumption . . . [and] benefits of fresh air'.

Additional material on Step 1, the general discourse, is found in the architects' own report on their competition submission (*UK City of Architecture and Design 1999* 1999: 4–5) which repeats many of the aspirations found in the brief: (a) 'defensible courtyard' (against railway noise), 'holistic spirit . . . landscaped surface to core environment, . . . passive, low energy, . . . natural lighting, . . . natural airflow/ventilation, . . . triple glazed, . . . sustainable, managed forest sources . . . reflect[ing] natural form and layout' (of the lecture space and hydrotherapy pool in the courtyard) . . . with 'planting and maintenance policy . . . to reinforce therapeutic ambience'.

Step 2, the establishment of categories and their classification, is found in the brief. There are four main groups – staff, patients, activities and processes, objects and spaces.

The *staff* categories are:

> Medical consultant
> Units secretary
> Doctor
> House officer
> Sister(s)
> Male(s)
> Female(s)

Nutritionist
Staff

The *patient* categories are:

Patients
Disabled (patients?)
Male(s)
Female(s)
Outpatients

The *activity* categories (written as both verbs and nominalizations of verbs) are:

Entrance (entering)	Reception
Reception (being received)	Waiting
Changing	Retail(-ing)
Uniform distribution	Consulting/examination
collection	Acupuncture
disposal	Preparation
Administration (administering)	Disposal
Education	Washing up
Treatment	Dining
Nursing	Manufacturing
Interview(-ing)	Circulation
Washing	Parking
Physiotherapy and rehabilitation	

The *object* categories are:

Locker	Single bed
Shower	Sluice
WC	Mobile X-ray machine
Washhand basin	Records
Staff uniform	Wheelchair

Step 3, the labelling of spaces, is done in the brief by labels based explicitly or implicitly on the categories of Step 2. It is worth quoting all the six parts of the schedule for Phase I of the project, especially to observe the grouping of categories. (Phase II is to add an extra lecture theatre, additional education and research offices, a hydrotherapy pool, an additional café area, and a pharmacy retail outlet and manufacturing area.)

Administration

Entrance and waiting
  area
Reception
Wheelchair bay
Male and female
  visitors' toilets
Locker changing area
Male and female
  washhand basins
Shower facilities
Staff uniform
  distribution
  collection/disposal
  point
Domestic service room
Medical consultants'
  rooms
Unit secretary's office
Seminar room
Library
Administration office
Store
Doctors' offices
Education offices
Laboratory
Patient education
  room

**Kitchen and staff
  dining area**
Kitchen
Store
Nutritionist
Staff dining area

Bed nursing section

Four bedrooms with day
  spaces
WCs and showers
Single bedrooms with
  day spaces
Bathroom (with assisted
  bath)
Preparation room
Sluice room
Disposal room
Treatment room
Ward pantry
Store
House officers
Sister
Nursing station
Interview/overnight room
Shared WCs and
  washing compartments
Wheelchair bay
Staff toilets (male and
  female)

Pharmacy
Dispensary
Wash-up
Store

**Day dining and
rehabilitation**
Dayroom/dining
Quiet room
Toilets for day area (male,
  female and disabled)
Mobile X-ray machine
Parking
Physical medicine
Physiotherapy and
  rehabilitation
OT kitchen
Office
Store

Outpatient department
Reception and records
  (included in
  administration)
Waiting area and tea bar
Consulting and examination
  rooms
Acupuncture room
Preparation room
Disposal room
Equipment room
Sister's office

Several significant points arise from this labelled schedule found in Step 3. First, the six sections make up groups which, we will see in considering Step 4, are, in the main, reflected in the clustering of spaces in the plan. Second, the radical, boundary-breaking aspirations of the general discourse (Step 1) are hardly reflected. It reads as would any schedule for an orthodox small hospital or clinic.

The only exceptions are the education spaces (though one would find these in any teaching hospital), and the future, Phase II, 'manufacturing area' of the pharmacy. There seems to be a conflict between the taxonomic conservatism of Steps 2 and 3, and the radical, boundary-breaking aspirations expressed in Step 1 which aim to span the divisions between complementary/orthodox medicine, patient's self-healing/outside intervention, and natural/artificial. It would appear that language has been used in a rhetorical and imaginatively innovatory way in the general discourse but was not seen as an instrument for change in the creation of categories and classifications. These are conventional, and hierarchically grouped and subdivided.

What could have been done? How could categories in tune with the aspirations have been created? For instance, the brief mentions several times 'self-caring' patients, and a 'therapeutic community'. This implies access by patients to a knowledge base, both about their own case and what is generally known about their condition and treatment, probably via the Internet. Such provision, in turn, implies computer stations and search assistance beyond what is implied by 'library'. A 'therapeutic community' might imply that the space for education be not labelled 'patient education room' with the implications not only of the conventional division between patients and professional staff, but also between patients and the community from which they come. Such a space would need to attract patients, friends and relatives, and professional staff, meeting during the day or in the evenings, with access to computer terminals, and provision for light refreshments. It might have been called exactly what the 'aspirations' section called it – a 'therapeutic community space'. Does the unorthodox approach to drugs, which involves advice and the 'acknowledge[ment] of the special properties of medical plants' not imply a space far beyond what is implied by 'dispensary' and 'shop' – one in which samples and information would be exhibited, where patients and pharmacists could sit down and discuss alternative 'whole person forms of care' in 'an harmonious interior environment which will help in the process of healing'? Could this not have been called a 'holistic drug centre'?

These suggestions for more appropriate labels are not merely cosmetic tinkering; with such labels the spatial relationships between individual spaces and blocks of spaces would need to be reconsidered, with important implications for social relationships.

The winning design (Step 4) faithfully interpreted Steps 2 and 3. The labels and the groups of spaces identified in the schedule of accommodation have been followed. Thus there are 'bed nursing', 'consulting', physical medicine', and 'administration/education' wings or blocks. There are a few indications that the architects actually tried to overcome the orthodoxy of the brief – for instance, in creating, and labelling on the plans, 'external patient day space(s)' which attempt to bridge the inside/outside, and the artificial/natural categories, and which are not specifically called for in the brief.

In conclusion, then, this example is one where a fresh vision has not been carried through, in linguistic terms, into categories, classification, and design. We know nothing about use (Step 5). It is quite probable that the actual therapeutic skill is fully in line with the 'aspirations' and that patients receive the benefits of the new approach. If so, however, this will be entirely the result of dedicated staff skilfully managing a regime whose spaces give little support to their activities, mainly because the power of language has not been grasped and used. Here there is a classic case of conflict of discourses; Step 1 is a radical statement of a new approach to medicine; however, the categories in Step 2, and the consequent space labels in Step 3, are much more conventional. The key authors of the brief were the homoeopathic medical practitioners. It appears that they were caught in a dilemma between the ideals of this radical form of medicine, and the need to make the project acceptable to the more orthodox practitioners and administrators on the major hospital site to which they were moving. Part of the explanation for this conflict between the discourses is perhaps that the financial resources to support the two forms of medical practice come from a common source.

INTENTIONS AND ACHIEVEMENT IN THE WORKPLACE

We have noted the case of all employees in an enterprise being labelled as 'associates'. In the introduction to a promotional brochure entitled 'Togetherness' about the new headquarters building for the Scandinavian Airlines System (SAS) completed in 1987 near Stockholm, our fourth case, the Chief Executive emphasizes the aim of giving liberty and responsibility to all employees (SAS n.d.). The introduction (Step 1) is called 'Good ideas spring from impromptu meetings' and its text claims that the new building was designed to generate 'good ideas . . . rarely created when you're sitting at your desk alone and tense, but during creative encounters between human beings'. There was clearly an agenda for change – '. . . something of a cultural revolution [which] may take a little time to get used to. We need . . . to get a different perspective on our work.' The key was to be 'encounters and dialogue'. Later in the brochure categories of activity (Step 2) are created: there is a 'buzz of conversation between people who meet on their way to work', emphasis on 'thinkfood [lectures, and art exhibitions] for inspiration', 'quiet deliberations', and 'sharing openness and teamwork . . . qualities that further excellence'. The office is described by a spatial label (Step 3) as an 'open facility for work . . . [dependent] on the creativity and ideas of its staff. For the ideas to flow there has to be space and incentive . . . It must be easy for people to establish contact with each other.'

The planning of the building aimed to achieve these objectives by creating a series of blocks, each with its own identity, linked by an internal two-level street which contains, or opens onto, the shopping, recreational, eating, medical and sports facilities (Steps 3 and 4). This street was designed to embody 'life . . . at

at the same spatial depth, if their functions are perceived as similar (for instance, the classrooms in a school) or at very different depths if their functions are seen as very dissimilar (for instance, the classrooms and the head teacher's room in a school).

In the fifth and final case which we now consider, clustering and boundaries are key issues. It is the new School of Jewellery established within the University of Central England in Birmingham, and opened in 1994. The courses offered are at various levels: MA, BA, Higher National Diploma, National Diploma, and City and Guilds and some of them are offered on a day-release basis (i.e. where employers release employees for study purposes during the day). The courses cover jewellery, silversmithing, precious metals and gemstones, gemology and horology.

The building is located in Birmingham's traditional jewellery manufacturing quarter. Our interest in this case is in how the brief first categorized activities and labelled spaces without grouping them, but then located the spaces on each of the building's four floors, thus achieving, *de facto*, both clustering and dispersion. To what extent did this locational strategy fulfil, and to what extent undermine, the stated, fairly radical, aims of the project?

The building combines new construction with parts of earlier structures built in the 1860s, 1891 and 1911 (*The Architects' Journal* (*AJ*) 23.3.1995). Conservation of portions of the earlier fabric formed an important objective of the brief.

Step 1, the general discourse, appears in the brief and in a professional journal (Core Briefing Documents 1990–91, collated September 2000, and *AJ*). In the latter the head of the School, the architect (Associated Architects) and an architectural critic (Marcus Field) amplify the objectives. First, 'high priority (was to be given to) . . . architectural heritage' (brief). Second, the sponsors were anxious to achieve a mix of students '. . . "superior enclaves" should be avoided when positioning BA studios. These should be interlinked but not focused in one zone' (brief). Despite this desire to avoid the creation of homogeneous classes of privileged and underprivileged students, some of the briefmakers expressed 'a preference for the focusing of BA/HND/MA studios towards the top of the building with more "transient" students lower down' by, for instance, moving day release students 'from the top to the basement thus elevating HND' by swapping their location with that of the day release students (brief).

Another set of aspirations concerned the deliberate breaking down of barriers. The head of the School wanted to '. . . forge links between traditional craft skills, modern technology and design, and encourage the involvement of the industry and community' (*AJ*). The architect aimed for integrating design with production and encouraging student interaction: '. . . by developing communal "process workshops" on each floor for heat and chemical treatment, the concept of adjoining studio workshops was introduced where both designing [at desks] and making [at benches] could take place. The sharing of process workshops and the use of glazed partitions encourages interaction between students and blurs the distinction between traditional craft skills [to create] . . . a coherent relationship between old and new'. One means of doing so was '. . . to create a fully glazed, double-height space [and provide] . . . clear views into the studio workshops [thus] link[ing] the building with the street' (*AJ*).

The architectural critic picked up several of these aspirations: '. . . making the action inside the building clearly visible from the street . . . is achieved by using full-height glazing to the workshops in the new wing and lowering the ground floor level . . . to meet the street'. He saw the '. . . new spaces [as] conducive to creativity . . . The transparency of the workshops and process areas, achieved by full-height glazed partitions, makes for good interaction and free exchange of ideas between students . . . The new glazed entrance is inviting and student activity is now very obvious from the street. Studios have transparent partitions for maximum student interactions and open directly on to process workshops' (*AJ*).

Thus there is a marked emphasis on breaking down barriers which separate traditional categories: 'town and gown'; inside/outside; old/new; prestige courses/ lower level courses; technology/craft; education/industry; design/production. There was a strong belief that this struggle against conservative categories would be achieved by the use of glass. We refer in Chapter 6 to a similar belief about glass and physical transparency at work in the debates surrounding the rebuilding of Berlin's *Reichstag.*

Step 2, the creation of categories and their classification, is a mixture of category types. In part it is part people based ('Head of School', 'D[ay] R[elease]', 'MA/BA students'); in part activity based, with the activities only *implied*, using words to move by a kind of shorthand directly to the Step 3 space labels ('casting shop' – implying the 'casting operation of production', 'studio' – implying 'design', and 'workshop' – implying 'production'); and in part object/material based ('horology', 'gemology'). In fact we need to consider Steps 2 and 3 together to get a clear picture of the categories and their classification. (Sometimes slightly different names are used within the brief, and between the brief and plans, for the same spaces). Examining the brief, the following main groups emerge:

1. Basic material production ('machine shop', 'electro-plating', 'casting shop' and 'process workshop[s]').
2. Precious object/material production ('gemology', 'horology', 'silver-smithing' and 'engraving').
3. Production/reproduction of knowledge/information/data ('seminar', 'CAD studio', 'lecture theatre', 'library' and 'computer').
4. Design ('studio', 'workshop/studio').

5.   Administration/control ('head', 'head of school', 'reception/administration', 'office', 'meetings', 'caretaker', 'staff accommodation' and 'staff').
6.   Recreation/nourishment ('common room', 'restaurant', 'café' and 'kitchen').
7.   Image projection ('exhibition hall', which only appears on the plan).

Another, cruder, way of grouping 1, 2, 3 and 4 is simply to divide them into the two cultural dimensions of material production and knowledge production.

Following the complete schedule of accommodation in the brief, it is broken down on a floor-by-floor basis. The resultant clustering thus prescribed for each of the four floors of the building has important spatial and relational effects.

The most evident attempt at boundary-crossing is the 'workshop/studio', which spans production and design. In parts of the brief, and on the plans, this becomes simply 'studio', though it is clear from its furnishings that it is intended to function in both ways.

In Step 4, the actual designed building, there is a more or less faithful reproduction of the labels of Steps 2 and 3, with slight but significant deviations, such as the disappearance of the only boundary-crossing label of 'workshop/studio'.

On Step 5, actual use and behaviour, there is, as usual, little information. It is significant, however, that in the *AJ* article on a building said to house nearly 600 students, published some five months after its opening, there are seven interior photographs, of which five show empty spaces, one shows a few people in the café, and one shows two people in a workshop. Whether this depopulation is because of the early phase in the building's life when the article was produced, or whether it represents a widespread lack of interest in social reality, reflected in the conventions of architectural photo-journalism, it is impossible to know.

In this case the actual planning of the building, and its subsequent adaptation, has been influenced by the classification in two ways.

First, some identical spaces have become widely dispersed, not only geometrically but topologically (in terms of spatial depth) too. Notably the twelve workshop/studios for the various types and levels of course are placed on three of the building's four floors, and their spatial depth varies from 4 to 15. This appears to be a successful response to the aspiration of avoiding clustering, such as 'design spaces', or 'student spaces' and a desire rather to create a local order for each group of students, identifiable and distinguishable from that of other groups.

Second, three sets of spaces are not dispersed but strongly clustered.

> One set is fairly obvious – it is that of the precious object/materials production spaces which are all located on one floor, the basement, except for the horology workshop on the first floor (the engraving studio [marked on the *AJ* plans] apparently having disappeared). Security considerations have given this cluster a formal and spatial coherence which will affect the sense of identity and the social relations of those who work there.

A second set is that of administration/control. This set is grouped on the ground floor, with its own, separate entrance, in shallow space (no more than four steps deep from the street) with the exception of a deep staffroom on the top floor. This cluster is located in the oldest part of the complex, dating from the 1860s. So apart from having an identity achieved by clustering, and being located at the strategically important spatially shallow zone, it is also given the extra validation of history and tradition. It a commonplace that in modern science and high-tech parks, built in the grounds of old country mansions, it is generally the director and central administration which are located in these prestigious monuments.

The third set of clustered spaces consists of those dedicated to knowledge production – the library, seminar rooms, computer aided design studio, and lecture room. Although these spaces occur on both the first and second floors, they are closely linked by a dedicated staircase, whilst the library is but a few steps away from the lecture and seminar rooms on the same floor.

The clustering of these three sets is a direct consequence of the floor-by-floor grouping in the brief.

The coherence and shallow spatial location of the administrative spaces should be read as a strategy for solidarity and control. The clustering of the knowledge-production spaces gives that group of activities also a coherence and identity which those related to design and material production, dispersed at all levels through the building, lack. Such clustering seems to undermine the close integration of theory and practice. (The library was, at one stage in the brief's development, located on the ground floor, and knowledge production was thus more widely distributed. In the event it moved up by one floor.)

Clustering therefore seems to have something to do with power. The activities which control and manage the programme of activities, and the theoretical and ideological formative processes which underpin the material production processes, are both nodes of power.

This case shows that labelling and classification, followed by the pre-design definition of groups by floor level, Steps 3 and 4, can successfully support those aspirations of the general discourse which aim at boundary breaking, but only for second-order functions which ultimately do not determine the social outcome of the institutions' activities. The risk of allowing first-order, control, activities to become 'invisible' by fragmentation and dispersion is too great; it would too seriously challenge the social and educational orders. So in steps 3 and 4 the sponsors and designers work together to subvert critical parts of the rhetoric of the general discourse, largely through the medium of language.

SO HOW DOES CLASSIFICATION SHAPE SPACE?

The examples we have chosen do not demonstrate the formative role of classification uniformly. In the case of the housing report and the art gallery there is
a fairly smooth transition from categories and classes to space. In the case of the
hospital there is a conflict of discourses, between radical aspirations and conservative categories. The jewellery school shows a different kind of conflict; here the
general aspirations are followed through in the various texts as long as they do
not undermine the conventional power structures which control both administration and intellectual formation. Where there is a danger of them doing
so, various strategies are used to undermine the general discourse, one of which
is to cluster by prescribing, early in the design process, locations (e.g. by floor
level). In the case of the airline headquarters the discourse is cohesive, maintained
throughout the various texts, but the conflict arises between the intentions of
these texts, as well as those of the design, and actual human behaviour. These
differences in the five cases should serve to alert analysts, like us, as well as
sponsors and designers, to the complex effects of categories and classifications
on space.

Chapter 4: Power

BUILDINGS, LANGUAGE AND POWER

The nature, genesis and scope of power are much-debated topics in social science and philosophy. While this is not the place to discuss in detail the numerous accounts that have been offered, it may be useful initially to distinguish some of the main forms power has been said by theorists to take. For example, power may be founded directly on force or the threat of it (e.g. military power, state-sponsored torture, or the right that exists in some societies to physically chastise such 'inferiors' as one's wife, children or servants). It may be an economic relation, in which those who possess material resources are able to coerce others who lack them (e.g. the exploitation of workers by capitalists in Classical Marxist theory). Or it may be exercised through various kinds of disciplinary apparatus – a body of codified, authoritative knowledge defines particular groups, like 'criminals', 'the poor', 'homosexuals', etc., as targets of disciplinary power and on that basis their members may be subjected to particular institutional regimes (imprisonment, the workhouse, aversion therapy). Power in this 'disciplinary' sense has an intimate relationship with the topic of Chapter 3, classification: though in order to make the material manageable we have separated the two phenomena and dealt with them in successive chapters, it will readily be seen that there is overlap between them.

In reality, it is often the case that unequal social relations are maintained by different forms of power operating simultaneously. Slavery, for example, is a form of economic exploitation which also involves the use of force (both to enslave people and to keep them compliant afterwards). In many cases it has also involved legal discourses regulating the trade in human beings, and other discourses, both popular and (pseudo) 'scientific', defining enslaved peoples as 'naturally' inferior. These ways of classifying and regulating persons, activities and relationships have served not only to make the institution of slavery work in an orderly manner, but also to legitimate it ideologically.

Power enters into the design of buildings in various ways (for a detailed theoretical and historical discussion, see Markus 1993). Perhaps the most

immediately obvious of these is the use of architectural form to symbolize particular kinds of power. In the case of economic power, for instance, one thinks of
the banks and exchanges that resemble cathedrals and temples, or of the
towering skyscrapers that house so many contemporary financial institutions.
These are metaphors, readily interpretable where a community shares the
assumptions they are based on (e.g. the equation of a building's height with its
importance). But the relation between buildings and power is not just a matter
of symbolism, and indeed we would argue that there are far more significant
manifestations of it than the symbolic use of form.

It is evident for instance that facilitating the exercise of power, particularly
in its 'disciplinary' forms, may be a building's main function. The prisons and
workhouses mentioned above are obvious examples. These are building types
which came into existence as a consequence of the emergence of certain disciplinary regimes (and which may subsequently go out of existence because
those regimes are abandoned, as has happened with workhouses). Conversely,
the regimes themselves may be dependent on the existence of the buildings. The
practice of imprisoning criminals or confining the insane, for instance, obviously
requires that there be designated spaces for the purpose, and those spaces must
have certain characteristics (e.g. it must be possible to secure them).

Yet it would be a mistake to suppose that relations of power are relevant
only in the obvious cases, like prisons, in which buildings have clear disciplinary
functions. The notion of disciplinary power belongs to a current of thought, associated particularly with the work of Michel Foucault (cf. Foucault 1980), in which
power is ubiquitous, and its workings are complex. There is no easy division of
people into 'the powerful' and 'the powerless', for the same individual may
occupy a range of social positions, and according to Foucault is 'always in the
position of simultaneously undergoing and exercising . . . power' (1980: 98). The
worker who is subjected to regulation and surveillance on the factory floor may
subject his wife and children to regulation and surveillance at home; incarcerated
criminals or 'lunatics' may threaten and terrify their keepers. In addition, power
engenders resistance. Those who exercise power fear that it may in turn be used
against them, as when exploited workers or slaves rise up in revolt against their
oppressors.

This notion of power has consequences for the way we think about the
connections between power and buildings. If power is ubiquitous, then we cannot
draw simple distinctions based on function between those buildings where power
is exercised and reproduced (e.g. disciplinary institutions like prisons) and those
where it is not (e.g. sites of domesticity and leisure such as homes, shopping malls
and nightclubs). Even where power is neither symbolized in the form of a building nor foregrounded in its function, it is always at issue in the articulation
of *space*. As Markus (1993) has argued, the articulation of space always embeds
relationships of power, insofar as it governs interactions between the users of a

building, prescribes certain routines for them, and allows them to be subjected to particular forms of surveillance and control. There are, then, no 'innocent', power-free spaces.

Of course, this is not to say that the power relations reproduced in buildings must always be oppressive, nor that they must all be so in the same way or to the same degree. Rather it is to argue against the view that power can ever be simply an *absence*; it is to resist the idealization of certain kinds of buildings as outside or beyond the workings of power. As an example of resistance to what was at the time a common-sense idealization, we could cite the feminist Betty Friedan. One of the earliest writers to draw attention to the plight of the economically dependent and socially isolated middle class housewife, Friedan shocked audiences by describing the affluent US suburban home as 'a comfortable concentration camp'. As she and other feminists saw it, the same space men regarded as a refuge was for women a place of (unpaid) work – also, for some women and children, a place of violence and abuse, which was often condoned because of the status of domestic space as 'private'. Undoubtedly, buildings generally considered 'benign', such as homes, hospitals, offices and museums, are *different* from institutions such as prisons, workhouses, military barracks and labour camps; but on closer examination it will be seen that they have their own regimes of power.

Finally in this brief discussion of buildings and power, it should be pointed out that the institutions of architecture and planning are themselves sites for the (re)production of what Foucault called 'power/knowledge' (power exercised not through brute force or pure economic exploitation, but through claims to expertise on various matters). The authoritative knowledge produced by professional architects and planners, and codified in such forms as building and planning regulations or design guides for certain building types, has enormous power to affect people's everyday lives. It affects, for instance, what kind of housing they live in and, for tenants of public housing, how much space is allocated to their household, what they see when they look out of the window, how far they must travel to work or to shop, what kind of education their children receive, and how readily they can construct and maintain social networks. The right to produce and publish texts in which this expert knowledge is contained, to choose the language of those texts, to teach them in educational or professional institutions and, not uncommonly, to back up their prescriptions with legal sanctions, is a significant exercise of power.

In what we have said so far, there is an implication that language, in the form of discourse, plays a role in the exercise of power generally, and also more specifically in the organization of space to construct and reproduce power relations. When architects design buildings – be they prisons, parliament houses, hospitals, offices or residential complexes – they will typically, as we have pointed out already, be working from prescriptive specifications which are embodied in texts. Texts such as briefs and design guides will discuss the functions of the building and the needs and characteristics of those who will use it. Relations of power will seldom be an explicit focus of this discussion, but on closer examination it will often become evident that they are implicitly represented. The *inexplicitness* of many architectural texts on the subject of power makes them potent vehicles for reproducing it, since assumptions which are not made explicit may pass unnoticed and unchallenged. In some cases, as we will see, the explicit message of a text is undercut or contradicted by other messages; what is concealed or mystified in such texts may also be concealed and mystified in the eventual design of the building.

The presence of heterogeneous or contradictory meanings and messages in discourse has been recognized as an important consideration for critical discourse analysis. In considering it, analysts often make reference to a notion borrowed from post-structuralist literary and cultural criticism, the notion of *intertextuality*. Critics such as Julia Kristeva and Roland Barthes pointed out that literary texts typically contain both direct allusions and indirect references to other texts, and consequently elements of those pre-existing texts' meanings are transferred into the new text. This, in fact, was part of the argument for the post-structuralist proposition that criticism cannot be a search for the 'one true meaning' of a text. Texts have multiple meanings, and these cannot be ascribed uniquely to their authors, since authors are always to some extent recycling material composed by other authors (who were also, of course, doing the same thing themselves). For critical discourse analysts it implies that when one seeks to uncover the workings of power in a text, it is not necessary, or helpful, to assume that the person(s) who produced that text had a conscious and deliberate intention to construct or perpetuate particular social relations, and that this will be made transparent in the language of the text. Rather, one is looking for the traces of diverse and perhaps contradictory discourses, in which certain social relations are taken to be 'natural', or presupposed as a matter of common sense. It may also be important to look for gaps and absences: what is *not* said in a text points the analyst to what is taken for granted, so that it does not need to be spelled out. Since interpretation is not just a matter of decoding the words, but of inferring their meaning *in this particular context* by setting them against a much larger store of background knowledge, propositions that are nowhere directly stated may in practice play a key role in the interpretation of a text.

The points just made are relevant to the present discussion for two main reasons. First, because texts about buildings are often intertextual 'hybrids': that is, they do not only contain or draw on ideas and propositions from the fields of architecture, planning, engineering etc., but also ideas drawn from other kinds of expert or professional discourse, on subjects relating to the building's proposed function. The brief for a prison will draw on current understandings of crime and punishment, that for a school will draw on ideas about education and child development, and so on. It is in this kind of discourse – discourse which defines and then makes statements about 'the criminal' or 'the child', for example – that Foucault and his followers locate the workings of disciplinary power in modern societies. So investigating the way power is figured in texts about buildings involves looking for the traces of other, non-architectural texts, in which power is also figured. Second, and following on from this, because the designer's task when interpreting a brief is in a sense the same as the critical discourse analyst's: to infer from the (inevitably limited) information actually given in the text what kinds of social relations or values the client assumes and wishes to see materialized in the building. Because of the 'hybrid' nature of many texts, this task is not always straightforward.

Our purpose in this chapter is not to discuss in detail *which* characteristics of buildings (re)produce power relations (again we refer the reader to Markus 1993 for a detailed discussion) but rather to show how *texts* are formative of those characteristics. We will illustrate, through a series of case studies, how various designers have gone about the task of 'reading' textualized power relations and translating them into spatialized power relations. In many cases, it seems unlikely that the designers were conscious of participating in processes of power/knowledge. They were simply responding to what they took as the overt meaning of the texts in which clients set out their specifications – supplementing the contents of those texts, no doubt, with their own common-sense understandings of social reality. In some cases, however, particularly since the self-conscious adoption of a social mission for architecture by modernists in the early twentieth century, architects have been more reflexive about their role, and have consciously set out to criticize, subvert or resist what they took to be prevailing structures of power. We will also consider the workings of power in some texts and buildings reflecting this more 'critical' orientation.

HIERARCHICAL BUILDINGS AND THEIR TEXTS

As we have pointed out already, some building types are centrally concerned with the exercise of power, and presuppose hierarchical relations – the prison is a good example. Here we will illustrate the movement from text to space in a 'hierarchical' building using the example of the Glasgow Lunatic Asylum designed by William Stark in 1807 (this case is discussed in more detail by Markus 1993).

In a book about the asylum by Stark (1807) there is a short text which represents a basic brief. The origin of this text cannot be attributed with complete certainty, but it was most probably composed by Stark himself, on the basis of consultation with interested parties such as the town council and local medical authorities. It takes the form of a taxonomy of the building's intended inhabitants, i.e. different categories of 'lunatics', and is shown in Figure 2. Though the

Glasgow Lunatic Asylum text is unusual in consisting of nothing but a taxonomy of the intended users, many briefs for institutional buildings with quasi-disciplinary functions (e.g. prisons, clinics, schools) contain such taxonomies; and this is not coincidental, for taxonomy is inherently a hierarchical phenomenon.

Constructing a taxonomy is a matter, not just of identifying relevant distinctions, but also of ranking these distinctions, and the categories produced by them, in relation to one another. Various principles may be used to do this: for instance, one could make a taxonomy of toy building bricks by dividing them first by size, then by shape and then by colour. The decision to rank differences of size as more fundamental than differences of colour, or the decision to put red above yellow in the representation of colour distinctions, would have no social or political implications. When the objects categorized in a taxonomy are human beings, however, both difference and hierarchy tend to be constructed along lines which are related to the power structures of human societies. In the analysis that follows, then, we will be interested in the nature of the hierarchies that are constructed in the taxonomy of asylum-inmates, and also in the extent to which these same hierarchies are expressed spatially in Stark's design for the building. If it is true that taxonomic hierarchy mimics social hierarchy, and if the textual hierarchy is translated directly into spatial organization, then the resulting building will reproduce hierarchical power relations. If we accept, further, that the way space is organized in buildings places constraints on the way people can operate in those buildings, the embedding of hierarchical relations in an institutional building will exert significant influence on the institutional regime.

The inhabitants of the asylum are classified in this taxonomy into two sexes, two classes (this distinction rested on whether or not inmates or their relatives

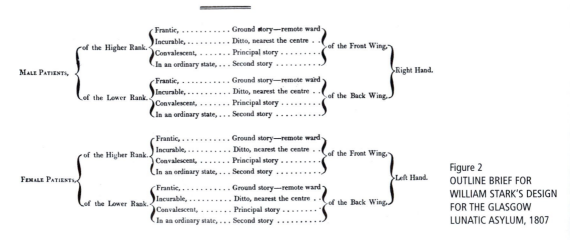

Figure 2
OUTLINE BRIEF FOR
WILLIAM STARK'S DESIGN
FOR THE GLASGOW
LUNATIC ASYLUM, 1807

could afford to pay), and four diagnostic categories. The classification system thus gives rise to sixteen classes defined by a combination of sex, rank and diagnosis. This system is faithfully materialized in the actual building design, which allots each of the sixteen classes a separate space (these are labelled on the plan). At the same time, the allocation of particular spaces to particular taxonomic classes is not random; it follows the hierarchical principles which structure the taxonomy itself.

The sex distinction, men versus women, is located on the left of the text. Since English is read from left to right, the leftmost distinction in a taxonomy will be understood as the primary, most general or most fundamental distinction. This understanding is reproduced in the architectural plan: Stark makes sex difference primary by locating women and men in the two wings of the building. This arrangement totally segregates the male and female inmates, since the entrance space which is the only connection between the two wings is not accessible to inmates at all. Social class is subordinate to sex both in the text and the building; in the latter it becomes a principal organizing space within each wing, where higher and lower ranking inmates are placed respectively at the front and the back.

In the allocation of spaces to different social categories of inmate, the design clearly draws on contemporary common-sense assumptions about social hierarchy, mapping oppositions between relatively favoured and disfavoured *groups* onto parallel oppositions between relatively favoured and disfavoured *spaces*. The ranking of the groups in the taxonomy reflects the same common-sense assumptions; although they are not actually stated in words, they are implicit in the vertical layout of the text, where men are placed above women and inmates of the higher rank above those of the lower rank – vertical placement functioning here as a conventionalized graphic representation of relative importance or status.

Diagnosis is the most 'delicate' categorizing device in this taxonomy: it is represented to the right of the two other distinctions, sex and rank, and it supports a four-way rather than binary contrast. In the plan for the asylum, diagnosis determines whether an inmate is nearer to or further from the building's centre and which floor s/he is housed on. 'Frantic' patients are housed in 'remote' wards; the most tractable are on the upper storeys and the least tractable on the ground floor. Interestingly, this arrangement does not follow the textual layout in the same straightforward way as the allocation of spaces by sex and class. In the text, the 'lowest' diagnostic category graphically is inmates 'in an ordinary state'. Despite their graphic positioning at the bottom, however, these inmates are actually at the top of the diagnostic pecking-order: they are not (or no longer) prototypical 'lunatics', and this is reflected in the space allocated to them. In fact, if position on the vertical axis of the taxonomy is taken to correspond to a group's status, the diagnostic category listing as a whole appears to be upside down. It is evidently arranged according to a different principle, where vertical positioning corresponds to something like 'degree of behavioural disturbance'.

The treatment of diagnostic category in the design makes clear that matters are not quite so simple as our earlier discussion suggested; taxonomic hierarchies in this case do not uniformly mimic social ones. This reflects the fact that there is more than one 'discourse' in play in the taxonomy of lunatics. On the one hand there is a 'social' discourse concerned with relations of gender and class, while on the other there is a 'medical' discourse concerned with the definition and management of mental illness, in which social status is less relevant than the degree of mental disorder an inmate exhibits. The whole taxonomy follows the principle that the vertical positioning of items is meaningful rather than simply arbitrary, but the actual meaning is different depending whether the classification represented is a 'social' or a 'medical' one. It is evident that Stark differentiated between social and medical hierarchies when he mapped the taxonomic categories onto spatial locations in the plan of the building. He was not just mechanically decoding the text according to a single fixed rule ('categories of inmate located higher in the taxonomy have more status than those located below them and should be allocated more favoured spaces'). Rather he was bringing to bear on the text knowledge which is not explicitly represented in the text – indeed, one might argue that it is actually obscured by the layout – namely that it makes sense both practically and symbolically to place the most disturbed inmates furthest from the interface between the asylum and the outside world. Practically, such an arrangement reduces the risk of 'frantic' lunatics escaping or being encountered unexpectedly by visitors who might find their behaviour threatening. Symbolically, it represents the distance between the seriously disturbed inmate and the normal, sane world from which s/he has sought 'asylum' (or from another perspective, been banished).

The point here is that architectural texts do not necessarily contain all the information which is necessary to interpret them, and on that basis to construct sensible building designs from them. We emphasize this point because in some treatments of the efficacy of discourse and the status of this or that reality as a 'discursive construct', the impression is given that language, or text or discourse, has the power in and of itself to *determine* extra-textual reality. This is, in our view, an oversimplified and finally untenable claim. The effects of texts in shaping reality do not occur directly (texts do not themselves have agency) but through the activities of readers making sense of texts and then acting on the sense they have made. This adds an additional layer of complexity, since the 'making sense' process involves more than just decoding what is explicitly said or written. It also involves mobilizing relevant background knowledge, e.g. about the class and gender relations of a given time and place or the management of mental illness, and using this knowledge to infer propositions that are nowhere actually stated in the text.

Texts may present quite complex problems of interpretation, leading to variability in the meaning readers make from them. We chose to begin with the Glasgow Lunatic Asylum because the taxonomy of inmates is a sparse and relatively straightforward text, and its relationship to the design for the asylum is also fairly straightforward. The text and the design in this case were probably produced by the same person, but even if they had not been, the text would have left the reader/designer with few puzzles to solve. To the extent this hypothetical reader had to infer messages about hierarchical power relations which were not directly contained in the text (for instance, concerning the 'naturalness' of gender and class hierarchies), these would have been widely shared and taken for granted as obvious. Arguably, however, this (relative) simplicity is not the typical case – particularly today, when briefs and other architectural texts have become far lengthier, more internally heterogeneous and complex documents. Frequently such texts require their architect-readers to grapple with internal contradictions, and to solve in their designs the puzzles those contradictions generate. Our next example is a case in point.

TEXTUAL CONTRADICTIONS: THE SCOTTISH PARLIAMENT BUILDING

As a consequence of the devolution of certain powers from the UK government based in London to Scotland, Wales and eventually Northern Ireland, a separate Scottish Parliament was set up in 1997, and this created a need for a building to accommodate it. Various possibilities were discussed, but eventually it was decided to commission a new building on a site in Edinburgh, selecting the designer by competition. This decision inaugurated an outpouring of public discourse on the subject of the new Parliament building, one major theme of which – unsurprisingly – was the need for the building to enable and symbolize the flowering of democratic self-government in Scotland. 'The architecture of democracy' was a recurring phrase, with all kinds of commentators expressing the hope that the building would be designed to affirm an 'openness' and 'transparency' greater than anything that had been achieved in the Palace of Westminster.

This theme also surfaced in the brief produced by the Scottish Office (the department which had administered Scotland on behalf of the UK government, and which remains in existence though some of its former powers have now passed to the new Parliament and Executive). However, the brief as a text contains a fundamental contradiction. Periodic references to openness, transparency and accessibility are both overwhelmed and undercut by a pervasive concern with *security*, which is an explicit or implicit focus of about half the sections in the document. 'Control of the various users must be provided. The interaction of Press and Public with MSPs [Members of the Scottish Parliament] is controlled by the discreet planning of the building and by security arrangements.' According to the specifications contained in the document, the public and MSPs must have separate entrances and car parks, occupy different floors and take separate routes through the building (public access to many parts of which will be barred). MSPs meeting their constituents must approach the spaces designated for that purpose 'without going through the public areas'. In addition the brief instructs designers to provide for extensive surveillance in the form of CCTV (covert as well as overt), intruder detection systems, perimeter intruder system, voice alarm system, door access control system, entry/exit barrier control system, under car screening (smell and visual), X-ray machinery, and security pass production system.

What we see in the Scottish Parliament brief is a clash between two discourses on power. One is a political/ideological discourse, whose keywords are *democracy, transparency*, *openness* and *accessibility* (of the people's representatives to the people). Power in this discourse is a benign and positive thing, which the Scottish people have wrested from the remote institutions of the English-dominated state, and which they will now exercise through their own elected representatives. There is no division between the people and their political institutions; this is what devolution is supposed to have accomplished. The other discourse, in stark contrast, is based on a hierarchical and statist idea of power as something exercised by the state *over* the people. The people are implicitly represented as a threat, so that their access to their representatives must be strictly monitored and controlled. There are some signs in the text that the Scottish Office has recognized the contradiction between democracy and control: throughout the brief, the noun 'security' is regularly modified by the adjectives 'discreet' and 'unobtrusive'. This suggests that the building should be made to *appear* democratic by *concealing* the mechanisms of control.

In Chapter 7, which deals with the relationship between language and images in texts about buildings, we discuss in more detail how the architects whose designs were shortlisted in the competition responded to the challenges and contradictions of the brief. Here we will make some more general observations on how architects might interpret texts in which there is a clash of discourses, and what they might go on to do with the interpretations they produce.

Communication works by inference, and interpretation begins from the assumption that what is said or written is said or written for a reason: however redundant, enigmatic, illogical or contradictory it appears on the surface, an attempt will be made to infer the reasoning behind it. Faced with a noticeable contradiction in a text, a competent reader will ask: 'what is the purpose of presenting me with this contradiction?' In this case, the most likely inference is that the contradiction is there to alert designers to a problem which their design is meant to solve: the problem of designing a building whose function is to house institutions of democratic governance, but which also requires stringent security measures controlling access and use.

Having identified the problem posed by the text, how might the architect try to solve it? One solution (and we will see that designers in this instance made use of it) is to set up a sort of division of labour between the formal aspects of the building and its spatial organization. In the Scottish Parliament case, for example, many of the control mechanisms which are specified in the brief require space to be organized in certain ways (the provision of separate routes through the building for MSPs and members of the public, say, is a spatial issue). This leaves form as a vehicle for communicating democratic values. An architect might propose to build a glass debating chamber as a sign of 'transparency', or to make the chamber circular to signify egalitarianism or a commitment to non-adversarial politics. The underlying contradiction is not resolved by this strategy, but one discourse – the one embodying the more positive, 'democratic' reading of power – is made visually dominant, while the 'control' discourse is submerged, made 'unobtrusive'.

In the text, the control discourse is not unobtrusive: on the contrary, the proportion of the text devoted to the subjects of security and surveillance is greater than that devoted to 'the architecture of democracy'. The reader can hardly help but be struck by the importance accorded to control. But the Scottish Office can rely on architects not to conclude from this that their designs should resemble fortresses or prisons, emphasizing control visually and ignoring democracy. It does expect the reader to grasp the importance of control, which is explicitly spelled out in the detailed lists of security measures and surveillance devices. But it implicitly expects other contextually relevant knowledge to be brought to bear on the text – for instance, that in the context of a parliament building, as opposed to, say, a military installation, democracy is a positive value whereas control is a negative one. In our later discussion of the shortlisted competition entries (Chapter 7), we will demonstrate that this message was understood by the entrants, and recycled in the texts and images they produced for public exhibition.

This discussion of the Scottish Parliament brief is intended to exemplify the general point that 'contradictory' texts drawing on conflicting or incommensurable discourses of power are not simply impossible to make sense of; rather they cue the reader to make a particular kind of sense from them. They both define what an architect will understand as the design problem and point the way to a particular solution. The solution is to represent one set of power relations in the spatial structure of the building and another in its formal details. The first set will have a stronger influence on how the building works spatially and socially, the second will have a stronger influence on how it is perceived visually. The architect will have more freedom with respect to the second than with respect to the first – especially in competitions, which, as Ellen Dunham-Jones has argued (1997: 21, n. 8), encourage the idea that what will be judged is an array of different formal solutions to the same pre-defined problem. Challenging the definition of the problem itself is not on the agenda – at least, not if you want to win the commission.

Here we might recall that in discourse analysis, questions are considered more powerful moves than answers, because the question always constrains the answer. Many kinds of institutional discourse (e.g. in courtrooms, classrooms and clinics) are characterized by an unequal distribution of questions – it is the more powerful party who asks more of them (in the courtroom, witnesses and defendants are actually forbidden to ask questions except for clarification). In the domain of architecture, the 'question' is in the text(s) that preceded a building; the building is an 'answer' to that question. But since many people use buildings, whereas few read architectural briefs, we are usually in the position of judging the answer without really knowing what the question was. This, too, may obscure the power relations which are relevant to the creation of a building.

Alternatively, the question may be defined textually in such a way as to mystify the power relations that are at stake in a particular building. In the next section we discuss a case of this kind, where discourse on architecture and design has acquired a particular significance in debates about the nature and workings of the 'new' (post-Fordist, globalized, hi-tech and service-oriented) capitalism. We will suggest that architectural discourse tends to presuppose as 'real' the new capitalism's own representations of itself as more enlightened and egalitarian than previous regimes. The producers of architectural texts – and of buildings which are shaped by those texts – thus become implicated in reproducing and legitimating new forms of power.

TEXTUAL SILENCES: 'THE HAPPIEST WORKPLACE IN BRITAIN'?

The texts we consider in this section pertain to the design of a particular kind of workspace, the 'call centre'. We will focus particularly on texts about one call centre building in Swindon (an industrial town in the west of England) designed by Richard Hywel Evans for Cellular Operations, a telecommunications company specializing in mobile phones. This building, nicknamed 'the glass torpedo', was completed in January 2000 and featured in *The Architects' Journal* (hereafter *AJ*) in March of the same year. (This and other texts relating to the building were kindly made available to us by the designer, whom we thank.)

The term *call centre* denotes a new kind of workplace which has come into being as a result of new communication technologies. Advances in telecommunications have enabled companies to locate sales and customer service functions at a central point which may be geographically remote from the customers themselves. Given access to a central computer database and a sufficient quantity of telephone lines, a business may deal with customers located anywhere in a sizeable piece of territory (e.g. a major urban centre and its surrounding suburbs, a province, a collection of neighbouring states, an entire small nation) from a single building located somewhere quite different – possibly even in a foreign country.[1] The customer calls the centre (at a special cheap rate) to make transactions, place orders, etc.; the call centre operator, who is equipped with a telephone headset and a computer terminal, ascertains the customer's needs by talking to her, calls up her details from a database and makes the appropriate adjustments. Services like banking and insurance, mail order retailing, travel reservations, telephone directory assistance and reporting equipment faults are now frequently provided from call centres. These are, in the jargon, 'in-bound' centres, where customers initiate contact and workers answer their calls. There are also, however, 'out-bound' centres, where the workers make (usually unsolicited) calls for the purpose of selling goods and services.

Call centres are a rapidly expanding sector of the new service economy, and in Britain it is estimated that by 2000 they employed about a quarter of a million people. Companies are increasingly choosing to shift sales and service provision to call centres largely because of the savings this can produce: there is no need to duplicate the same functions (and the associated labour and equipment costs) in every town or region. In addition, since customers do not require physical access to call centres, they can be placed in the most economical rather than the most accessible locations – on out-of-town sites rather than in expensive city centre property, for instance, and in regions where costs, including wages, are low. Nor is it necessary to spend money on making call centres attractive and welcoming to customers who cannot actually see them.

These considerations have influenced the design of call centre buildings, many of which, at least in the early period of the sector's development, were spartan sheds resembling factories or warehouses. Over time, however, the design (or non-design) of call centres has come to be seen as a significant problem. This is because the call centre industry has suffered throughout its short history from extremely high rates of staff turnover. Customers may not be affected by the dreary surroundings of the average centre, but it has been concluded that those surroundings do affect employees. The need for better workplace design to enhance recruitment and retention has become a recurring theme in discourse on call centres, both in specialist 'trade' literature and in publications addressed to a broader general audience, such as newspapers.

The UK media have, in fact, taken a surprisingly strong interest in the rapidly developing call centre industry over the last few years: in public debates that industry seems to function as a symbol of the 'new' capitalism more generally. The tone of media coverage has often been critical, with call centres portrayed as alienating and oppressive institutions. Predictably, management spokespeople who are approached by journalists for quotable comments have developed a response aimed at deflecting this kind of critique. It involves acknowledging that call centres have had problems in the past, and hinting more or less delicately that some of the speaker's competitors still have problems, while stressing that the speaker's own organization has spared no effort to make its call centres more humane and enlightened places. The specific issue of call centre *design* takes on particular significance here: the improved layout and appearance of the physical space of the call centre becomes the outward and visible sign of a more general, inward and spiritual enlightenment.

A good example of design being invoked for this rhetorical purpose is found in a feature that appeared in the *Independent on Sunday* in 1998 (17 May: 9). A call centre operations manager in Falkirk, central Scotland, is quoted saying that 'Many [call centres] still involve rows of people in low ceiling environments reciting the same words day in and day out. I was adamant . . . that this would not be our approach.' The feature also quotes a designer from BDG McColl, the architectural practice responsible for the Falkirk centre. 'The challenge', she explains, 'was to create an unfactory-like atmosphere.' The reporter continues by describing this designer's response to the challenge: 'Unlike the usual serried ranks of operators, the Falkirk teams sit in groups. The most striking innovation is the "sensorama", a passageway through which all call-handlers pass daily to the accompaniment of bright sunny yellow lighting.' The centre handles calls for a travel agent selling package holidays, and has been provided with appropriate décor: 'Bright murals of exotic locations cover the walls. The ceilings are painted an exotic Mediterranean blue, and a running stream wanders through the middle.'

The text constructs a set of oppositions between past bad practice and present good practice, which could be represented like this (the phrases below are direct quotations):

Old call centre (bad)	**New call centre (good)**
Rows of people	Unfactory-like atmosphere
The usual serried ranks of operators	Teams sit in groups
Low ceiling environments	Ceilings are painted an exotic Mediterranean blue
Warehouse on the dingy outskirts	Bright murals of exotic locations
	Bright sunny yellow lighting

These contrasts provide the material for a narrative of 'enlightenment' in which employers have recognized that using design to create a more attractive working environment is not only humane, but also makes good business sense. (That humanity and profitability go together rather than conflicting is one of the key axioms of new capitalism rhetoric in general, as a number of commentators have noted (cf. Rose 1990: 56).)

A similar narrative structures texts about the 'glass torpedo'. A short summary of the 'Design Brief' made available to us by the architect sets out the problem thus:

> In one of the UK's fastest-growing towns with unemployment currently running at 2%
> Cellular Operations decided to invest in design to create a landmark building with

excellent working conditions, providing optimal temperatures and natural light as part of their drive to recruit and keep valuable Staff.

The implication here is that the employer, Cellular Operations, has been driven by economic circumstances (such as low unemployment in the area) to treat staff as a valuable resource and invest in their satisfaction by providing 'excellent working conditions'. A certain kind of relationship is presupposed between capitalists/managers and workers/employees, in line with the general new capitalist axiom that in the new economy of service and knowledge, people are a company's most important asset. Rather than being subordinate, oppressed and downtrodden, therefore, workers are seen as equal partners in the success of a business, and by implication moreover as individual free agents who, in the context of Britain's current economic growth and near-full employment, have considerable power over their employers. If they do not like their conditions of employment, they can simply take their valuable knowledge and skills elsewhere.

In the *AJ* feature on the building, once again the 'enlightened' strategy of Cellular Operations in recognizing employees' needs and their value to the company is contrasted with the less enlightened practice of the past. 'The reputation of such "offices" [i.e. call centres] is very poor. They have tended to be stuck on cheap out-of-town sites, bearing an uncanny resemblance to the kind of shed that sells DIY ['do it yourself', i.e. home improvement] products. They also have a very high turnover of staff who, on average, stay for only six months in a job often associated with a grim working environment' (*AJ* 2000: 35). Here the implication of causality (staff turnover is high *because* the working environment is grim) is even stronger than in the *Independent* feature. More narrowly focused than the newspaper on design issues, *AJ* does not mention any other possible reasons for high staff turnover, whereas the *Independent* also mentions low pay (basic annual salaries for operators run at around £10,000, about $15,000), and having to perform extremely repetitive tasks ('reciting the same words day in and day out') under pressure from demanding productivity targets.

In the design of the Cellular Operations building, various approaches have been taken to the problem of the typical call centre's grim 'working environment'. Some solutions are technical: attention has been given to the control of lighting, temperature and the ergonomic properties of workstations. Some are organizational: a 'breakout space' has been provided for workers to take the regular breaks to which, as VDU operators, they are entitled under health and safety regulations, and refreshments are dispensed from a roving trolley. However, the strategy to which most prominence is given in the text is described in the architect's summary of the 'Design Solution': 'The interior of the building is choreographed as a series of visual entertainments from the coach-built reception desk to the organic pre-cast stairs, themed WCs and lift-linked water feature.' The *AJ* feature makes much of the staircase, 'a curious cast-concrete spine that has the quality of a prehistoric skeleton . . . the glass treads, which are underlit, provide the possibility of an interesting ascent' (p. 37), and even more of the lavatories, about which the architect is quoted as explaining that 'each one is different so you can decide which one you want to visit'. Three of the cubicles are the subject of colour photographs – one clad in blue mosaic, one detailed in timber and one in stainless steel with coloured telephone handsets embedded in a Perspex toilet lid (Figure 3).

On the 'visual entertainment' approach overall, *AJ* comments:

> It is the sense in which the architecture is playful that accounts for its success . . . the premise was to create an environment that made the workforce feel good. The references to popular culture, to the kinds of bars, nightclubs and shops that many of the young workers visit, reinforces the belief that a building can be more than just a place to work . . . At Cellular Operations, creating a context and landscape that juxtaposed the ordinary working experience with the extraordinary experience of the building has resulted in a synthesis of function and form.

The last sentence quoted above is particularly interesting. Its syntax and vocabulary suggest a progression from cause to effect:

Cause: creating a context and landscape that juxtaposed the ordinary working experience with the extraordinary experience of the building
Effect: has resulted in a synthesis of function and form

Yet on inspection the logic is obscure: the effect does not obviously follow from the cause. Indeed, one might argue that the juxtaposition referred to in the first clause has precisely the *opposite* effect from the one proposed in the second clause – it produces not a *synthesis* between function and form, but a significant *disjunction* between the two. Functionally the building is a place of work, or production; formally, however, it borrows features from the architecture of spaces dedicated to consumption, leisure or 'play'. The *AJ* notes that Richard Hywel Evans's practice has designed a number of spaces of this kind, such as juice bars and sportswear shops, and that the design of the glass torpedo has drawn on that experience. It is a workspace that *looks*, at least in some respects, like a play space, and this is intended to make the workforce 'feel good', to persuade them that Cellular Operations is indeed 'more than just a place to work'. According to the architect's own textual material, the building has had the intended effect: staff turnover has fallen to around half the national average for call centres, and the building has been 'celebrated in National Press and TV – "the happiest workplace in Britain" '.

We do not wish to deny the merits of the Cellular Operations HQ building, which is undoubtedly a superior example of call centre design (particularly in the attention paid to non-superficial issues like lighting and ergonomics, where other companies are content to paint the ceiling blue). We do wish to point out, however, that there are some significant gaps and silences in the texts which shape our perception of the building as an unqualified success; and we also want to

suggest that one effect of the gaps and silences is to obscure and mystify the power relations that are operative in call centres.

The *AJ* feature describes Cellular Operations as a context in which the 'ordinary working experience [of call centre operators]' and 'the extraordinary experience of the building' are juxtaposed to create some kind of synthesis. But they are not synthesized in the text itself, for whereas the 'extraordinary' characteristics of the building are described in detail, almost nothing is said about the 'ordinary working experience' of its users. The actual work performed by operators is strikingly absent from both text and images. The first, full-page illustration shows the 'breakout area', and since this is located adjacent to the working area, we also see some workstations at the right-hand side of the frame. But only one of them has anyone sitting at it, and since he wears no headset, he is obviously not engaged in handling calls. Three other colour illustrations feature exterior shots of the building taken from varying distances and angles, in daylight and in darkness; a further four show the architect's 'visual entertainments' – the cast concrete stair and three of the lavatories. It could not be deduced merely from the illustrations that we are looking, specifically, at a call centre, and only one of the illustrations, the first one showing the 'breakout area', even suggests we are looking at a workspace – the external shots and photos of the lavatories could as easily be showing something like a new multiplex cinema, from the point of view of filmgoers rather than staff. In the breakout area shot, as noted already, the employees are with one exception shown at leisure (talking and drinking coffee), not at work.

Of course these illustrations are not presented or processed in isolation from the text; the meaning of the feature depends on both of them, in interaction. The text does make clear that the building is a call centre, but it gives few details of what goes on there (it alludes in passing to the presence of workstations and of VDUs, and to the fact that the building is used on a 24-hour cycle). Though the *AJ*, as a professional journal, has much to say about lighting, temperature control and other technical issues, it makes no mention of the hi-tech telecommunications infrastructure which makes the work of a call centre possible – and which certainly has implications for the design of call centre buildings.

These are not just random silences. They reflect the purpose of the text, which is to tell a particular story about call centres – the narrative of enlightenment mentioned before, in which employers who initially sought only to save money by cramming hundreds of operators into dingy sheds have now seen the error of their ways. By employing skilled designers they have transformed at least one call centre into the nation's 'happiest workplace'. The issues on which the texts are silent (the nature of the work and the technology that supports it) are precisely those which hint at a different story – one in which call centre workers are not powerful free spirits and all their problems cannot be solved by a brighter or more 'playful' working environment.

Call centres have attracted critical attention from both journalists and social scientists, because, as we mentioned above, they can be seen as particularly advanced exemplars of the disciplinary practices of the new capitalism. It is no coincidence that the Falkirk centre discussed by the *Independent on Sunday* specifically asked a designer to create an 'unfactory-like atmosphere', because in truth a call centre is in many ways more like a factory than like the office it superficially resembles. The work is clerical, involving the manipulation of words and symbols rather than physical objects, but it is organized on production-line principles of the kind associated with the early twentieth century time-and-motion expert Frederick Taylor, or with the contemporary fast food industry as described by sociologist George Ritzer (1996). Tasks are broken down into components and workers instructed in the 'correct' performance of each (in the call centre context this often means they are given scripts for common transactions). There are time targets for each task (e.g. four minutes to process a travel reservation, 32 seconds to deal with a 'standard' directory assistance call), and if the targets are not met, the operator or team of operators may lose bonus payments. In most centres today, an 'automatic call distribution' (ACD) system is used to ensure that calls are immediately routed to the first operator free to take them; at the same time there are always more lines for incoming calls than operators on duty. The result is that operators often have to take calls continuously: as on an assembly line, the rhythm of work is dictated by machines. Most studies have found that the main cause of disaffection cited by call centre employees is the stress and boredom engendered by the relentless pace of the work combined with its extremely repetitive character.[2]

The other major source of disaffection with call centres is the degree of surveillance their operators are subjected to. Telephone systems are set up so calls can be monitored by supervisors without the operator knowing; many centres also record calls for later appraisal, and some employ 'mystery callers' to pose as genuine customers and then report back on the operator. As well as being able to listen in to calls, supervisors can access computer-generated performance statistics on individual operators and teams of operators: how many calls they have taken, what the average duration of their calls has been, when and for how long they have been away from their workstations during a shift. (This might prompt a sceptical view of the themed WCs at Cellular Operations – 'each one different so you can decide which one you want to visit'. While we concede we have no specific information about the work regime at this particular call centre, some centres require employees who need to visit a WC to key in a special code before they go, so that supervisors know where they are and can assess whether their absence is unreasonably long. In such centres, employees would be wise to visit whichever cubicle is nearest, and not linger too long over its visual entertainments.)

Because of the level of surveillance in call centres, facilitated by the same technology that makes the 'communication factory' itself possible, researchers have dubbed the typical call centre a 'virtual panopticon' (Sewell and Wilkinson 1992: 283). Operators must conduct themselves on the assumption that they are under continuous surveillance; supervisors could be listening in at any moment, any caller could be a 'mystery caller', and the computer which logs performance statistics is never inactive or distracted from its task. But the virtual panopticon, unlike its non-virtual original, has no all-seeing eye located at a single, central point. Information on workers' behaviour and performance is gathered instead by hi-tech means which do not require any particular spatial organization. There is, indeed, no need for workers in a call centre to be arranged in 'the usual serried ranks' – technology frees designers to get rid of the visible spatial signifiers of regimentation and surveillance, while at the same time it enables managers to maintain or intensify control over employees. For the *AJ* to comment on this, however, would pose problems for its preferred narrative, which represents modifications in call centre design as concessions made by enlightened managers to their 'valuable staff'.

The *AJ*'s feature on the Cellular Operations call centre was written after the completion of the building: its purpose is not to shape the design itself, but to influence the way it will be perceived by a readership of professional architects. In soliciting readers' admiration for the 'glass torpedo' as an outstanding example of contemporary workspace design, the *AJ* uncritically retells the 'enlightenment' story and avoids posing more critical questions about the way power works in call centres, or more generally, about the relation between power and workspace design. It does not ask whether the staff turnover problem might go beyond dissatisfaction with the 'grimness' of the prototypical call centre environment, and it does not discuss or depict those aspects of call centre regimes (e.g. hi-tech surveillance) which might prompt readers to ask that question themselves. There is, of course, a fairly simple explanation for this: as a professional journal for architects, the *AJ*'s brief is to deal with building design, and not to digress into the sociology of work or the power structures of the new capitalism. Arguably, though, in defining its scope so narrowly, and considering workplace power relations in such superficial terms (as a matter of whether employees 'feel good'), the *AJ* ends up – no doubt without consciously intending to – allying its own point of view with that of the new capitalist/managerial class.

The *AJ* might object that the building under discussion is genuinely popular with those who work in it, and that this is reflected in reduced rates of staff turnover. We do not dispute that: it is hardly surprising if many or most workers would prefer to work in a 'playful' and visually entertaining environment like the 'glass torpedo' rather than sitting in rows in some anonymous, low-ceilinged, factory-like shed. It is not surprising either that Cellular Operations should represent its investment in a new architect-designed building as a sign of its enlightened commitment to the wellbeing of its workforce. Nevertheless, asymmetrical power relations remain fundamental to the regime of the

call centre. As commentators have noted, however, the new capitalism is practised in using language to accentuate the positive, to soften or conceal the
workings of power. A rhetoric of enlightenment, of managerial approaches based
on valuing and empowering workers, of work itself as (like consumption) a
domain of individual creativity and self-expression, very often coexists with disciplinary practices, mechanical routines and technologies of control and surveillance
which bear comparison with the most oppressive industrial regimes of the nineteenth century. As the sociologist Richard Sennett summarizes (1998: 10): 'the
new order substitutes new controls rather than simply abolishing the rules of
the past – but these new controls are also hard to understand. The new capitalism is an often illegible regime of power.' The architectural text we have
analysed here belongs rhetorically to that regime, and plays a part in maintaining
its 'illegibility'.

CONTESTING POWER

We noted at the beginning of this chapter that some architectural texts (and
indeed some buildings) are produced with the overt and conscious goal of
contesting prevailing assumptions about power. There is a strand of discourse –
especially prominent in the twentieth century but not confined to it – which
represents architecture as one means for intervening in social relations and
processes. A 'better' built environment, according to this discourse, has the
power to change the behaviour of those who inhabit it, and so produce a 'better'
society. (This of course is also the assumption behind 'enlightened' workspace
design, as in the case we have just discussed; in that case, however, there is no
grand social/political programme: 'better' is defined in terms of capitalist goals
such as increased productivity and staff retention.)

The most ancient and arguably the 'purest' discourse genre in which the
project of contesting power architecturally is pursued is that of utopian writing.
People who founded utopian settlements (like the socialist Robert Owen and his
followers in New Lanark, Scotland, and then New Harmony, Indiana), as well
as those who wrote about imaginary utopias, often embodied their sociopolitical ideals in texts describing (among other things) the ideal arrangement of the
spaces used by the utopian community. In some cases these texts became
the basis for actual buildings.

In the introduction to this chapter we made the crucial point that there
are no 'power-free' spaces. It follows that utopian texts and building designs do
not *eliminate* power relations: rather they inscribe those relations differently, in
accordance with political ideals that diverge from current mainstream common
sense. Of course, not all utopias are based on egalitarian ideals: Plato's *Republic*,
for example, is a description of an ultra-rational city-state, but not, in the modern
sense, an egalitarian one. But even utopian designs which do aim to eliminate

or reduce social inequality necessarily prescribe certain social roles and ways of life. We say 'necessarily' because prescription of this kind is an inevitable concomitant of any kind of rational spatial planning: to organize space, particularly on a large scale, it is necessary to make assumptions about its users and its uses. In utopian plans, which are informed by their authors' commitment to a consistent set of values, these assumptions may result in a higher degree of constraint than would be imposed by non-utopian planning.

In a paper on feminist utopias, for example, Markus (1999), following Dolores Hayden (1976) describes a plan by Alice Constance Austin for a radical socialist feminist city of 10,000 inhabitants, Llano del Rio (1916). One goal of this utopia was to eliminate domestic drudgery, which Austin considered an obstacle to gender equality since it entailed 'the maiming or fatal, spiritual or intellectual oppression . . . [of] each feminine personality'. Accordingly the houses of the city, organized around courtyards and constructed using the latest technology, had no kitchens. However one judges it politically, this design decision obviously constitutes a prescriptive intervention in family life: its effect is not to put absolute freedom in place of constraint, but to replace one constraint with another. The absence of a kitchen in a house favours certain social structures and routines – for instance, public or communal meals – just as the presence of a kitchen favours others – for instance, the traditional division of labour whereby food is prepared for a single household by women family members and/or domestic servants. The two arrangements are different, and one is more 'radical' in the sense of breaking with established tradition, but they are both underpinned by particular (and disputable) assumptions about social and power (especially gender) relations.

As Markus notes, a key question that arises in relation to utopian designs such as Austin's is whether, in their efforts to undermine or subvert conventional power relations, they impose alternative social arrangements in a way that can itself be seen as authoritarian and 'totalizing', unresponsive to variation in community members' own habits, expectations and desires. The problem of totalization becomes especially acute when the utopian impulse is applied not to an imaginary city like Llano del Rio or a small settlement for a pre-existing utopian community, like the Owenites' New Lanark, but to a public project whose intended beneficiaries are ordinary citizens – often, indeed, those citizens (like tenants of public housing and residents of state institutions) who have least personal control over their environment. In the following section we examine the textual representation of one such project, a public housing scheme in Gifu, Japan, whose architect used the commission to make a feminist intervention in the conventional power relations of the Japanese family. Our aim in the analysis is not directly to evaluate the feminist claims of the building, but rather to explore some characteristics of the discourse in which *critics* evaluate those claims. On what grounds is a building represented as 'radical' or 'subversive'?

What assumptions about power and politics inform critical discussions about the potential of architecture to make a difference?

'WASHBASINS IN THE SUN'

In 1994 the Prefecture of Gifu City approached Arata Isozaki to co-ordinate the development of a new public housing project. Isozaki commissioned four women architects, each of whom designed one block of flats intended to be occupied by low-income families. In an essay on one of these, the block designed by Kazuyo Sejima, Akira Suzuki (1999) proposes that Sejima has deliberately engaged in 'reversed planning by gender', by which Suzuki means that her design is a feminist intervention in the power relations of the traditional family. The key to this, according to Suzuki, is the placement of the washbasin: 'It is installed at the south side of the flat, facing a large front window. You wash your face, apply your make-up and dress while facing this large opening' (Suzuki 1999: 138). Although at this point Suzuki has not yet explicitly said so, it is clear from his description of what goes on at the washbasin, which includes the clause '[you] apply your make-up', that the implied user of the washbasin is a female rather than male family member. He goes on (1999: 139–40):

> The washbasin in the sun is stunning. Standing in front of it feels like you are standing in front of the whole world. In reality, there is another block opposite, which means the user is, in effect, facing society. Washing your face used to be done behind closed doors. This activity is now on full view and brought to public attention. Thus lies the importance of Sejima's strategy: the housing block has been designed around the activities of the 'daughter', who is treated, through the plan, as the principal person in the family.

Although the essay quotes no words spoken or written by Kazuyo Sejima herself, it is implied that she has drawn on an explicit theory of gender relations within the institution of the (Japanese) family, and that she has sought deliberately to subvert the hierarchical gender relations identified by that theory. Her subversiveness is expressed in a decision to foreground the family member who would traditionally be understood as least important or powerful, the 'daughter' who is made subordinate both by her gender and by her generation.

This strategy does indeed show the influence of feminist discourse about the family, but the point we would want to make here is that feminist discourse is not a single homogeneous set of ideas or statements. The kind of feminist discourse endorsed in the Gifu project, and in Suzuki's account of it, is one that permits what is perceived as problematic, the subordinate positioning of women (especially daughters) in families, to be addressed architecturally on a purely symbolic level. The solution of moving the washbasin from its 'normal' location in a disfavoured (small, closed, private, hidden, dark) space to a location where it becomes public, highly visible and salient implies a certain definition of the problem being solved. Apparently that problem is not the association between women and washing in itself,[3] but the low visibility and value accorded in patriarchal societies to this and other 'womanly' activities, which is routinely expressed in the usual organization of both public and private domestic space. The proposed solution, 'the washbasin in the sun', is a symbolic counter-move affirming the centrality of women's activities: it does not question the underlying division of activities into 'women's' and 'men's' (which in this case is a symbolic division anyway, since presumably both sexes wash and dress).

In fact, Suzuki stresses that the project eschewed the kind of radicalism (exemplified in a lot of modern(ist) architecture and planning, as well as in much earlier utopian schemes) that would raise suspicions of authoritarian social engineering – of trying to change people's behaviour by changing their environment. 'Sejima's revolutionary plan does not try to rule or force its residents to change their lifestyle' (Suzuki 1999: 140). In thus representing what Sejima has done, though, Suzuki seems entirely to overlook one respect in which her symbolic solution to the problem of gender inequality *does* in fact force residents to change their lifestyle – it compels them to wash 'standing in front of the whole world'.

We do not know, because the issue is not raised even once in Suzuki's discussion, what the working class residents of the block, and especially the women whose activities it symbolically celebrates, think of an arrangement which places the washbasin in front of a large window. But there are obvious criticisms of that arrangement which other kinds of feminist discourse would be likely to emphasize. One would be that it potentially exposes women engaged in washing themselves to the unwelcome voyeuristic attentions of men outside the building. Another would be that feminism as a practice (as opposed to a type of avant-garde theory) demands that architects should ascertain and then address the concerns and preferences of the *real* women who use their buildings (as opposed to designing for abstract theoretical constructs like 'the daughter'). Perhaps women who were prospective residents of the Gifu project would have been enthusiastic about 'washbasins in the sun'; very likely they would have had a view on the ideal placement of washbasins, even if it did not coincide with the designer's. But since Suzuki does not tell us whether anyone consulted these women, we gather that he considers their opinions irrelevant to any assessment of the feminist credentials of Sejima's design.

Both Suzuki's text about Gifu and the discourse on gender which informed the design itself arguably exemplify what the critic Tania Modleski (1991) dubbed 'feminism without women' – that is, 'feminism' becomes a highly abstract discourse on gender appealing (and indeed, intelligible) mainly to a theoretically sophisticated avant-garde. Meanwhile its ostensible subjects, actual, historical and socially situated women, are hardly even referred to by the producers of the discourse, let alone given a role in articulating their own interests. Modleski's critique of 'feminism without women' is a critique of certain tendencies within postmodernism, which she sees as promoting theoretical complexity at the expense of practical politics. Sejima's washbasins in the sun might well be seen as manifesting the same tendencies in the sphere of building design. As a theoretical gesture, the message of the washbasins is 'women are important', but as a practical intervention in women's domestic lives, they accomplish something – bringing the act of washing to public attention – which, so far as one can tell, has never been articulated as a political goal by anyone.

TEXTUAL AUTHORITY: SUBJECTS AND OBJECTS

The question we have just raised could be glossed, crudely, as 'do women in Gifu really want to wash in front of the world?' Similar questions could be asked about our other textual examples. If asked about their design priorities, would call centre workers mention visually entertaining toilets? Might the Scottish public, on mature reflection, prefer its parliament building a little more accessible and a little less secure? Such questions might seem to take us beyond the scope of a discussion about buildings, language and power, but in fact they point to an important, and often neglected, aspect of the workings of power in discourse. In critical discourse analysis it is always worth asking the question: 'who may speak to whom, about whom, and on behalf of whom?'

Discourse on architecture, like other kinds of expert discourse, very often involves an expert speaking to other experts about groups of people whose own voices are not represented in the text, and who are not directly addressed by it either. This generalization applies, in fact, to all the cases we have examined in this chapter. The taxonomic text relating to the Glasgow Lunatic Asylum is *about* the inmates, but it is not addressed to them, and certainly does not incorporate their voices. The brief for the Scottish Parliament is more complicated: it seems at times to speak *on behalf* of the Scottish electorate, but it also represents them from the viewpoint of the state, as objects of surveillance and control. *The Architects' Journal* feature about the 'glass torpedo' has much to say about the workforce, but no worker's opinion is quoted: the voices most prominently represented in this text are those of the designer, the company chairman and the feature-writer himself. Finally, an article by a male architecture critic praising the feminist designer of Gifu's 'washbasins in the sun' speaks on behalf of the woman architect and about the women users of the building, while the women themselves remain mute.

The relationship between subjects and objects of discourse – those who speak and those who are spoken about, or spoken for, by others – is a fundamentally asymmetrical one, and we would argue that in the domain of architectural discourse that asymmetry can have far-reaching consequences. If, as we have claimed, buildings exist in discourse before they exist in physical reality, and if, after their construction, their meaning is ongoingly interpreted through discourse, it becomes a matter of consequence *whose* discourse we are dealing with, and conversely, whose voices we never hear. Typically, we are dealing with the discourse of authorities – professional, institutional, economic, political. Their discourse may be 'enlightened', 'progressive', 'utopian', 'egalitarian', 'radical'; but to the extent they retain a monopoly on the definition of those concepts, speaking for and about others, not to them and not with them, their discourse both reflects and reproduces their authority and power.

Chapter 5: Value

INTRODUCTION

The central argument of this book is that our experience and understanding of buildings are always and inevitably mediated by language and discourse (i.e. language used to make meaning in particular contextual conditions). This chapter is concerned with the kind of discourse whose purpose is to form taste and pass judgement: *evaluative* discourse.

Evaluation is an important dimension of our response to buildings and the built environment. We are not just passive inhabitants of that environment, but are apt to make judgements on whether a building, a housing estate, a shopping mall, a city centre, etc., is 'good' or 'bad' and whether we ourselves 'like it'. Language is the main medium in which our judgements are circulated and recorded. Especially when they are written down (because of the potential for writing to reach more people over a longer time), those judgements have an important role in shaping subsequent judgements, as people expand on, or take issue with, judgements already in circulation.

The judgements in circulation about a particular phenomenon may also shape responses to it in material reality. It is not uncommon for people to encounter evaluations of certain buildings – especially ancient, monumental and otherwise notable ones – before they have any direct experience of the buildings themselves. Conscientious tourists, for instance, often prepare to experience the architectural monuments they plan to visit by reading a guidebook in which those structures are not only described but (positively) evaluated. The decision to visit a particular site may well have been made on the basis of a guidebook's evaluation of it as important. And the text will have set up a framework of beliefs and expectations into which the tourist must fit his or her own judgements of the building. In other words, the value of the building has been constructed for the tourist in discourse in advance of any actual encounter with it. This is bound to affect the nature of the encounter and shape the form of the tourist's own eventual judgement on the building – not in the sense that s/he must automatically agree with the guidebook, but in the sense that s/he is likely to measure actual experience against the judgement contained in it.

In the case of important new built structures, it is increasingly difficult to encounter them physically for the first time without reference to prior textual judgements about them, because so much public discussion and debate on their merits takes place in advance of their completion. One extreme example of this tendency might be Zaha Hadid's competition-winning design for an opera house in the Welsh city of Cardiff, which has generated volumes of evaluative comment *pro* and *con*, though no one either has experienced or ever will experience the building directly. The design was ultimately rejected (it was this that sparked public controversy about its value) and it remains unbuilt.

The Cardiff opera house example reminds us of an important point. No discussion of evaluative discourse on buildings can overlook the key role it plays, not just in deciding the worth of existing structures but in actually determining what gets built. This is particularly obvious in cases where the contract to design a building is awarded on the basis of a competition, with entries evaluated by a panel of judges. The panel's discussions are examples of evaluative spoken discourse; and when the judges have made their decision, they will also produce a piece of evaluative written discourse which explains for the record why the winning entry was considered superior to the others.

Occasionally, evaluations may also be solicited from the public during a competition. For instance, during the competition for a new Scottish Parliament building in 1997, the shortlisted designs were displayed publicly in several Scottish cities, and interested visitors were invited to write comments which would be passed on to the judges. It is unclear what impact these comments had on the final outcome of the competition. But for the purposes of our argument in this chapter, what is interesting about the Scottish Office's democratic gesture in soliciting lay opinions is the common-sense assumption it makes manifest: that lay people as well as experts are capable of producing, in the medium of language, evaluations of building designs.

Thus far we have mentioned a number of different kinds of evaluative discourse on buildings, including discourse produced by guidebook writers, by architectural competition judges and by laypeople whose opinions are being solicited in a process of democratic consultation. We might also have mentioned the writing of academics such as architectural historians, which also often has an evaluative dimension (though compared to, say, the guidebook genre, academic writing has a fairly narrow circulation). Nor should we forget that evaluative discourse plays a role in the training of architects via the 'crits' to which student projects are regularly subjected.

But there is another kind of evaluative writing about the built environment which has become increasingly widespread and salient in recent years (it figured prominently in the controversy over Zaha Hadid's Cardiff opera house design, for example). This writing is done by journalists; it appears in upmarket newspapers and in the style magazines which were among the most notable publishing success stories of the 1990s (in 1999, for example, the monthly circulation of the British edition of *Elle Decoration* was 300,000). The style magazines are strongly oriented to stimulating consumption among their affluent readers, and most are more concerned with interior design than with buildings as such – though they often carry biographical features on great architects living and dead. The 'quality' newspapers, on the other hand, treat architecture on a par with art forms such as cinema, theatre, opera and dance – which is to say, they give it a weekly slot in the features section and employ a regular 'architecture critic'. Just as the key function of a newspaper's film critic or its theatre critic is to evaluate recent film releases or theatrical openings, so one important function of its architecture critic is to evaluate new buildings or plans for new buildings.

In producing this sort of evaluative discourse for newspapers, writers are hoping to exert influence in at least two ways. First, they hope to have an impact on future policy and practice by influencing important actors and opinion formers such as architecture and design professionals and their clients. A content analysis of architectural criticism in the *Independent* newspaper during 1996, for instance, reveals a quite sustained effort on the part of its then-critic Jonathan Glancey to persuade the UK government – a major client for new buildings – to adopt a more adventurous policy in relation to building design. The assumption here is that politicians and other establishment figures are sensitive to media criticism, and that one function of the media in democratic societies is, precisely, to subject the decisions of these powerful social actors to critical scrutiny. Second, journalists who write about buildings (like those who write about cinema or literature) see it as part of their function to educate public taste. Reading the opinions of a well-informed and experienced judge is meant to influence the judgements of less well-informed people.

In the specific case of architecture journalism, at least in Britain, there is a certain missionary zeal about this quasi-educational project. Architecture criticism in newspapers is a more recent innovation than film or literary criticism, and it seems to be assumed that whereas readers of film and book reviews are already quite knowledgeable and confident in their own tastes, people are less sure what kinds of buildings they like, and less convinced of their ability to tell a 'good' from a 'bad' building. Allegedly, British educational and cultural traditions have produced a nation of design illiterates, who therefore need to be shown how to discriminate good from poor design. One of the things this entails is giving people access to a linguistic register in which the relevant distinctions are conventionally encapsulated.

Here it might be asked why people need to become familiar with a particular register of language in order to form or express opinions on buildings. It is a commonplace belief that taste is 'subjective', so that value judgements on matters which fall under the heading of taste should not be bound by fixed conventions. But while it is obvious that people do not all make the same judgements on the same objects – their evaluations differ, and may conflict – it does not follow that evaluations can be expressed in any way speakers and writers choose. They may express any *opinion* they choose, but whatever opinion they put forward has, at the minimum, to be intelligible to others involved in discussion *as* an opinion. There are also conventions for explaining and justifying one's opinions. Someone who insists that a particular object is worthless, and who is challenged to justify that statement, cannot simply refuse to elaborate, or say merely 'because it is', or 'because I hate it', and still be seen as making a valid contribution to an evaluative discussion. Evaluating objects is a particular kind of 'language game', to use the Wittgensteinian phrase, and in order to play it is necessary to understand the rules. Value judgements will lack authority and validity if they are not expressed in a form which is recognized as appropriate by the relevant interpretive community.

Consider, for example, Prince Charles's widely publicized comment on a proposed extension to the National Gallery in London's Trafalgar Square, which he likened to 'a monstrous carbuncle on the face of a much-loved friend'. This metaphor – comparing a new addition to an older building to a boil on someone's face, i.e. an unhealthy excrescence which ought not to be there – is clearly evaluative, but it deploys a kind of ordinary, populist language of value, rather than using the terms in which 'expert' judgements are typically couched. So although the criticism may have struck a chord with sections of the lay public, it was contemptuously dismissed by experts as ignorant, philistine, reactionary and subjective. That is not to say that the Prince's interventions in this debate or other debates about architecture have been inconsequential, for on the contrary, his status as a public figure has given him considerable influence (we discuss some of his contributions to recent architectural debate in more detail in Chapter 7). Our point, however, is that he is widely thought not to deserve that influence; his authority to make judgements on buildings is seen to derive from who he is rather than what he knows. And that is in part a consequence of the fact that he is either unable or unwilling to use the evaluative language that has authority for the community of 'people who know about buildings'. By contrast there are critics who share Prince Charles's distaste for certain architectural styles, but whose unfashionable opinions command more respect, even among those who strongly disagree with them, because they are expressed in a more 'appropriate' language.

In this introductory section we have suggested that evaluation is an important function of discourse about buildings, and we have drawn attention to a number of contexts (e.g. professional training and practice, academic scholarship, tourism, journalism) in which evaluative discourse on buildings is regularly produced and consumed. We have pointed out that evaluating buildings is a kind of 'language game', successful instances of which must conform to certain linguistic conventions. Undoubtedly, these conventions will not be identical in every context – journalism and scholarship, say, may well differ in terms of what is considered appropriate. At the same time, evaluative discourse has certain general characteristics which recur across contexts and text-types. Later we explore how some of these characteristics are realized in evaluative discourse about buildings. First, though, we will give some attention to the prior issue of *which* buildings are selected for the evaluative treatment.

EVALUATIVE DISCOURSE: SELECTION OF OBJECTS

One characteristic of evaluative discourse is that it selects its objects. Not every object is worth evaluating: choosing which objects to evaluate is itself an act of evaluation. It need not imply that the selected object is necessarily 'good', but it does imply that this object is in some way significant – that it matters whether or not it is judged to be good.

Of course the selection criteria will vary depending on the context and the purpose of evaluation, and here we cannot hope to encompass the whole range of possibilities. We concentrate, in the first place, on the selection of buildings for *public* evaluation. People are continually making value judgements on all kinds of things, but most of these do not enter the public domain, or they may enter a very limited public domain: thus we may remark on the ugliness of a neighbour's new garage or write to the local press deploring plans to demolish the factory round the corner, but neither of these buildings is likely to feature as the object of expert evaluation in a guidebook, a newspaper article or a feature in a style magazine. A somewhat different example of a 'limited public domain' is the world of specialist scholarly or professional debate. Buildings whose value would not be seen as a matter of wide public interest may be discussed at length in a professional journal because of, for instance, some unusual technical feature. In the following discussion we will leave such cases aside and focus on the reasons why buildings are featured in evaluative discourse produced for a relatively large 'general' audience, in, for example, newspapers, magazines, exhibition catalogues, coffee-table books and guidebooks.

Probably the most obvious criterion on which buildings are selected as objects of evaluation concerns the identity of their designers. A new building by a well-known architect will be extensively featured in newspapers, magazines and, eventually, guidebooks covering the area where it is sited. Buildings made in the past by a famous designer are less likely to be discussed in newspapers (though they may be mentioned as points of comparison for new buildings), but retrospective assessment is not uncommon in style magazines, which quite often run features on the work of canonical figures such as Frank Lloyd Wright, Alvar Aalto and Le Corbusier. Such figures are also regular subjects for museum exhibits and guidebooks. If the designer is a celebrity, his or her whole output is considered worthy of judgement. A 'star' designer adds value to building types which are normally given scant attention, such as car parks and office blocks, and drawings or models for buildings which were never built, like Zaha Hadid's Cardiff Opera House, may be displayed and reviewed as art objects in their own right.

Another criterion is the type and status of the building. This criterion works differently in different textual genres: for instance, style magazines concentrate overwhelmingly on private residential buildings (often using the identity of the owner as a criterion for featuring their home – the homes of celebrities, including celebrity architects, are featured frequently). In other text-types, private residences are much less common subjects. In a sample of (British) newspaper writing about architecture whose content we analysed,[1] most attention was given to large new public buildings of a high prestige type, such as museums and galleries (e.g. the Guggenheim museum in Bilbao) and buildings designed to house the institutions of state (e.g. the Scottish Parliament building and the Reichstag complex in Berlin). Another significant category was that of historic buildings undergoing restoration, alteration or conversion to new uses.

While the attention given to institutions of high culture and state power is particularly intense, museums and parliament houses are by no means the only buildings considered worthy of evaluation. As an illustration, we may consider the contents of a book titled *Vertigo: The strange new world of the contemporary city* (Moore 1999), which was produced to coincide with an exhibition of the same name in Glasgow during that city's year-long festival of architecture and design. The book contains ten essays: their subjects are the Tate Modern gallery in London, the redevelopment of Berlin as reunified Germany's capital city, Chek Lap Kok airport in Hong Kong, the Yokohama port terminal, Lake Las Vegas resort, a public housing project in Gifu, Japan, the Shanghai World Financial Centre, the Millennium Dome in London, the Landschaftspark in Duisburg and the Ontario Mills shopping centre in California. The objects selected as exemplary in relation to the theme of 'the contemporary city' are a city centre, two 'cultural' buildings, two devoted to commerce and two to transport, two tourist developments and one (public) housing development. And they are not only 'exemplary' in the sense of providing a snapshot of the contemporary urban environment; all are treated seriously as examples of design.

Many of the buildings featured in *Vertigo*, though not all, are designed by well-known architects. The 'status of building' criterion is in practice not unrelated to the 'identity of designer' criterion, because the commission to design a high profile new building is so often won by a 'name' architect. Thus many of the most intensively evaluated projects are deemed worthy of attention on both grounds: the Bilbao Guggenheim, for example, is of interest both because it is a high-prestige building (an art museum) and because its designer is a 'star' (Frank Gehry).

The Bilbao Guggenheim also fulfils a third criterion: buildings attract evaluation when their designs are seen to be in some way 'extreme'. In Gehry's case the 'extreme' features have to do with shape and materials, but the most striking illustration of this principle, arguably, is the attention accorded to very tall buildings such as the Petronas Towers in Kuala Lumpur and the Shanghai World Financial Centre, even when they are not particularly innovative either formally or technically.

The list of criteria above is very general and not intended to be exhaustive, but it does suggest that the vast majority of the buildings used most often by most people are rarely or never the subject of public discussion about their value. Factories, offices and functional public buildings such as schools and hospitals, will seldom attract the interest of those who write about architecture and design for a general audience, since they tend not to have famous or even named designers, they do not belong to prestigious types and they are not often (though they are sometimes) innovative or 'extreme' in their design. We noted in the introductory discussion that media writing about architecture is intended to educate public taste; the criteria on which journalists select their subjects would suggest, however, that this is not necessarily a question of developing people's capacity to judge the quality of their immediate environment. Style magazines might be said to educate people's judgements of domestic design, but what of their workplaces, their children's schools, the public facilities they use every day?

In fairness we should note that some architecture writers do occasionally venture into the territory of the everyday: in August 2000, for example, the architecture critic of *The Guardian* newspaper devoted his weekly column to reviewing (seriously and positively) a bus station in Walsall. The design is credited to a practice rather than a single well-known architect; the location is provincial and unfashionable; the function (sheltering buses and passengers) is hardly prestigious (whereas the port and airport featured in *Vertigo* have the glamour of international travel and trade). Selecting this particular structure for extended evaluation is thus a marked and deliberate departure from the usual criteria.

Having established what kinds of buildings evaluative discourse is typically about, let us now turn to some of the characteristics of the discourse itself.

EVALUATING BUILDINGS IN DISCOURSE: SOME CASES IN POINT

We begin by reproducing four extracts of evaluative discourse on one or more buildings, each of which represents a different genre of public writing about architecture, produced with a particular audience in mind. (A) is an extract from the introduction to an exhibition catalogue (the *Vertigo* book, whose contents are briefly summarized above). The implied reader is not necessarily a professional in the field of architecture, planning or design, but s/he is clearly constructed as someone with an informed interest in those fields. The essays in the book are short, and broken up with large full-colour illustrations, but they are also fairly 'academic' in tone and style. Contributors include academics, museum curators, specialist journalists and practitioners: the author whose text we reproduce is a curator. Extract (B) is an example of the weekly architecture criticism feature in the arts section of an upmarket newspaper (in this case *The Guardian,* a paper which locates itself on the liberal left of the UK political spectrum). The implied reader is more of a 'generalist' than the one constructed in *Vertigo,* and the style of writing is typical of arts journalism addressed to an educated lay audience. Extract (C), by contrast, is taken from a British weekly publication specifically for architects, *Building Design*. It is more of a newspaper than a specialist technical or academic journal, but can take for granted that its readers are knowledgeable about the issues it covers. Finally, extract (D) is from *Homes & Gardens*, one of the numerous monthly style magazines dealing primarily with interior design. This particular title is relatively conservative, addressed to an older and less 'trendy' audience than, say, *Elle Decoration* or *Wallpaper*. Like all the style monthlies, though, it has an overt promotional agenda which the other three sources do not. It is full of advertisements, and the features too function to stimulate consumption, giving sources and often prices for the objects they show.

Obviously, four examples of evaluative discourse – from each of which we take only a short extract for analysis – do not constitute a representative sample. Discourse analysis can, of course, be applied to much larger corpora, but since it is a micro-analytic technique, a great deal of space would be needed to do justice to the outcome. Given that the space available to discuss them here is limited, we chose these particular examples as indicative case studies for several reasons. First, as noted above, they represent a number of different textual genres and audiences for which evaluative discourse about buildings is produced; there is thus some potential for interesting similarities and differences to emerge in analysis. They may also point to similarities and differences associated with the kind of object being evaluated. Extracts (C) and (D) both deal with private residential buildings designed by well-known architects; (B) is a much more 'marked' choice, assessing a bus station in a provincial town; (A) assesses a whole category of objects, namely 'new Asian building'. (A) is also the only example of a *negative* evaluation; the other three are all positive. Though we have made no statistical analysis, it is clear impressionistically that in the genres we are considering, positive evaluations are commoner than negative ones. (This one would predict from the predominance of the work of acclaimed architects.) Finally, and most importantly, we have chosen our examples to illustrate certain features of discourse which we consider particularly salient in the kind of writing we are discussing. Again, our aim is not to make statistical claims about the frequency of these features, but to point them out, explore how they work and consider what effects they produce.

Texts

Note: bold type indicates a heading, small capitals an editorial introduction (most probably written by a subeditor and not the writer whose by-line is on the piece) and [. . .] indicates where material, either text or illustration or both, has been omitted.

A: Source: Editor's introduction to Vertigo, *topic: 'the new orientalism' (Moore 1999: 28).*

> [. . .] Most new Asian building can fairly be described as hideous. In Shenzen, architects challenge the sanctity of artistic authorship by trawling the world's architectural magazines and copying what they find, with due adjustment of scale, on to the elevations of their buildings. The result is a skyline in which a not-quite Norman Foster jostles with an almost-Arquitectonica and a just-Cesar Pelli [. . .].

B: Source: The Guardian *newspaper, arts section, weekly architecture column, topic: a new bus station in Walsall, 21 August 2000 (Figure 4).*

Give me shelter

IT'S NOT CONCRETE, IT'S NOT DEPRESSING AND IT'S NOT BRUTALIST. **JONATHAN GLANCEY** ON A BUS STATION WITH A DIFFERENCE.

Figure 4
WALSALL BUS STATION,
ARCHITECTS ALLFORD HALL
MONAGHAN MORRIS
copyright of, and permission
from, News Team, Birmingham;
photograph by Mike Scott

[. . .] The finished item consists of a forest of steel trees holding up a sprayed-concrete roof like a flattened umbrella or parasol over a rounded wall of glass. Open, light and attractive, it has the feel of an exhibition pavilion and draws, perhaps unconsciously, on a plethora of public transport buildings that have been designed in the round across Europe over the past 70 years. Its stretched drum-like form and overhanging canopy, or eaves, call to mind the handsome, geometric architecture established in both London (Arnos Grove tube station 1932) and Berlin (the Olympic Stadium U-Bahn station, 1936) [. . .].

C: Source: Building Design *(weekly newspaper for architects), 'Rostrum' feature, topic: Rem Koolhaas's design for a house in Bordeaux, 20 February 1998.*

Quite simply the best . . .

KESTER RATTENBURY ENTHUSES OVER A STUNNING DESIGN BY REM KOOLHAAS.

[. . .] And it's utterly amazing; a latter-day billionaire La Tourette; excavated and carved basement rooms and staircases; a totally startling ground/first floor plan with astonishing clear span, seemingly unsupported glazing; and sliding aluminium walls which make an occasionally open-air room.

On top of this was a massive cantilevered upper storey cut through with circular holes and shutters making sun spot patterns. It also featured a fabulous bathroom, stairs like a castle, bookcases, metallic ceilings, the lot.

Oh, and just at the end, he explained that the centre of the house is a huge lift section – itself the size of a large house – which can move from the basement right up out on to the roof, designed for the disabled client but used by the whole family, and which totally changes the house's configuration.

This is certainly one of the great seminal houses of the century [. . .].

D: Source: Homes & Gardens *(monthly style magazine), topic: apartment in south London, September 2000: 71–3.*

Star attraction

DAVID COLLINS' GLAMOROUS INTERIORS HAVE BEEN GIVEN THE SEAL OF APPROVAL BY MADONNA. AND THE APARTMENT HE CREATED FOR RICHARD ROGERS' MONTEVETRO BUILDING IN SOUTH LONDON LIVES UP TO HIS SHIMMERING REPUTATION, WITH METALLIC FINISHES THAT REFLECT MASSES OF LIGHT.

[. . .] Glass, glass and more glass. One of architect Richard Rogers' latest projects, the Montevetro apartment building on the south side of the Thames in Battersea is the epitome of modernity. It is part of the regeneration of London of which Lord Rogers is at the forefront, and if you want to jump into 21st century living, here would be a good place to start. The curvaceous edifice of the block capitalises on its location, with all the apartments benefiting from panoramic river views.

Surprisingly, this does not mean shunning all that is warm, friendly and familiar. The 'cold' materials of the building – predominantly glass and metal – take on a life of their own in the context of the river [. . .].

VOICES OF AUTHORITY

Evaluative discourse aims to persuade its audience that the judgements it offers are sound ones, and this typically requires that the person doing the judging should be seen by the intended audience as a credible or authoritative source. How is authority/credibility established in the four texts above?

One device which is used in three of them is the presentation of the writer's judgement as a matter of acknowledged fact:

1. Most new Asian building can fairly be described as hideous. (A)
2. This is certainly one of the great seminal houses of the century. (C)
3. The Montevetro apartment building . . . is the epitome of modernity. (D)

In all three of these sentences, the judgement has an impersonal, definitive quality because of the absence of any identifiable agent standing behind it. In each sentence the grammatical subject is the building itself (or in the case of (2), a pronoun standing in for it), and the predicate contains a proposition about the building (that it is 'hideous' or 'seminal' or 'the epitome of modernity'). The judgement delivered thus seems to encapsulate not someone's opinion but a self-evident, consensual truth, like 'water boils at 100 degrees centigrade'.

The most interesting case is (1), because in order to make the building the subject of the sentence and get the effect of impersonal, consensual judgement the writer has had to employ the passive. The corresponding active sentence would require explicit mention of *who* describes most new Asian building as hideous. Even if the identity of this agent were left fairly vague (e.g. 'commentators have described . . .'), the sentence structure would still call attention to the status of the judgement as *someone's* rather than everyone's and no one's.

Another interesting feature of this sentence is the use of the adverb *fairly*. This marks the apparently very harsh criticism contained in the sentence as being nevertheless judicious: the judge has deliberated on the matter and concluded that 'hideous' is a just description, rather than an unwarranted slur. Similarly, the writer hedges by referring to '*most* new Asian building', a formulation which allows for the possibility that some new Asian building is not hideous. In fact, the sentence is full of hedging and mitigation (that is, linguistic devices whose function is to weaken the speaker's implied commitment to a given proposition). Below the relevant parts of it are underlined:

> <u>Most</u> new Asian building <u>can fairly be described as</u> hideous.

If all the writer wanted to do were to predicate 'hideousness' of 'new Asian building', he could have made the bold statement 'New Asian building is hideous'; and indeed, it might seem that this would be *more* authoritative than the mitigated version. However, in certain fields (academic discussion being one), credibility may be undermined by generalizing in a way that is perceived as too sweeping, or judging (especially negatively) in terms that are seen as exaggerated or hyperbolic. If you choose a word like *hideous* (which is marked as communicating a 'strong' reaction by comparison with semantically related alternatives like *ugly, unattractive*), it may well be prudent to mitigate the force of the negative judgement in some other way. The judge in sentence 2, who is making a strongly positive judgement on Rem Koolhaas's Bordeaux house, does not have this problem: she uses an adverb ('*certainly* one of the great seminal houses of the century') for the opposite purpose – to intensify rather than mitigate the strength of the assertion.

Another way in which judges construct authority and credibility is by displaying expert knowledge. In the texts we are considering, the most significant way in which this is done is by comparing the building(s) under discussion to other buildings, thus displaying the judge's status as someone well acquainted with canonical traditions in modern architecture. For example:

4.   The result is a skyline in which a not-quite Norman Foster jostles with an almost-Arquitectonica and a just-Cesar Pelli. (A)
5.   it . . . draws, perhaps unconsciously, on a plethora of public transport buildings that have been designed in the round across Europe over the past 70 years. Its stretched drum-like form and overhanging canopy, or eaves, call to mind the handsome, geometric architecture established in both London (Arnos Grove tube station 1932) and Berlin (the Olympic Stadium U-Bahn station, 1936). (B)
6.   a latter-day billionaire La Tourette. (C)

The writer of (5) scores particularly well here for the extensiveness and relative obscurity of his references: here, we are invited to think, is a critic who knows his stations. Interestingly, (6), from the specialist publication *Building Design*, shows the least preoccupation with displaying expert knowledge: the reference to (Le Corbusier's) La Tourette is the only invocation of any canonical building, and the text as a whole is sparing in its use of technical vocabulary: phrases like 'cantilevered upper storey' and 'unsupported glazing' appear alongside 'a fabulous bathroom' and 'stairs like a castle'. The description of Koolhaas's design as 'a latter day billionaire La Tourette' is immediately preceded by a much less 'expert' evaluation: 'it's utterly amazing'. One might ask whether the display of expertise becomes redundant in the context of a publication whose readers are all experts themselves (though later on we will suggest another possible reason for the very informal tone of text (C)). In the case of *Homes & Gardens* (D), by contrast, it appears that authority and credibility do not lie in membership of the community of experts on architecture, nor does one establish the worth of a new building by comparing it to the work of Norman Foster, Cesar Pelli, Le Corbusier *et al*. Instead the editorial introduction informs us, 'David Collins' glamorous interiors have been given the seal of approval by Madonna.'

In some cases, at least, the text flatters the reader by assuming s/he too is knowledgeable, sufficiently well informed to recognize and make sense of the allusions to canonical designers and their buildings. In the *Building Design* example, this assumption is likely to be accurate, but in the other two cases individual readers will vary considerably in how much they know about the subject. (4) is a particularly interesting example, for it implicitly demands that the reader use her or his familiarity with the real thing to imagine 'a not-quite Norman Foster . . . an almost-Arquitectonica and a just-Cesar Pelli'. Addressing the reader as an equal, someone who shares in the writer's knowledge and expertise, constructs a relationship of collaboration and solidarity between writer and reader, thus maximizing, arguably, the reader's willingness to accept and agree with the judgement being offered – in this case that the 'not-quite' versions of acclaimed architects' designs are 'hideous'.

CONSTRUCTING VALUE: COMPARISON AND CONTRAST

As well as establishing the credentials of the author to present an evaluation of the object under scrutiny, evaluative discourse must present grounds or criteria for judging the object in a particular way. In our four texts we have one negative and three positive evaluations of buildings: how is their value, or lack of value, constructed in the terms of the discourse?

One answer has already been given in the discussion of authority: a building's value can be asserted or denied through a favourable or unfavourable comparison with some other building that is already established canonically as valuable. The Walsall bus station is compared to classic modernist underground stations in London and Berlin; Rem Koolhaas's Bordeaux house is compared to Le Corbusier's La Tourette (though the nature of the resemblance is not even hinted at); the work of architects in Shenzhen is compared (unfavourably) with the work of Norman Foster, Arquitectonica and Cesar Pelli – though once again, we are not told what differences between original and copy, other than 'adjustment of scale', make the former 'good' and the latter 'hideous'.

We might conclude that in these texts, both 'tradition' and 'originality' are presented as criteria for assessing buildings, much as they are criteria for assessing other works of art in the modern age. A 'good' building should bear *some* resemblance to good buildings that preceded it – that is, it should be part of an identifiable tradition – but if the resemblance is too great, if it results from merely copying (and particularly from imperfect copying), it is no longer a good building.

(B) exemplifies this principle, not only in the passage reproduced as (5) above, but also elsewhere in the text, where we see the comparison strategy applied in reverse. One of the criteria on the Walsall bus station judged to be 'good' is its *lack* of resemblance to other buildings with the same function, which are represented as generally bad. This is what readers are invited to infer from the introductory statement:

7. *It's not concrete, it's not depressing and it's not brutalist.* **Jonathan Glancey** *on a bus station with a difference.*

According to the principles of pragmatics, the study of utterance interpretation, one of the default expectations with which language-users approach any utterance is that it contains as much information as is required to understand the speaker's intentions, and no more. When that expectation is violated by an utterance that seems to contain too little or too much information, hearers will take it that the under- or over-informativeness of the utterance is itself intended to be meaningful, and try to infer what the speaker intended to communicate by flouting standard expectations. (7) sets the reader just such a pragmatic puzzle, for it contains a listing of three things the building under consideration is *not* – information which might be considered unnecessary and irrelevant. But the purpose of giving this information is to alert the reader to the possibility that there is something especially significant about the object's not being concrete, depressing and brutalist. As s/he reads on, the reader discovers that the object is a bus station 'with a difference'. The puzzle is solved. The first sentence of the introduction is intended to communicate that bus stations as a class of objects are typically concrete, depressing and brutalist. This one stands out as 'different' because it does not share the negative attributes of its class. Though it participates in a noble tradition of public transport buildings, it breaks free from the specific (and grim) traditions of bus station design, and in that sense is original.

Of course, we would not wish to claim that the same criteria are operative in all evaluations of buildings, or that there is no debate about the status of tradition and originality in relation to architecture. Actually, the fact that there *is* debate on these issues is relevant to the question of how text (A), in particular, works. Consider the sentence 'In Shenzen, architects challenge the sanctity of artistic authorship by trawling the world's architectural magazines and copying what they find, with due adjustment of scale, on to the elevations of their build-ings.' In this context the sentence clearly signals disapproval of the Shenzen architects: since the previous sentence asserts that 'most new Asian building can fairly be described as hideous', the next statement will be read as providing support for the negative judgement, along the lines of, 'their buildings are hideous because they copy what they find in magazines'. Yet it is not hard to imagine an alternative context in which the assertion *architects challenge the sanctity of artistic authorship* might be uttered with approval (perhaps by an enthusiast of postmodernist pastiche or an advocate of Asian resistance to West-ern notions of art). Indeed, the phrase 'challenging the sanctity of X', where X denotes some conventional belief or traditional institution, often has positive connotations of scepticism and resistance to mindless conformity. Knowing that might point the reader of text (A) towards an 'ironic' reading (the author is hav-ing a dig at postmodernist pretensions by writing 'challenge the sanctity of artistic authorship' in a context where he will immediately reveal that what he actually means is 'copy' or 'plagiarize'). This is a good illustration of an important principle: in discourse, language in use, meaning does not reside in isolated propositions, and it cannot be revealed by simply decoding the words. 'Architects challenge the sanctity of artistic authorship' is capable of being taken a positive or a negative judgement, or indeed as a statement of fact or a slogan, depending on what precedes and follows it, and also on what background knowledge the reader can bring to bear on it. While the reader of text (A) would have to be very obtuse to miss the writer's negative atttitude to the Shenzen architects, s/he could easily fail to grasp the irony if s/he did not know something the text itself does not spell out – that there are critics who do not regard cut-and-paste design as deplorable, but rather celebrate it as fresh and iconoclastic.

Buildings are not only compared to other buildings in evaluative discourse, however. It is commonplace for writers to describe them using comparisons to non-architectural phenomena which the reader is assumed to be able to picture easily. For instance, Enric Miralles's winning design for the Scottish Parliament building was almost universally described in news reports on the competition outcome as looking like 'an upturned boat'. A design by Norman Foster for a new financial building on the site of the Baltic Exchange in the city of London has been widely decried as looking like 'an erotic gherkin'. Comparisons of this kind are usually based on some point of physical resemblance between the terms, but they are obviously not just descriptive: the comparison is also implicitly an evaluation. In the case of the 'upturned boat', the evaluation is positive because of the object's associations with a mythical Celtic past symbolizing, like the Parliament itself, the continuity of Scotland as a nation. These associations were explicitly emphasized by Miralles in the text of his competition entry (see Chapter 7). The 'erotic gherkin' comparison, by contrast, expresses a negative judge-ment of the building, because there is something either ludicrous or perverse about the juxtaposition of gherkins and sex – and neither seems an especially appropriate reference for the building in question.

Comparisons of buildings with objects other than buildings, then, are rarely intended simply to provide concrete descriptive information. The object or phenomenon to which a building is likened may indeed resemble it in some particular way, but it is also selected for the associations it carries outside the domain of architecture. Metaphors which are less concrete – for instance, the description of Norman Foster's Millennium Bridge over the Thames as 'a blade of light' – are also loaded with evaluative meaning. The phrase 'a blade of light' is not only a metaphor for the bridge, but also a metaphor itself (light is likened to something extended, sharp and metallic, like a sword). 'A blade of light' is more rather than less difficult to picture concretely than a bridge: the effect is less to evoke a definite image than to overlay our perceptions of the bridge with the associations of light and of sharp, clear lines.

Unsurprisingly, there are many non-architectural comparisons in the four texts we have selected for analysis. Here we focus on a theme that is common to several of these comparisons, exemplified by the following passages:

8.   The finished item consists of a forest of steel trees holding up a sprayed-concrete roof like a flattened umbrella or parasol over a rounded wall of glass. . . . Its stretched drum-like form and overhanging canopy . . . (B)
9.   The 'cold' materials of the building – predominantly glass and metal – take on a life of their own in the context of the river. (D)
10.   . . . a totally startling ground/first floor plan with astonishing clear span, seemingly unsupported glazing; and sliding aluminium walls which make an occasionally open-air room. (C)

Each of the above examples contains one or more comparison figures (that is, metaphors and/or similes) in which an architectural structure is related in some way to a natural phenomenon. The most straightforward case is (8), where the bus station is likened to a 'forest of steel trees'. The writer goes on to note that it is overhung by a 'canopy': the word does denote an architectural entity, but it can also denote the top level of a forest, and this association is arguably prompted by the earlier 'forest' metaphor. In (9), the metaphor is of a glass and metal structure becoming 'alive' through its juxtaposition with something natural, the river (this is later clarified as a reference to the way light is reflected from the water onto the building). The building is not directly compared to the river, but the river is represented as an essential part of its design. In (10), there is both juxtaposition and resemblance. The description of Rem Koolhaas's ground/first floor plan emphasizes the apparent lack of boundaries between inside and outside: the clear span, unsupported glazing and sliding walls make the juxtaposition between the building and its surrounding environment unusually close. Then comes the paradoxical metaphor of the 'open air room', which likens the experience of being in the room to the experience of being in the open air. Literally speaking, these experiences are opposites, since by definition a room is an enclosed space.

The evocation of nature in architecture, and the harmonious juxtaposition of buildings with natural objects, are both well-worn themes in architectural criticism, and from examples 8–10 it appears that a building's ability to incorporate the positive connotations of nature remains relevant to the question of its value. In (8), for instance, the value conventionally associated with the 'natural' is transferred through the 'forest' metaphor onto a building – Walsall bus station – whose urban setting and function could hardly be more remote from nature. Only a long tradition of idealizing nature could make the idea of a fleet of buses 'shaded' by a 'forest of steel trees' self-evidently pleasing rather than just incongruous. The other two buildings are more 'fortunate' in their settings, and their architects are praised not so much for managing to suggest natural associations as for managing to exploit the pre-existing natural resources of water, light and air in their designs. Rather similarly, the judges of the 1970 competition to build the Burrell Museum in Glasgow's Pollok Park praised the winning design, remarking that it 'has managed to insert a large building into the site without losing its idyllic qualities'. The metaphor of 'insertion' suggests that in the judges' view, a good design would seek to blend with the 'idyllic' natural setting rather than trying to overshadow it.

EVALUATIVE DISCOURSE AND PROMOTIONAL DISCOURSE

As we noted in the first chapter of this book, critical discourse analysts have made the general claim that since the 1980s, many kinds of public speech and writing have shifted noticeably in the direction of 'marketized' or 'promotional' discourse. Texts whose primary purpose is to inform or advise – an example might be the kind of health education materials available in doctors' surgeries – increasingly address readers as if they were consumers, borrowing modes of address and rhetorical techniques from the genres of advertising and public relations. These genres are, of course, strongly evaluative. The ultimate goal of advertising – persuading the reader to buy the advertised product or service – is accomplished, typically, by representing the product as desirable and/or as particularly good of its kind (i.e. better than competing products). PR discourse has the goal of creating a positive image for a client – an individual, company, government or other institution. It is of interest to ask, then, whether evaluative discourse on buildings shows the same 'promotional' tendency as other kinds of discourse have been claimed to do, and whether it draws on the linguistic conventions of advertising and PR.

We have pointed out already that at least one fairly widespread textual genre in which the value of buildings is a recurrent concern – the style magazine genre – is overtly promotional. The boundary between advertising and the editorial content of style magazines is not sharply drawn, and many features are essentially displays of products, not uncommonly including the services of named (though usually not [yet] celebrated) architects and designers, which the reader may wish to purchase. The style magazine text we have selected for analysis here, (D), is not directly promoting its subject, the Montevetro building, or indeed the services of Richard Rogers and David Collins, whose clients (like Madonna) need to be exceptionally wealthy. It is more of an 'aspirational' feature, showing the reader a model of (allegedly) good taste. Nevertheless, and whether or not it is deliberate, the text has features of more than one kind of promotional discourse:

11. David Collins' glamorous interiors have been given the seal of approval by Madonna.
12. The curvaceous edifice of the block capitalises on its location, with all the apartments benefiting from panoramic river views.

(11) uses a traditional advertising technique, the celebrity endorsement. (12) recalls, at least for British readers, the distinctive linguistic register in which estate agents describe properties for sale. In estate agents' details, houses almost invariably 'benefit from' something: recent improvements, closeness to local schools and shops, or as in this case, panoramic river views.

The presence of promotional features in the discourse of *Homes & Gardens* is not, of course, surprising (though the resort to estate agents' prose is more so, given the almost universal ridicule this particular register provokes). A more interesting question is whether similar tendencies can be found in the other three texts, whose purposes are less straightforwardly commercial. Consider, for instance, the following:

13. The result is a skyline in which <u>a</u> not-quite <u>Norman Foster</u> jostles with <u>an</u> almost-<u>Arquitectonica</u> and <u>a</u> just-<u>Cesar Pelli</u>. (A)
14. <u>And</u> it's <u>utterly amazing</u> . . . a <u>totally startling</u> ground/first floor plan with <u>astonishing </u>clear span, seemingly unsupported glazing; and sliding aluminium walls which make an occasionally open-air room . . . It also featured a <u>fabulous</u> bathroom, stairs like a castle, bookcases, metallic ceilings, <u>the lot</u>. (C)

In (13), buildings are labelled with the names of their designers, which are preceded by articles: *a Norman Foster, an Arquitectonica, a Cesar Pelli*. In ordinary usage one can rarely do this with personal names; here the designers' names are used like brand names and their works become branded commodities. The same commodifying usage is familiar in relation to valuable works of art ('recent acquisitions include *a Rembrandt and a Van Gogh*'), but also to more mundane consumer products such as cars ('I'd really like *a Porsche*, but I'll have to settle for a *Volvo*'). In architecture, the 'brand name' usage seems less established, and in some cases dubious: could one refer to St Paul's cathedral as *a (Christopher) Wren*? Undoubtedly, buildings have always been commodities with a market value. But perhaps the architects who design buildings have not always been represented as commodities.

The features of promotional discourse that are discernible in (14) are informality and hyperbole (instances of which are indicated by underlining). These are common devices used in advertising to convey enthusiasm and produce (or more exactly perhaps, simulate) intimacy between advertisers and consumers. Here, the writer eschews the measured prose of, say, text (B), in which the Walsall bus station 'has the feel of' this and 'calls to mind' the architecture of that, in favour of a more immediate and personal response (that is, focusing on the reaction the building evokes in the writer as opposed to the building itself). Koolhaas's design is 'utterly amazing', 'totally startling', 'astonishing', 'fabulous'. These terms of approbation are both strong (in some cases made even stronger by intensifiers like *utterly* and *totally*) and colloquial in tone. The last sentence is a heterogeneous list, mentioning the bathroom, the stairs, the bookcases and the metallic ceilings before concluding with 'the lot', a colloquial summarizing formula which suggests the speaker's enthusiasm outstrips her ability to express it in words. The word *speaker* might seem misplaced here, but it does call attention to an important characteristic of this text's language: like a good deal of written (and pre-scripted spoken) advertising, this is writing which mimics the spontaneous quality of speech. It is not easy to reproduce in writing the rhythms of unplanned spoken discourse, and where the impression of spontaneity is achieved it is the product of deliberate craft.

None of the texts is actually selling any tangible product, so what is the significance of the 'promotional' elements that surface in three of them? Perhaps it is not coincidental that the three texts in question all discuss the work of famous name architects, whereas the one that is least promotional deals with a building by Allford Hall Monaghan Morris, no doubt a well-respected practice in professional circles, but not a household 'brand' name like Norman Foster or a cult figure like Rem Koolhaas. Promotional discourse in texts (A), (C) and (D) seems to be symptomatic, more than anything, of the cult of celebrity in relation to modern/contemporary architecture. Celebrity, in any field, has an impact on evaluative discourse. For one thing it generates quantities of discourse in which the creator rather than the creation is the real object of evaluation (the notion of '*a Norman Foster*' both minimizes the contribution of partners in Foster's practice and tends to imply that all Foster's buildings are of equivalent merit). For another, it encourages a form of evaluation in which the author is positioned more as a fan than as a critic or a judge. The subeditor of *Building Design* is not wrong to preface text (C) with the words 'Kester Rattenbury *enthuses* over a stunning design by Rem Koolhaas'. Without disputing that the enthusiasm may be warranted in a given case, we do not think it would be a positive development if evaluation became synonymous with enthusiasm.

AESTHETIC VALUE AND SOCIAL VALUE

One general observation that might be made on the sort of evaluative discourse we have discussed above is that it tends to approach architecture as an art form rather than a technical or social discipline. Architecture criticism appears in the arts-and-lifestyle pages of newspapers, for example, not the science and technology pages or the sections devoted to social commentary. Texts which reflect the tendency towards a 'cult of celebrity' also draw their ways of talking about buildings from the traditions of art criticism with its focus on individual creativity.

One consequence is to privilege certain aspects of buildings over others as 'natural' subjects for evaluative discussion. The most readily available languages of value, those which circulate in 'popular' texts such as newspapers, magazines and guidebooks, are heavily focused on the formal and aesthetic characteristics of buildings. They give less attention to function, and very little to spatial characteristics.

This point is illustrated in our analysis of four texts. The new Asian buildings assessed in text (A) are damned as 'hideous' and formally unoriginal; no consideration at all is given to how people use them and whether they serve their intended purposes well or badly. The evaluation of Rem Koolhaas in text (C) does mention the fact that the client is disabled and the design will give him greater mobility, but what most impresses the writer is its formal and technical brilliance – the lift which allows the client to move freely around the space is admired not for that, but for 'totally chang[ing] the configuration of the house'.

Text (D) exemplifies a somewhat different approach to the question of value. An apartment in the Montevetro building is presented as a desirable commodity, less because it is beautiful to look at than because it reflects well on the person who owns it, or desires to own it. It displays not only the putative owner's wealth, social position and good taste in A-list designers (shared with such icons of celebrity as Madonna), but also his or her readiness to 'jump into 21st century living' and to participate in the 'regeneration of London' spearheaded by Richard Rogers, now a member of the House of Lords. In short, the Montevetro building is evaluated as a status symbol: while the particular kind of status it symbolizes may be a twentieth/twenty-first century construct, there is nothing new or even modern about valuable art objects (buildings included) having this function.

Text (B), on Walsall bus station, is different again, though its agenda only emerges from a reading of the whole article and is not immediately evident in the extract we have analysed. Jonathan Glancey's objection to the typical concrete, brutalist bus station is a social as well as aesthetic one: 'why do they look, for the most part, as if they were designed to depress and demean those who use them?' Buses are the cheapest mode of public transport, and many users of bus stations are poor people: the Walsall bus station appeals to Glancey because part of its meaning, from his perspective, is to affirm poor people's need for, and right to, good architecture. A well-designed bus station conveys that bus passengers deserve no less respect than the more affluent users of, say, Hong Kong's new airport. But although this is a 'social' argument, the grounds on which the bus station is judged to be well designed are entirely conventional aesthetic ones. Glancey's positive evaluation is supported, as we have noted already, by appeals to the canons of modern architecture and by analogies with nature. His description of the bus station is entirely formal. Nothing is said about whether the design encourages or deters unplanned interactions among users, what technologies of surveillance and control are deployed in it, how safe it feels to spend time there, what seating or other facilities are available, etc. The photograph accompanying the text is taken from outside the structure, which is seen from a distance; this accentuates the 'forest of steel trees' effect while entirely obscuring the interior. In sum, there is no attention to social/spatial issues, though to the average user these are probably more pressing concerns than whether looking at the bus station from afar 'lifts the spirits' or recalls other examples of 'handsome' public transport buildings.

We are not trying to suggest that evaluative discourse about buildings should have nothing to say about their form and appearance; rather we are pointing out a tendency for writers to concentrate, or at the extreme to confine themselves exclusively, to those aspects of a building. If this is a valid observation, it has implications for the educational project of developing laypeople's critical faculties in relation to building design. People may be acquiring a language in which to make more informed judgements about how buildings *look*, but they are not gaining the means to make more informed judgements about how buildings *work* as social spaces.

In his book *Words and Buildings,* the architectural historian Adrian Forty devotes a chapter to the history and present state of descriptive vocabulary for talking about social aspects of architecture. A theme that runs through his discussion is the relatively impoverished nature of vocabulary in this domain: 'Rich though architectural vocabulary is in terms for the perception of the physical properties of architecture – "depth", "plasticity", "transparency", "articulation", "texture" and so on – attempts to define its social qualities immediately reveal the poverty of the language' (Forty 2000: 103). Until the nineteenth century, Forty says, evaluative discourse on the social properties of buildings was confined to 'limited discussions round concepts of utility, *convenance* and "fitness" ' (2000: 103). John Ruskin and William Morris introduced the rather vague approbation terms 'living' and 'organic', which encapsulated the view these thinkers shared that a building had social value to the degree that it expressed 'the vitality and freedom of those who had built it' (2000: 104). Twentieth century architects and planners were more interested in the potential of the built environment to express social values and shape social relations, but the terms they employed to talk about this laudable goal, such as 'community' and 'urbanity' (as well as the already-available 'living', 'organic', 'vitality') suffer, in Forty's view, from a lack of precision. An alternative, the coining of new terminologies like Hillier and Hanson's 'convexity', 'axiality' and 'integration', is problematic for a different reason, namely that the currency of these unfamiliar terms is limited. Forty comments:

> In general, in the attempts to describe the 'social' aspects of architecture, language has let architecture down. Language's particular strength – the creation of differences – has been of limited value in this domain; while the task of making evident a relationship between two such utterly disparate phenomena as social practice on the one hand and physical space on the other has proved to be largely beyond the capacity of language. (2000: 117)

In our view more has been achieved by scholars like Hillier, Hanson, and others who have sought a suitable language in which to talk about social qualities of the built environment, than Forty acknowledges. Even so, we would not dispute that the language of social evaluation in relation to buildings is impoverished by comparison with the language of aesthetic judgement (for a historical discussion of how this came about, see Markus 1993). A more fundamental point on which we disagree with Forty concerns his suggestion that language, as such, is the source of the problem. In the passage just quoted he seems to be asserting that language is good at making the kinds of distinctions that are useful for discussing form, but largely incapable of representing the complex relationships between social practice and physical space. For all kinds of reasons, we find this line of argument misguided and unconvincing. The 'language' Forty invokes is clearly an idealization in the tradition of Saussure's *langue* (it is autonomous, decontextualized and ahistorical), and while idealization may be useful for some purposes (e.g. determining the phonological system of a language) it becomes seriously misleading when applied to an issue like the elaboration of aesthetic terminology relative to social terminology.[2] This is an issue, not of *langue*, but of what Saussure called *parole*, or what we have been calling *discourse*. In other words the question is not about what language can or cannot do, but about what its users have or have not done with it.

From this point of view, to ask why the architectural discourse community has not developed ways of discoursing on the social to the same extent it has developed ways of discoursing on aesthetic value is really to ask about the historical, social and cultural conditions in which certain discourses arise (and others do not, or attain only very limited currency). Relevant questions here might include: what purposes and/or interests does a discourse on such-and-such serve? Who is recognized as possessing the authority to produce such a discourse? On what kinds of knowledge would it draw, and who has access to that knowledge? Is there an audience or a market for it? Are there media through which it could be circulated?

A 'social' language of value does occasionally manifest itself in a seemingly unlikely source. Figure 5, for example, is an extract from a feature in the style magazine *Wallpaper* (September 2000) on the phenomenon of 'gated communities'. *Wallpaper* is among the most upmarket of the monthly style magazines available in the UK: it has a very high cover price, both editorial and advertising content are targeted to an audience of affluent and fashion-conscious consumers, and more space is devoted than in competing titles to architecture as distinct from interior design. The feature on gated communities comprises three linked reports on developments in the USA, South Africa and Britain. It is clear that the feature takes a critical stance in relation to gated communities, which are seen throughout as morally repellent because they reproduce social segregation (by race in the USA and South Africa, and by class in Britain) in a particularly extreme and explicit way. Essentially, this is a *social* critique which focuses on the *spatial* characteristics of the gated community. 'Undesirable' groups of people are not just prevented from living there by lacking the economic means to purchase property, as is in practice the case in many other residential communities; the walls, locked gates and other security devices prevent outsiders from penetrating the space at all, as well as discouraging insiders from venturing beyond the gates to encounter the other people who are nominally their neighbours.

In two out of the three reports, the representation of gated communities as obnoxious morally and socially is carried forward mainly by way of an *aesthetic* critique. The benighted views of the inhabitants and developers are signified by their preference for design which is conventional, backward looking and vulgarly ostentatious. The houses in one US development are described, for example, as 'cookie-cutter Charleston garden town houses and custom neo-Georgian trophy mansions that can make even new money look old. Well, kind of.' The reader is invited to infer the moral ugliness of gated communities from their physical ugliness, and the objectionable social values of the residents from their appalling taste in architecture. The strategy is somewhat reminiscent of allegorical paintings or medieval morality plays where vice is portrayed as ugly and virtue as beautiful: it is a familiar convention that we all know how to interpret. But in the report that comes from South Africa, the naturalness of the equation between goodness and beauty is called into question. The reporter quotes a professor of urban planning and architecture in Cape Town:

> To David Dewar . . . any walled compound, regardless of architectural merit, is
> 'absolutely terrible' and 'all the same' . . . 'There is a profoundly anti-urban ethos here.

THE GATE'S CLOSED

The gated community is the fastest growing property-development trend in the world. Forget about loft conversions and inner-city townhouses, if your new digs don't have a phalanx of guards and spiky fencing around the perimeter you might become part of the defenceless majority. Our correspondents in the States, Britain and South Africa, however, reckon they'd rather be on the outside

Figure 5
FIRST PAGE OF ARTICLE ON GATED COMMUNITIES FROM WALLPAPER MAGAZINE, SEPTEMBER 2000
Copyright of, and permission from, Art Department, London and New York; artist Jordi Labarda

We have never celebrated the urban experience. These things [i.e. gated communities] are heavily marketed as "the good urban life" where you can find peace and tranquillity and security in every sense of the word.' Dewar posits that this sprawling, 'cocooning suburbia' is illegal. The benchmark Development Facilitation Act introduced in 1995 just after the ANC came to power was meant to implement 'wealth, race and spatial integration'. Edited communities are unlikely ever to achieve this. Not surprisingly he refuses to countenance 'good' examples of what he sees as a sad

116 □

phenomenon. 'Once you have gone through the act of putting a wall round something, it ceases to be a design problem, because the wall destroys the relationship with the community at large. It's an absolutely awful idea all round.'

In this text, there are two distinct 'voices'. One is the writer's voice, which is 'dominant' insofar as it carries the institutional authority of the magazine and all other contributions are framed by it; the other is David Dewar's. In the first sentence, the writer's voice expresses the conventional idea that 'architectural merit' is a non-social matter, determined by formal and aesthetic criteria; a walled compound might in principle possess this kind of merit, even if it were judged on other (social) criteria as 'absolutely terrible'. But this separation of architectural value from social or moral value is rejected by Dewar himself, and the distancing between his voice and the writer's, which is clear in the first sentence, becomes progressively less marked. For example, the text reproduces quite lengthy quotations in his voice, without editorial comment (e.g. lines 2–5 and 10–12). In other passages, the writer's framing of Dewar's views suggests a degree of sympathy with them. For example, the proposition 'he <u>refuses to countenance</u> "good" examples of <u>what he sees as</u> a sad phenomenon' clearly attributes the relevant views to Dewar, but the preface <u>not surprisingly</u> suggests that the writer considers Dewar's position justified and invites readers to take a similar position. In the sentence 'edited communities are unlikely ever to achieve this [i.e. wealth, racial and spatial integration]' the writer appears to have aligned herself with Dewar; the sentence is not marked as a quotation but rather renders his views in her voice. In the next sentence 'good' is placed in quotation marks, suggesting that the two voices have now changed places completely: here the unmarked and dominant voice is the one which rejects the possibility of a gated community's being 'good' architecture, while the voice which acknowledges that possibility has become (quotation) marked. The passage we have quoted is the last paragraph of the report, so the writer also gives Dewar the last word. The remarks which are selected to occupy this significant position in the text contain an explicit challenge to the assumption with which the writer began the paragraph, that one can separate the question of 'architectural merit' from the social issue of segregation/integration. In this report, at least, we would say that the 'social' voice ultimately prevails over the 'aesthetic' voice – though in the feature as a whole the relationship is more complicated.

Adrian Forty's argument about language's (in)ability to represent the social in architecture is pitched at the level of vocabulary: he deplores, in essence, a lack of words analogous to *depth, transparency* and *plasticity* but referring to social rather than physical qualities of buildings. Certainly no such lexicon is apparent in the discussion of gated communities which we have quoted above. Dewar's terms of disapprobation, not unlike Kester Rattenbury's terms of praise for Rem Koolhaas in text (C), are mainly colloquial formulae such as 'absolutely awful/terrible'. On the other hand the piece contains some striking metaphors, such as 'cocooning suburbia' and 'edited community', and one technical phrase, 'spatial integration', which in this context clearly denotes a sociopolitical rather than formal/aesthetic goal.

The reference to context in the last sentence points to an aspect of meaning whose importance Adrian Forty seems to us to underestimate: the way meaning emerges from an interaction between a text and a reader in particular contextual conditions. It is not located only in the words, and therefore need not be undermined by a lack of specific vocabulary. In the gated communities text, for example, the meaning of what David Dewar says depends in part on our knowledge that he is talking about South Africa, and our understanding of that country's recent history. In the South African context, the opposition between segregation and integration is imbued by an accumulation of previous discourse with a very particular significance. When another architect is quoted in the piece describing South Africa's gated communities as 'walled cities of denial', we do not have to be told what the inhabitants are 'denying'; we understand that it is the ending of apartheid in South Africa and the advent of democracy. We also understand that a consensus exists that apartheid was a bad thing while democracy is a good thing. Those South Africans who choose to live in 'walled cities of denial' are segregated not just physically from the surrounding population, but also morally from the wider global community. This does not have to be said in so many words to be part of the meaning we can make from the text.

The *Wallpaper* text challenges, however partially and equivocally, the conventional criteria of evaluative discourse on buildings. If the conventional criteria usually prevail, it is not because language is inadequate to challenge them, but because in many contexts a challenge is not in the interests of dominant groups. Here we are not necessarily talking about economic or political élites, but about people whose influence is dependent on being able to claim expert knowledge about the value of buildings: architects, scholars, teachers, museum curators, critics. These experts have been trained and socialized to understand the value of buildings in essentially non-social terms, and it is not surprising that this understanding is expressed in the kind of evaluative discourse they produce – or that they should protect their position as experts by minimizing engagement with alternative discourses where others might have a competing claim to expertise. Hence, for example, the propensity of critics to couch moral and social judgements in aesthetic terms – brutalist concrete bus stations stand for the contempt with which their users are regarded, vulgar imitation Georgian mansions stand for the reactionary social attitudes of the *nouveaux riches* who own them.

There is a vicious circle here: since the discourses available to us now shape the understandings from which future discourse must necessarily begin, a discourse to which there is no credible alternative easily becomes self-perpetuating. But in the right contextual conditions, other discourses may break through. In South Africa, for instance, current political realities create a space in which architecture can readily be seen as a key social practice, and someone like David Dewar who refuses conventional value-judgements can exert influence where it counts. *Wallpaper*, which defines its implied reader as intelligent, cosmopolitan and perhaps a little unorthodox, can afford to give some space to alternative discourses – though aestheticism and consumerism remain dominant in the magazine as a whole, they do not have to occupy the unchallenged position they do in, say, *Homes & Gardens*, whose readers are imagined as less self-confident people with more conventional attitudes and tastes. In sum, it takes more effort to challenge dominant discourses and the interests they serve than it does to reproduce those discourses; but there is no reason to think that the task is 'beyond the capacity of language' – or beyond the wit of its users.

Chapter 6: Heritage

TIME, SPACE AND THE PAST

'The past is a foreign country' is a metaphor that works by extending the meaning of distance and borders from space to time. To get to a foreign country, far away or not, one has to cross over one or more spatial barriers. To make a journey through time apparently also involves crossing borders, and landing in a strange place. We usually call this retracing of steps though time 'history'. In what way is that different from 'heritage'?

On the front of an envelope enclosing a recent appeal for funds by English Heritage is the slogan 'Without your help, England's heritage could simply become history' alongside a colour picture of a sixteenth century mansion, Kirby Hall in Northamptonshire, framed by wild flowers in the foreground (Figure 6). The appeal leaflet inside asks the recipient to 'Help us [English Heritage] conserve the nation's heritage . . . [evidence of] England's rich and fascinating history.' What do these two short texts and images say about heritage and history?

First, they simultaneously distinguish between the two terms and conflate them. Second, they place history in an inferior position to heritage by implying that if, through lack of (costly) maintenance, Kirby falls into ruin, and maybe entirely disappears, instead of the past being experienced in a tangible, material form, it becomes a memory captured in what is merely ('simply') 'history'. Though there may be a colloquial sense to this – becoming history being equivalent to being forgotten – another reading is that if all that remains is a written text or (more rarely) a spoken account, the normal media of history, this would be a diminution. And third the flowers 'naturalize' the built heritage, using an image which sets the building into a natural landscape. This makes two related ideas concrete. One is that buildings share with nature the property of 'innocence' – of having no social context. The other is that buildings, like natural elements, are not (or should not be) subject to the historical forces of change and degeneration.

The English Heritage texts bear out the contrast between time and space implied by the 'foreign country' metaphor, in presenting the move from time to

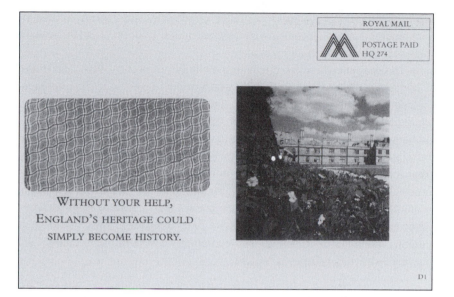

ROYAL MAIL

POSTAGE PAID
HQ 274

WITHOUT YOUR HELP,
ENGLAND'S HERITAGE COULD
SIMPLY BECOME HISTORY.

D1

ure 6
VELOPE OF ENGLISH
RITAGE APPEAL LEAFLET

space as a move from history to heritage. It is a move to material specificity, to the localization of narrative in space. All space is articulated by material objects which are either the contained, *in* space, or are the containers, *of* space. So both small objects in display cases, or large ones such as buildings, are the natural medium of heritage. But material objects are capable of multiple interpretations. To select one or a few in order to narrow the interpretation into some preferred channel, to turn history into heritage, requires language. So although the history/heritage distinction may appear to be one between linguistic representations of the past (the spoken and written texts of 'history') and non-linguistic, material objects which directly embody the past ('heritage'), it turns out that things are not so simple. Language is required, not only for the production of history, but also for the creation of the shared meanings which turn material objects into 'heritage'. It is also to a large extent language that establishes the addressee's relationship to a certain 'heritage' and defines the context in which objects are experienced as meaningful. In this chapter we consider these functions of language in relation to 'heritage' buildings and their sites.

There is a multiplicity of relevant text-types – oral recitals, books, articles, travel brochures, posters, printed or spoken guides, lectures, inscriptions and labels, advertising in print or on television, and information from the Internet. The subjects addressed in these texts have multiple identities of gender, class, age, ethnic group, culture, education, and they have multiple purposes in visiting, viewing, or reading about, heritage sites. There is a multiplicity of contexts – home, school, museum, or tourist site. The texts position us as women or men, scholars or students, children or adults, domestic consumers or 'foreign' visitors, professionals or laypersons, rulers or subjects, and persons of wealth or of modest means. The context may be study, tourism, education, conservation, entertainment, commerce or investment.

The distinction between the texts and material objects of history and those of heritage is blurred and unstable. David Lowenthal (1996) in *The Heritage Crusade and the Spoils of History* notes: 'Critics who confuse the two enterprises condemn heritage as a worthless sham, its credos as fallacious, even perverse. But heritage, no less than history, is essential to knowing and acting' (xi). For him the relatively recent dominance of heritage over history, at least in the popular experience, is marked by a shift in the purpose of understanding the past; history focusing on knowledge, heritage 'enlist[ing] the past for present causes' often by emphasizing the similarity between the present and (a possibly fictional) past. Moreover, he argues, though history 'cannot avoid being incomplete, biased, and present-minded' (115), it nevertheless 'conform[s] to evidence accessible to all' and, above all, this evidence is testable.

> Heritage is not like that at all. It is not testable, or even a reasonably plausible account of some past, but a declaration of faith in that past. Heritage is not history, even when it mimics history. History seeks to convince by truth and succumbs to falsehood. Heritage exaggerates, omits, candidly invents and frankly forgets, and thrives on ignorance and error . . . [and] is immune to critical reappraisal because it is not erudition but catechism; what counts is not checkable fact but credulous allegiance (121).

CREATING IDENTITIES

For buildings to become heritage objects, visitors must be induced to feel that in some sense they belong to the 'inheriting' community – that the building is somehow 'theirs'. Since buildings on their own cannot induce this sense of community and ownership, establishing it is a recurrent function of heritage texts. Yet the issue is more complex than it might appear at first glance. Many heritage sites are visited by a considerable range of people (maximizing this range is, unsurprisingly, one of the aims of the heritage tourism industry) and visitors must therefore be addressed in ways which do not exclude and alienate some in the process of making others feel they 'belong'.

Consider, as a small example, the way potential donors are addressed in the English Heritage text on Kirby Hall. This text strikingly does *not* use the inclusive first person plural (*we, us*) as a way of specifying *whose* heritage is at stake. It refers to *the nation's/England's* heritage and history, addresses the reader as *you* and reserves the pronoun *us* to refer to the institutional author of the text, namely English Heritage. There is a fairly obvious motivation for these linguistic choices. If the addressee were constructed specifically (exclusively) as a member of the community whose heritage needs to be preserved – that is, as *English* – then non-English readers (such as the Scottish resident to whom our copy of this text was sent) might be deterred from making a donation. We might detect a small and subtle gesture towards English readers in the use of the phrase *the nation* (like *this country*, it presupposes that readers are insiders to the entity in question: it exemplifies the phenomenon Michael Billig (1995) has dubbed 'banal nationalism', in which nationalism is not overtly ideological, but is invoked as an everyday reference point). Otherwise, however, the text positions the reader non-specifically. Interest in preserving England's heritage does not have to depend on belonging to the category of 'the nation'. The point about inclusiveness is not only relevant to texts whose function is to solicit money; it would equally apply to the texts found *in* Kirby Hall. Clearly, 'England's heritage' is marketed as a tourist attraction to foreigners as well as to the English themselves, and heritage attractions must be presented in a way that makes available positions for both 'native' and 'foreign' visitors.

Apart from 'native versus foreign', other kinds of social differences are relevant to the positioning of visitors to heritage buildings. The meaning of heritage is not confined to questions of national identity but may also relate to, for instance, ethnicity, class, age, religion, culture and gender. In a building like Kirby Hall, for example, even most English visitors are not obviously and unproblematically members of the community whose heritage the building represents, since what is preserved is the possessions and the lifestyle of a highly privileged class: the average visitor is more likely to be descended from the servants than the owners. Despite an increasing concern to preserve the material culture of poorer people (some examples of which we consider below), many heritage buildings are monuments to past wealth and power. Textual representations of their significance as 'part of the nation's [= everyone in the nation's] heritage' may try to downplay this by keeping silence on the whole issue of class (though obviously class differences were salient within aristocratic households and on the estates where they were sited). This silence can easily go unnoticed, since innumerable cultural practices (from studying novels with upper class protagonists at school, to consuming a diet of royal trivia in popular magazines) have 'naturalized' the habit of identifying 'the nation' with its most privileged members.

In other cases, however, the issue of difference is not glossed over, and the experience of visiting a site is designed on the assumption that for many visitors what is being presented is not merely distant in time, it is a past which they are unlikely to consider 'theirs'. One strategy for dealing with this is to encourage the visitor to identify imaginatively with one or more members of the group whose past experiences are commemorated. The visitor to the museum of immigration on New York's Ellis Island, for instance, follows the same path through the space as the actual immigrants who landed there: essentially s/he is positioned *as* an immigrant. Visitors to museums dealing with enslavement or the

Holocaust may work their way around the exhibits following the narrative of a specific historical slave or prisoner. While for some visitors this identification with the original inhabitants or users of a building will reinforce a prior identification (e.g. with ancestors who were themselves immigrants to Ellis Island, or slaves, or inmates of Nazi camps), for others it allows them to make connections that are absent from their own personal histories.

Clearly, the means whereby visitors are enabled to enter into others' experiences are fundamentally *linguistic*. Without explanatory text positioning the visitor as X, Y or Z (and signage to regulate the visitor's progress through the space), a building could not be experienced in the intended way: all kinds of experiences, and positions from which to experience, would be available to the visitor – while conversely the experience of 'becoming' one of the original inhabitants would be unavailable. Language narrows the range of possibilities, and in the cases just cited lessens the potential distance between the visitor who already identifies with a particular group like 'immigrants' and one who does not. (Interestingly, we do not know of any heritage attraction which tries to *increase* that distance, for instance by encouraging white visitors to a museum of slavery to identify with a slave trader or plantation overseer: identifying with the oppressed is considered educational, but the alternative, while it might also be educational, would be considered offensive and shocking. This says something about the liberal ideology underlying even the more radical presentations of heritage. It is acknowledged that visitors are of many nations, classes, races, ages, ethnic groups and religions, but they are addressed as a homogeneous group *ideologically* – 'we all agree that X [racism/slavery/fascism] was abhorrent'. This also carries the implication 'we are not to blame'. Any challenge to that presupposition is unspeakable in the context of 'heritage'.)

The techniques of address just discussed are very often used in connection with the heritage of 'minority' groups, and are adopted both to emphasize the specificity of minority experience and at the same time to make it accessible to others, so that ultimately 'their' heritage can be recognized as part of 'ours'. But the technique of imaginary identification is also used in more banal ways, to recreate a past that is merely distant rather than potentially divisive and painful to contemplate. In Robert Owen's, the social reformer, two hundred-year-old World Heritage industrial village of New Lanark in Scotland one can take a chair ride 'back in time' with the ghost of an 1820 millgirl in the 'Annie McLeod Experience', to the accompaniment of a spoken commentary. In the Hitchin British Schools Museum in Hertfordshire, England, children can dress up in mid-nineteenth century school clothes and be taught a Victorian lesson by a teacher also dressed in appropriate costume, speaking a carefully designed text. In Virginia's Colonial Williamsburg costumed actors make barrels and visitors can meet a live Thomas Jefferson. The visitor to Williamsburg is prepared for these encounters by guidebooks which claim that here 'history is alive . . . so to speak free of dust . . . (here one can) experience what it was like to be alive on the eve of the American Revolution . . . personal encounters like these are anything but virtual reality. They involve all the senses and stimulate the minds of adults and kids alike'. In all such cases the multiple possible interpretations of what is seen and heard are narrowed by language.

The examples just discussed challenge conventional approaches to 'national heritage' in which there is a preoccupation with constructing, for the benefit of both 'native' and 'foreign' visitors, a more unitary and less problematic version of 'national identity'. It should not be thought, however, that this project is obsolete. A major conference on Museum and Cultural Identity (Edinburgh 1999) was called 'Shaping the image of nations'; the Director of the National Museum of Scotland wrote that the (new) Museum of Scotland '. . . must [also] provide an opportunity for Scots to reflect upon their national identity'. This has to be seen in the context of Scotland's circumstances and aspirations at the time – the opening of the new National Museum came shortly after devolution had brought Scotland a significant degree of political autonomy from England, and questions of national identity were highly salient in many domains.

One connotation of the 'past is a foreign country' is that of borders; boundaries which separate 'us' and 'them'. The business of creating an inheriting community, through texts attached to real objects, spaces and places, involves the creation of boundaries, within which we are, and outside which the Other is located. The boundaries are legal, ideological or political, and may involve the creation of mythological pasts, sometimes alternative pasts in which the same events are seen from the positions of communities in conflict. The creation of identities and the drawing of boundaries between them are underlying aims of heritage creation, no matter what the intrinsic value of and interest in what is being preserved. And this process is always a social construction achieved through language. But the boundaries are also material and spatial, as in the enclosure that marks a workstation, house, compound or village, the markers and gates of ghettos or city limits, and national territorial or marine borders. These physical and spatial markers interact with the language of the texts.

Frequently the texts deliberately obscure the distinction between history and heritage in order to create an identity. The former legitimizes the knowledge of the past, the latter puts it to present political use. It is so obvious that it may go unnoticed that the buildings themselves are quite incapable of doing this. For example, the late eighteenth century Kilmainham Gaol in Dublin is where the leaders of the 1916 Easter Rising were imprisoned and executed. It is now a museum where one can read the final messages written on the cell walls by those prisoners. The Irish National Monuments and Historic Properties Service looks after the gaol, and its website states that it is responsible for the *heritage* functions of the government, indeed for 'Ireland's built *heritage*', which it promotes by '*heritage* publications', and by organizing an annual '*Heritage* Day' through its 'Heritage Services'. But, at the same time, by opening a new exhibition building at the gaol financed by the National Lottery, the service claims to be preserving 'the integrity of a . . . historical site' (our emphases). A popular Dublin tourist guide speaks of Kilmainham as 'offer[ing] a panoramic insight into some of the most profound, disturbing and inspirational themes of modern Irish history'; another speaks of it as 'a museum to the struggle for Irish independence'; a third speaks of 'the [prison's] political and penal history'.[1] This conflation of heritage and history serves the specific purpose of 'naturalizing' the political perspective in the interests of nationalism.

At a time when the north-south division of Ireland is still a live and bitterly contentious issue, such texts, and such sites, have an important political role. It may even be that, as The Guardian reported (4 January 2000: 5), the infamous Maze prison in the UK province of Northern Ireland – formerly known as Long Kesh – once it is closed down, will become a museum. It remains to be seen what kind of history a Maze museum will tell, and what kind of heritage its guidebooks will celebrate.

These examples of prisons becoming heritage sites are useful reminders that not all heritage deals with religious worship, genteel life in country houses, dynasties of Chinese emperors, farmwork, industry or rural life. The violence embedded in narratives of political oppression, imprisonment and executions is materially present on grim sites; and even more so when the entire project which is commemorated is extermination in the name of ethnic or political cleansing. The former Nazi concentration camps and Cambodia's 'killing fields', which are now museums, are national heritage sites. We discuss these episodes a little later.

COMMODIFICATION

Today an economic dimension of investment and profit has become an over-riding consideration in the creation of heritage. This involves the commodification of history. The economic arguments over capital investment and the generation of revenue come into the sharpest focus when important architectural monuments can only be conserved by finding new, economically viable, uses for them. In the late 1990s London's Royal Naval College at Greenwich became a classic case. The building stands on the site of a major Tudor palace, replaced in the seventeenth century by a new palace, which was eventually turned into a seamen's hospital and later into the Royal Naval College. England's most celebrated architects were involved at Greenwich – Inigo Jones, Christopher Wren, Nicolas Hawksmoor, John Webb and James Stuart. When the tenure of the complex was put up for sale the agents published a splendid glossy colour brochure (Knight Frank & Rutley 1995) lavishly illustrated with fifteen colour plates (one a magnificent, double page reproduction of Canaletto's painting of the buildings), as well as a block plan and a map. (But, as Jonathan Glancey pointed out in the Independent (25.9.95), there were no

floor plans; so neither the spatial structure nor the functional potential of the buildings was evident.) The two Secretaries of State of the day, of Defence and National
Heritage, described the complex in the Preface, as 'a magnificent group of buildings of outstanding cultural and heritage importance . . . a unique part of our
national heritage. Prospective tenants will need to be able to demonstrate enduring long term proposals sympathetic to the character of the site. Furthermore, the
Government is considering an application to UNESCO to designate parts of
Greenwich as a World Heritage Site.' The brochure also emphasizes the adjacency
of other historically important buildings and sites – the National Maritime Museum,
the Queen's House, the famous sailing ship the *Cutty Sark*, and the Royal
Observatory (with its zero longitude location). And of course since the complex was
offered for sale, the ill-fated Millennium Dome has been built, and London
Underground's Jubilee Line and the Docklands light railway have been completed.

The superlatives – 'magnificent, outstanding, unique' – and the emphasis
on the historic importance of the site would certainly be daunting to a prospective developer. If that were not enough, English Heritage in 1994 gave the
Ministry of Defence their views, as stated to the Department of National Heritage.
'In principle our advice to the Department is aimed at the preservation of the
maximum amount of historic fabric and finishes of the buildings and attempting
to ensure that if change of use and alterations can be proved necessary, they are
achieved with minimum impact on the overall integrity of the architecture'
(Knight Frank & Rutley: 10).

The emphasis on the, mainly royal, history of the site, on minimum alteration, on the need to 'prove' any need for change, and on the idea that buildings
constructed over a period of almost four centuries have an 'integrity' in which
anything added will be an intrusion, all combine to construct a strongly conservative policy. Though in the context of architectural heritage the ideological
underpinnings of such a policy are only implicit, other bodies dedicated to
heritage make their political and economic conservatism quite explicit, though
they generally remain silent about architecture. In the USA the Heritage
Foundation was founded in 1973 with a mission to 'formulate and promote
conservative public policies based on the principles of free enterprise, limited
government, individual freedom, traditional American values, and a strong
national defense [sic]' (website http://www.heritage.org). So whilst in political
projects such as this 'heritage' explicitly connotes conservative policies, in architecture the word functions implicitly.

The elevated language of conservation and heritage sits uneasily alongside
that of real estate, which the agents for the sale of the Royal Naval College
inevitably had to use. The buildings are several times referred to as 'property';
there are discussions of 'rack-rent at full market value', 'ground rent', 'repairing
liability', and the 'assets [and] trading accounts' of interested bidders. The buildings offered 'potential for a range of appropriate uses', which were identified as

institutional (but not residential) housing, a museum, art gallery or public exhibition hall, hospital, nursing home, residential school or training centre. Of course, this language is inevitable and necessary for real estate dealings. However since it is used in all such transactions, it diminishes the claims that are also made for the uniqueness and splendour of the site.

Not surprisingly there was a well-articulated public debate when this sale was first announced, especially against its privatization. Glancey, in the *Independent,* contributed under the headline 'Pile 'em high, flog 'em cheap? Not this time, Westminster' (23.10.1995). Whilst he agreed with the agents' evaluation – 'this magnificent group of buildings ranks among the greatest of the Renaissance world . . . of international standing', he condemns the government's 'asinine' attempt to sell the buildings 'as if they were any piece of lucrative real estate . . . promiscuous behaviour . . . divid[ing] up and flog[ging] off what remains of our public realm . . . the tacky way in which our architectural, historical and cultural heritage is being proffered for sale for what could well be a mess of potage at Westminster's equivalent of a car-boot sale'. He proposed imaginative new uses for the old buildings and the construction of new buildings – 'the very latest, and the very finest art, architecture and craftsmanship money [can] buy'.

In the event the outcome was less crude than Glancey had feared. Much of the site was acquired by the University of Greenwich for campus buildings, some by the Trinity College of Music, and apart from major restoration work, formally and technically imaginative additions and changes were made. Glancey still hankered after a 'world class institution . . . [rather] than a university college with such local roots . . . [such as] a world academy of music or architecture or philosophy'. In this case it is clear that the entire debate was not only carried out by means of texts – government directives, planning rules, estate agents' literature, and the press – but that the outcome was shaped by them.

Another aspect of commodification is that cultural tourism has generated enormous sectors of investment and employment in this major sector of the global economy. The production of books, souvenirs, reproductions and trinkets, has created a vast manufacturing, publishing and printing industry; whilst airlines, travel and advertising agencies, television and radio production, commercial art and photographic studios, guiding, teaching and running franchised sales outlets, hotels and catering enterprises, have created an equally vast service industry. The material products and the services on offer are merely the visible aspect of commodification, and the way historic buildings or ruins are used to yield the maximum income is a key issue.

All the printed architectural heritage materials we have looked at devote a substantial proportion of their texts to the promotion of souvenir and gift shops, hotels, leisure activities and restaurants. And business sponsorship, as in sports, has become essential for survival. The process has caused some critics such as Hewison (1987) to see the heritage industry, with its creation of a past that never was, as totally bogus, malign, and as evidence of economic decline which is debilitating to authentic culture. But the arguably corrosive effect on heritage of commodification and sponsorship, aspects of the global economy, have to be placed alongside the benefits: keeping alive folk traditions and narratives; the conservation of intrinsically interesting, sometimes valuable, vulnerable buildings and objects which would otherwise vanish; education; and the affirmation of identities which are not always chauvinistic or aggressively exclusive, but may represent struggles for freedom from oppression. And many heritage experiences are undoubtedly enjoyable.

DEPOLITICIZING THE PAST: THE CASE OF WIGAN PIER

'Interpretations of the past', say Gero and Root (Gathercole and Lowenthal 1990: 19), 'play an active function, a *political* function, in legitimating the present context, naturalising the past so that it appears to lead logically to present social practices and values'. One political function is to *de*politicize the past. This is nowhere clearer than in cases where the past is already explicitly politicized, as George Orwell, social critic and writer, politicized it in his 1937 description and critique of working class northern British life – *The Road to Wigan Pier*. This classic is still one of the most graphic accounts in the English language of disease-ridden urban poverty, squalor and misery. It is an especially powerful representation of, and argument against, class divisions. Wigan Pier, one of many loading stages along the Leeds and Liverpool canal running through the industrial North, was used for tipping coal from railway trucks into canal barges. It became a joke made famous in early twentieth century music halls by stage and film comedian George Formby. Orwell in fact only mentions it once (1962: 68) and then to lament its disappearance. It was demolished eight years before Orwell wrote his book.

What is remarkable is that as a result of its appearance in the title of his book, a non-existent phenomenon, nationally notorious only as a subject of humour and ridicule, became world famous and, in 1982, prompted the idea of regenerating this part of Wigan as an industrial heritage site. Four years and £3.5 million pounds later it opened to the public. It has grown a lot since then. Today its eight and a half acres include a conjectural replica of the Pier (nobody knows exactly what it looked like), restored mills and warehouses, including the Trencherfield Mill where one can find what is promoted as the world's largest working mill steam engine, The Way We Were heritage centre, representing the life of miners, textile workers and mills owners in 1900, and Opie's Museum of Memories, in which newspapers, magazines, comics, toys, music, entertainment, fashion, food, design and domestic life of the entire twentieth century are cele-brated. One mill houses the reconstructed Victorian School room, complete with teacher; another the Orwell public house and restaurant. The Way We Were

Centre has a Palace of Varieties which 'has been uniquely themed to capture the special atmosphere of Wigan Pier and the theme of Victorian music-hall'. The waterbuses which cruise along the canal are 'Wigan's answer to the *Parisian Bateau Mouche*'. The Parlour at the Pier, the George Formby Lecture Theatre, the Mill at the Pier, the Pantry at the Pier, and the Palace of Varieties offer facilities for conferences, business functions, seminars, weddings, 'Murder Weekends and Evenings', product launches and 'floating meetings' – using the canal boats (Figure 7). There is an education service which offers a variety of workshops under such titles as 'Washday Blues', 'Box of Memories', 'A is for Apple', 'Home Sweet Home', 'Spare the Rod', 'Towpath Sleuths', and 'Privy, Poultice and Piles', each equipped with teachers' and children's materials, and all geared to the recently introduced model for learning in the state's schools, the National Curriculum. And of course there is a gift shop.

If one has to single out one concept which recurs throughout the battery of guides and promotional leaflets it is *memory*. Apart from Opie's Museum of Memories – where a day out (is one) 'you and your group will never forget' – one is encouraged 'to take a trip down memory lane'; to meet 'the characters of yesteryear, re-discovering those items which shaped history, coming face to face with local heritage, and sharing with others memories of the past'; and to 'explore the fascinating world of memory – discover how memory works and listen to the memories of others'. A heading proclaims that the 'old days were the best'. The images are of old teddy bears, a *Mickey Mouse Annual*, a record cover of 1950s folk idol, Lonnie Donegan, singing to his guitar, and a smartly dressed family group in front of a harmonium. And of course selling fake and reproduction objects allows you to 'take home more than just a memory' after 'browsing around the Wigan Pier Shop for gifts and souvenirs'.

The 'memory' that is invoked in these texts is a curiously selective one, however. Platitudes like 'the old days were the best' are in marked contrast with Orwell's depiction of the old days which was based not on memory but on direct observations he made at the time. He first observes the work down the mines, where the miner works '. . . a thousand feet underground, in suffocating heat and swallowing coal dust with every breath, [walking] a mile bent double' (28). Work which he says would kill him (Orwell) in a few weeks, under constant danger of explosions, and which results in accidents, maiming, disease (such as the chest diseases caused by coal dust, and nystagmus of the eyes), and premature death. The working time for a fifteen year old miner with whose family he stayed, from leaving home to returning, taking travel into account, was eleven hours. He observed that allowing for washing, eating, dressing and sleeping, his 'leisure time' was four hours a day.

He then continues with graphic and detailed descriptions of the industrial towns, the housing and conditions within the houses, in which his feeling of disgust is dominant. 'As you walk through the industrial towns you lose yourself

in labyrinths of little brick houses blackened by smoke, festering in planless chaos round miry alleys and little cindered yards where there are stinking dustbins and lines of grimy washing and half-ruinous WCs' (46). Houses without running water, mostly over sixty years old, 'poky and ugly, and insanitary and comfort-less . . . [are] distributed in incredibly filthy slums round belching foundries and stinking canals and slag-heaps that deluge them with sulphurous smoke' (46–7).

131 □

He analyses the wages and living costs of typical families, the payment for gas by penny-in-the-slot meters (which then, as now, was more expensive than by quarterly bills or, today, by Direct Debit from your bank account), the extortionate rents charged by rapacious landlords, and the debts. Overcrowding, with ten people in a three-bedroom house, or 'four beds for eight people', results in 'squalor and confusion . . . a tub full of filthy water here, a basin full of unwashed crocks there, more crocks piled in any odd corner, torn newspaper littered every-where, and in the middle always the same dreadful table covered with sticky oilcloth and crowded with cooking pots and irons and half-darned stockings and pieces of stale bread and bits of cheese wrapped round with greasy newspaper' and a congestion 'in a tiny room where getting from one side to the other is a complicated voyage between pieces of furniture, with a line of damp washing getting you in the face every time you move and the children as thick underfoot as toadstools!' (54).

Orwell was well aware of the possibilities of romanticizing and camouflag-ing reality through language – for instance, in speaking of the caravan dwellers along the canals – where the word caravan 'conjures up a cosy gipsy-encampment (in fine weather, of course) with wood fires crackling and children picking black-berries and many-coloured washing fluttering on the lines' (56). The real caravan-dwellers of Wigan, according to him, live along the 'miry canal . . . [on] patches of waste ground on which caravans have been dumped like rubbish out of a bucket' (57). Some are old gypsy caravans, but more are old single-decker buses, wagons with canvas roofs less than six feet high and measuring from six to fifteen feet in length, with damp floors, wringing wet mattresses, and bitterly cold. Like all writers of creative imagination Orwell suffers under the inadequacy of lan-guage; his descriptions he regards as mere 'reminders . . . [enabling him] to bring back what [he has] seen . . . but they cannot in themselves give much idea of what conditions are like in those fearful northern slums' (52).

The descriptions in *The Road to Wigan Pier* are not only remarkably similar to the conditions described by the urban reformer Edwin Chadwick, the radical observer and theoretician Frederick Engels and others, almost a century earlier, but remarkably *dis*similar to the texts produced at Wigan Pier. These bear out Orwell's suspicion of language which romanticizes and camouflages. His account – making allowances for the fact that it is certainly slanted and possibly exag-gerated – nevertheless presents a convincing picture of misery, harshness, poverty, fatigue, and destructive and unequal economic relations. In contrast the heritage texts from which we have quoted, despite their reference to a 'back breaking day down at the pit' and the Miners' March, emphasize play, joy, colour, stability and solid working class virtues.

The Wigan Pier heritage site does not of course display large passages from Orwell's text, or historical material; probably the organizers feared that the audi-ence it addressed might not find this stimulating. But it offers, instead, restored buildings, machines and boats, music, pictures, life-size human models and live, costumed, actors. This is a rich battery of representation which can easily out-weigh any lingering literary or historical knowledge in the spectator's mind. For instance, Orwell's caravan dwellers along the canal disappear, replaced by canal cruises (coloured image – a bright, glass-roofed barge under a tree-lined bridge) and 'leisurely strolls along the banks of the canal or in one of our waterway gardens'.

The image of the famous Trencherfield Mill steam engine shows a polished and painted machine; this is exactly how machines were presented at the time they were still in use, in London's 1851 Crystal Palace. The contemporary engrav-ings of the Crystal Palace show immaculate, white-clad machinists, and silk top-hatted men and crinolined women, as visitors amongst the machines.

Much of the Wigan Pier promotional text addresses the reader directly – 'you', and uses the first person plural – 'the way we were' – inviting the reader to enter directly into the presentation of him-/herself. Besides the Victorian school room (which is obviously in a mill, with its cast iron columns, and not in a purpose-built classroom) there is a good deal of emphasis on children, children's games and toys (images of hopscotch, spacehoppers, sweets and Boy Scout magazines). By a barely noticeable sleight of hand instead of presenting the lives of children in the working class culture described by Orwell and, ostensibly the focus of Wigan Pier, specific objects, customs and images have been transposed from contemporary middle class culture.

So in this presentation by texts and images, dressing up, play acting, the use of innocent themes such as humour, childhood and nature, the heritage project rewrites history. Camouflage, romantic nostalgia, transposition and selec-tive silences combine not only to fabricate a mythical history, but to promote a modern message about production, honest hard work, education, and play. This is what Gero and Root (1990) mean by heritage 'play[ing] an active function, a *political* function, in legitimating the present context, naturalising the past so that it appears to lead logically to present social practices and values' (19).

GRIM EPISODES

We have already hinted at the chasm which separates Orwell's graphic depiction of working class life in the North of England in the 1930s, from what was made of it in the 1990s in the sanitized version at Wigan Pier; and we have also referred to what has been done at Kilmainham Gaol in Ireland. The role of grim episodes in memory and heritage is a perennially fraught issue, both theoretical and prac-tical, for heritage creators, conservators and curators.

These issues are starkly highlighted in action and debates about the former Nazi World War Two concentration camps and the Holocaust. The best known is Auschwitz I (with the adjacent Auschwitz II, Birkenau) in Poland, where probably

1.5 million men, women and children perished in gas chambers and other executions, and from medical experiments, work-exhaustion, disease and malnutri-
tion. Here the camp sites, with their huts, gas chambers and crematoria have been
in part preserved, and a museum and reflection centre has been established. This
was receiving over half a million visitors a year in the late 1990s; publishes two
Pro Memoria Information Bulletins (of over one hundred pages each) a year, carries
out a substantial programme of research, is accumulating an archive and a library,
carries out building conservation and repair work, organizes exhibitions, and produces educational material. We have used a *Bulletin* on the website (A), a small
printed guide (B: 1985, Figure 8) and some of the *Pro Memoria Bulletins* (C) for
our analysis and interpretation.[2]

'The camp . . . has tremendous significance for understanding the mechanisms of genocide. [It] also has a clear moral dimension. It is a place for reflection, contemplation and prayer, and for honouring the memory of the victims
whose ashes are scattered across the fields of Brzezinka – Birkenau – the largest
cemetery in the world' (A).

'That visitors can reflect upon the fate of the people who suffered and died
here . . . requires appropriate spatial and legal solutions which can be difficult to
reconcile with the interests of the city of Oświęcim [Auschwitz] and its inhabitants' (A). The use of space and the law as instruments for achieving and preserving the museum's abstract objectives hints at some ongoing conflicts and
debates of the time. In one, the authorities were strenuously opposing the
conversion of a building opposite the gate into a supermarket. In another, they
had recently refused permission for a demonstration on the site by the Polish
National Community/Polish National Party. The reasons for this opposition by the
museum are in its title and in much of the texts we have used, which emphasize repeatedly the reflective, commemorative nature of the site. 'In view of the
exceptional and sacred nature of this place, it is not to be exploited for any sort
of demonstration with a goal other than that of remembering the victims . . .
gatherings and demonstrations cannot take place on the grounds of the former
camp for any purpose apart from commemoration' (A). Other issues which generated religious and political polemics had previously been the focus of debate: the
presence of a Carmelite convent on the site, conflicting claims about the numbers
who died here (including 'instances of conscious distortion and even downright
mendacity' (A)), and the erection of crosses on the field full of ashes.

The commemorative and reflective objectives and activities, and the non-
polemical, calm and factual nature of the texts, stand in stark contrast to the
descriptive words, phrases, and metaphors used to describe what actually went
on here: 'a gigantic and horrifying factory of death . . . [Auschwitz] devoured
human life . . . voices from the abyss . . . cynical inscription ["Arbeit macht frei"
over the gates]' and so forth (B). Repeatedly the text describes 'premeditated anni-
hilation, murder, eradication, death, flogging, whipping, corpses, confinement,

ure 8
ONT COVER OF AUSCHWITZ-
RKENAU GUIDEBOOK
pyright of, and permission
m, Lidia Foryciarz
otographer and owner
the copyright)

toil, torture, execution, hanging, mass crime, beatings, shooting, punishment, gassing, incineration, burning of corpses, gallows, and suffocation'. In the face of these descriptions of sadism, the maintenance of a non-polemical balance was, and remains, difficult to attain, for it raises the question, as all heritage sites do, with whom is the visitor encouraged to identify? What identity is s/he asked to adopt? The text (A) recognizes this: '. . . visitors will learn through specific images that the camp's victims were people like us'. It makes no bones about distinguishing between history and emotional experience, unlike the texts of most heritage literature we have looked at, where this distinction is deliberately blurred. 'This part of the exhibition [photographs, documents and other images in the Sauna building] aims more at an emotional effect than at the conveying of information as in a typical historical presentation' (A).

The texts and images have to answer another question. How can the boundary be drawn between camouflage, on the one hand, and voyeuristic realism on the other, so as to transmit an authentic, accurate message? In some versions of the narrative there is a deliberate attempt to suppress the most graphic presentation of the horror in order to make the experience bearable at all. Wanda Jakubowska, film director and Auschwitz survivor, in her 1947 film about the camp *The Last Stage* explains why the reality of '. . . human skeletons, heaps of corpses, lice, rats and different outwardly disgusting diseases' was not represented. 'Shown on the screen, this reality would certainly have inspired fright and also revulsion. Elements that were indeed authentic and characteristic but unbearable for the postwar viewer had to be eliminated. Aesthetics imposes demands on the screen and must be heeded for every subject if the film is to fulfil its role' (C, No. 9, 1998: 84).

In one sense the answer to 'whose identity' is obvious – those who perished here. But World War Two and Holocaust history is more fraught than that simple answer would suggest. Who exactly were *they*, and who are *we* – with whom are we asked to identify? This site is in Poland; many Polish prisoners of war and civilians, not only Polish Jews, perished here. Thus in the Guide (B) the history of the camp opens with the arrival of seven hundred and twenty-eight Poles in 1940, and in the Museum text, for Block 4, the first sentence reads 'Auschwitz was the biggest Nazi concentration camp for Poles and prisoners from other countries.' And this part of the narrative is continuous: 'Polish political prisoners were being deported here till the camp ceased to exist' (B). Yet the guides dwell on the rapid expansion of the inmate population to others: Jews, Sinti and Roma people ('gypsies'), military and political prisoners from Nazi-occupied territories as well as from countries allied to Germany such as Italy and Hungary, and from Russia, members of resistance groups, homosexual men, people with learning difficulties, and Jehovah's Witnesses. The fate of Jews is particularly highlighted and the greatest part of the exhibits, photographs, objects and guidebook texts is devoted to it. This has to be seen against a pre-war, wartime and post-war history of anti-Semitism in much of eastern and central Europe, and Russia, on the one hand, and the slanted propaganda of international Zionism and what has been called 'the Holocaust industry' on the other hand. The creation of a Polish national identity has also to be seen against a background of deep hostility to both German and Russian occupation. So establishing an identity of victims, unlike that of Irish republican nationalism at Kilmainham, is no simple matter. In all the texts there is a constant thread of caution about avoiding 'accents [sic] that would aggravate patriotic, national or racial feelings' (C, No. 7, 1997: 98). How many official, state-sponsored heritage sites aim, positively, to undermine national and patriotic feelings?

The texts show a recognition of this complexity. The Polish government in 1996 ratified a programme of 'extensive architectural and town planning modernisation of the town and the commune of Oświęcim' with the following goals:

> to secure due homage to the place which commemorates the Jewish Holocaust and the martyrdom of the Polish Nation and other Nations [our emphasis];

> to make proper conditions for paying tribute to the victims of genocide and for learning about problems connected with the legacy of the war;

> to arrange and to improve the aesthetics of the protective [protected?] zone around the former concentration camp;

> to create the Educational Centre as an institution of international character.

The solution which has been attempted here has two main strands. First, the pursuit of scholarship, research, archival records and education. Second, to recognize the multiple identities of both victims and visitors. On both sites there had been some spatial and institutional segregation in the camps by type of prisoner, country of origin, and ethnic group. But at Auschwitz I the museum now reinforces the multiple identities by creating separate exhibits in separate blocks for Russians, Poles, Czechs, Yugoslavs with Austrians, Hungarians, French with Belgians, Italians with Dutch, and Romas. Though many of these victims were Jews, one additional block is dedicated to Jews as a group. And the text of the guide (B) follows this spatial classification. The *Pro Memoria Bulletins* (C) devote substantial space to non-Jewish themes; one issue (C No. 10, 1999) is entirely devoted to Sinti and Roma issues.

It is surprising to us that the inherent conflicts about history and heritage, information and ideology, appear to be best resolved on a site of the most deeply disturbing kind. So might we find guidance here as to what to do in conserving housing, or the representation of urban or rural slums? In representing the mills of the industrial revolution, how do we keep alive, relive, the physical danger, exploitative working conditions, harsh discipline, monotony, exhaustion, sweat, noise, vibration and dust which were the common lot of mill workers? Of course violence, disease, squalor, danger and death are quintessential pieces of history – just as they, or analogous ones, are for us all in our personal histories. Silence, suppression, camouflage and rewriting of such episodes not only has its well-known destructive effects in the lives of individuals, but creates analogous pathologies in the life of society. So the theoretical questions concern not only the objects selected for conservation, but the balance to be achieved within the context of social and political history; and the purpose of such conservation, if it is to be neither sanitization nor sadistic voyeurism. And language, as at Auschwitz, is the main instrument for doing this.

The practical issue is that inanimate objects mean little without the presence of human beings; this has been recognized by the dressed-up actors at Beamish Open Air Museum near Newcastle-upon-Tyne in England and also at Colonial Williamsburg. Obviously no one would argue for the preservation intact of, for instance, a damp, overcrowded, rat infested tenement, inhabited by real occupants, as a piece of housing history, nor would the Auschwitz Museum contemplate using emaciated actors in vertically striped prisoners' clothes. Photographs, pieces of descriptive text (bearing always in mind the dangers of extensive and fatiguing reading tasks), models, and collections of objects and original texts can go a long way to create striking and memorable knowledge and experience. At Auschwitz there are not enough resources, nor the intention, to reproduce sensations such as sounds or smells (as, for instance, at the Yorvik Viking Museum in York), and of tactile effects, as has been done elsewhere. Modern technology could, and has, in other places, come to the curator's aid. Laser holograms, virtual reality simulations, high quality visual and aural representations, film and videos, and computer simulations have all begun to find a place. But it is easy to forget, when dazzled by these technological possibilities, that the problem of representing pain remains. Auschwitz, and such messages as Wanda Jakubowska's, serve as a warning that the very technology of simulations may block such representations, in a way which can be avoided when the medium is natural language – spoken and in texts.

ARCHITECTURE, HERITAGE AND NATIONAL IDENTITY

Among the words with which heritage most frequently collocates in discourse are *nation* and *national*. All kinds of cultural artefacts and practices, from basket making to rocket technology, may be discussed in terms of what they 'say' about the 'imagined community' of the nation (Anderson 1983), but this tendency is especially marked in relation to architecture, reflecting the status of buildings as relatively permanent and highly salient features of the landscape: they persist over time, they stay in the same place, and compared to many other cultural phenomena (e.g. literary works or styles of dancing) they are highly obtrusive. They also tend to show their age in their outward appearance (their form and style, the materials they are made of, the various signs of wear and tear they acquire). Buildings thus function as everyday, material reminders of our location in time as well as space; and 'the nation' is of course a construct based precisely on the conceit of a population sharing both spatial location and history.

The buildings we associate with this shared experience of space/time may come to be regarded as emblematic of national character or culture, of the values a nation subscribes to, of particular social arrangements and historical events. A familiar and banal example of buildings being treated as national emblems is the way certain built structures can be used metonymically to denote the nations in which they are located – the Parthenon means Greece, the Statue of Liberty stands for the USA. It is also striking how historic buildings are treated as important symbols in the aftermath of revolutions and other major upheavals in the life of a nation. Reappropriating old buildings for new uses (as in the case of the Louvre, transformed from a palace to a museum following the French Revolution) is not just a practical solution to the problem of what to do with obsolete or redundant structures, it is a clear and powerful ideological statement about the nature and principles of the new regime.

In this section we look at some discourses in which debates on national identity and history are played out in discussions about architecture and the built environment. We focus on a case where something akin to revolution has made national identity a subject for explicit and very public discursive contestation in recent years, and where large-scale reconstruction has given questions of architectural heritage (what to preserve and what to destroy) a particular urgency. This is the case of post-unification Germany, and especially its capital city, Berlin.

National identity is both a particularly salient and a particularly difficult issue in Germany, because of the country's recent history – an unhappy history of humiliation in 1918, swiftly followed by the period of fascism which ended in military defeat, partition in 1945 and reunification in 1990. This is a narrative of the nation with which most Germans now are extremely uncomfortable. And their rejection of recent history as a basis for a contemporary German national identity entails, among other things, strongly negative attitudes to certain buildings and architectural styles.

These attitudes are especially marked in relation to Berlin. It is obvious why: Berlin was, both actually and symbolically, the centre of the Third Reich (it was also the site of its final defeat); subsequently it became the main symbol of postwar partition. Though geographically it was wholly located within the eastern communist state, the German Democratic Republic (GDR), the city itself was divided, and this division was materialized in a built structure, the wall. Now the wall is gone (literally: the only remaining traces of it are underground), and Berlin once again serves, as it served before partition, as the seat of national (federal) government for Germany as a whole. But architecturally, it is felt to be 'tainted': full of monuments to totalitarianism, both Hitler's fascism and the GDR's state socialism. There has thus been concern that something should be done to ensure that the built environment of the new, unified Berlin signifies a different (democratic) form of German national identity.

There is not, however, consensus on how this is to be accomplished. To demonstrate the point, we turn to a specific text: a radio programme which was broadcast by the BBC on 30 November 1997 under the title 'Reinventing Berlin', and featured contributions from local architects, planners, commentators and residents. Their remarks (they were not talking to one another but to the BBC presenter) can be analysed to show that debate on Berlin's architecture and its relationship to German history and identity is organized around a series of meaningful linguistic contrasts – a semiotic system in the sense explained in Chapter 1. The overarching binary opposition is political, between authoritarianism (Hitler's or the GDR's) and democracy. This key political distinction also underlies many debates on architecture, where it is signified by a series of contrasts relating specifically to the qualities of the built environment. We can show the system of contrasts schematically like this:

Authoritarian	*Democratic*
stone	glass
planned urban space	'bricolage'
preservation	new building
	demolition
	'covering'

We must stress that what is shown here – based on the analysis of a particular text – is a system of meanings that has emerged in particular circumstances, and is specific to its (spatial, temporal, cultural and historical) context: it is certainly not a universal code. To make sense of the system it is necessary to unpack the underlying assumptions and claims which it has become shorthand for. With that in mind, let us consider each contrast in turn, starting with the stone/glass opposition.

Obviously, stone and glass are not straightforward antonyms like 'big' and 'small'; they become opposites only on condition that we are able to refer to certain underlying assumptions which are context-specific. In this particular semiotic system stone and glass take their opposed meanings from the political terms for which they are symbols or metaphors. Because stone was the favoured building material of Hitler's architect, Albert Speer,[3] it conventionally signifies authoritarianism. A term that has been used extensively in German discourse to denote the political ideal which is opposed to authoritarianism is *transparency* (German *durchsichtigkeit*). In political discourse 'transparency' stands for the value of open government as opposed to the secrecy and terror associated with the communist regime in the GDR (and before that, with the Nazis). In the architectural context it has come to connote a preference for extensive use of a 'transparent' building material, namely glass. What we have here is a metaphor for a metaphor: 'transparency' as a term for a way of governing uses the physical properties of certain materials (the fact that you can 'see through them') as a figure of resemblance (obviously you cannot literally 'see through' a system of government), and when architects translate that as a prescription to use glass in new buildings, they are trying to symbolize the figurative meaning of 'transparency' (here, as it happens, by going back to its literal meaning).

A second contrast which is attested in the 'Reinventing Berlin' text is between 'planned urban space' and 'bricolage' (meaning roughly an *ad hoc* patchwork of types and styles). The former is seen as 'authoritarian' on the grounds that centralized planning of large areas of urban space, with the intention of filling that space with stylistically homogeneous buildings, is strongly associated with the fascist and communist regimes of the city's pre-unification past. 'Bricolage' was the term used by an urban planner to describe the favoured 'democratic' alternative. Interestingly, however, he did not mean it to have positive connotations; he himself expressed impatience with the contemporary mistrust of organized planning. He complained that despite the opportunities offered by the extensive reconstruction work in Berlin, it had become politically suspect and thus impossible for planners and architects to try to make any kind of bold or unified statement with space. 'Bricolage' was now considered more 'democratic', signifying the absence of central control (and the opposite of Hitler's monomania). The fact that at least one individual invoked the planning/bricolage contrast to take issue with the idea that planning is authoritarian and bricolage democratic underlines an important point about the workings of meaning. When an analyst proposes an underlying semiotic system like the one we have summarized above, this does not imply that everyone necessarily subscribes uncritically to the meanings or values it expresses. The claim is rather that these meanings are shared in the sense that they are intelligible to the relevant community of language-users: they do not determine the outcome of debate, but they do define the parameters within which debate can occur.

The opposition whose first term is 'preservation' is particularly relevant to this chapter's main subject, heritage, since it relates not to new buildings but to the issue of how Berlin's existing buildings should be integrated (or not) into a historical presentation of the city and the nation. This would appear to be an especially complex and contested issue, for analysis of the 'Reinventing Berlin' text suggests that 'preservation' does not have either a single meaning or a single opposite. It can be discursively opposed to demolition, or to the construction of new buildings, or to what we have glossed as 'covering', which means modifying an existing building so that certain objectionable features are covered up (literally or figuratively). Furthermore, 'preservation' is not always identified as an 'authoritarian' move implying celebration of a past that ought properly to be condemned. Some kinds of preservation may be reinflected with 'progressive' meanings to do with acknowledging, self-critically, those parts of Germany's heritage that many Germans would rather forget.

An example may help to clarify this, and the obvious one is the Reichstag. Younger German architects were heard in the BBC feature expressing great unhappiness that the Bundestag (national/federal parliament) was to be located in this building with its strong and, for them, intolerable resonances of Nazism. No one actually suggested demolishing the Reichstag, but it was suggested that a new building should have been constructed to house the Bundestag, leaving the old Reichstag building to serve another purpose or even remain symbolically empty (this would be an example of 'self-critical' preservation). There was also some comment on the architecture of the surrounding site: the Bundestag cannot function with just one building, and a competition was held to design a new complex, incorporating the Reichstag. One design, by the British architect Norman Foster, would have put up a large canopy over the whole area, but this was not pursued. In 1997, however, Foster *was* building a glass dome over the Reichstag (Figure 9), which was commended both as a symbol of 'transparency' and as a way of 'covering' the old associations of the building. Two years later, with the structure complete, Holger Kleine remarked in an article in *Architecture Today* based on an interview with Foster: 'one could hardly express the relationship of government more vividly than with this dome, which allows the public to walk over the heads of the elected representatives . . . The long debate about whether stone or dome are necessarily fascist can be buried' (Kleine 1999). 'Covering' in this case appears to be seen as a way of both acknowledging recent history (rather than obliterating it, as has been done with the Berlin wall) and at the same time 'burying' residual anxieties about that history under a layer of new, democratic meaning.

'Covering' is one answer to the question of whether to preserve 'problematic' monuments like the Reichstag: the monuments stay, but something is added to them to make the point that history has not stood still – one can use contemporary architecture to comment on the architecture of the past. A somewhat similar strategy is exemplified by Daniel Libeskind's Jewish Museum with its concrete 'void' dedicated to the memory of the Holocaust. The museum's zinc-covered structure in the form of a 'disturbed' star of David is both visually juxtaposed and structurally joined to the Baroque architecture of the Berlin city museum. Speaking on the BBC radio feature, Libeskind explained that he meant his design to be understood as a comment on the older building – visitors were being invited to ponder the contrast between the Enlightenment symbolized in the architecture of the city museum, and the horrors commemorated in the Holocaust void.

ure 9
ASS DOME OVER THE
CHSTAG BUILDING, BERLIN.
RMAN FOSTER AND
RTNERS, ARCHITECTS
pyright of, and permission
m, Norman Foster
d Partners; photographer
el Young

The BBC feature also discussed a very different answer to the preservation question: using architecture to affirm a historically-based German identity which is not, however, dependent on recent history, but involves a return to a more distant past. Given that Berlin's older building stock has suffered such extensive structural damage in recent decades, this may entail not preservation in the ordinary sense of that term, but the construction of replica buildings whose originals have been destroyed. Unsurprisingly, this approach to architectural heritage has not met with universal approval. At the time the BBC programme was made, for instance, there was controversy about whether to demolish the old GDR's parliament building and construct on the site a replica of the Prussian *Stadtsschloss*. This plan encountered objections from some former citizens of the GDR. One objection was that it appeared to affirm Prussian culture – regarded as hierarchical and militaristic – as a model for the new Germany. Another was that the demolition of what one Berlin pensioner described as a 'people's palace' to make way for the *Stadtsschloss* would constitute a symbolic celebration of aristocracy and privilege at the expense of the working class and socialist values espoused (at least symbolically) by the old GDR. Interestingly, however, other (West) Berliners spoke of Prussian architecture as a kind of national heritage which was neutral or positive for them, in a way twentieth century buildings could not be; and they also welcomed what they saw as a new openness to German history as such. Since 1945, constructing Germany (or more exactly, the Federal Republic)

143 □

as 'democratic' has entailed a massive, embarrassed silence on the subject of history, and a flight from nationalism or conventional patriotism. One architect explained: 'every people needs a national identity . . . but in Germany it has been banned from political discussion'. The architecture of old Prussia provides, for some at least, an acceptable way to reclaim some notion of German heritage and of a national architectural idiom, whereas the buildings of the Third Reich are wholly unacceptable for that purpose.

But some interviewed people dissented, in general, from any attempt to construct a partial or selective version of German history, whether by constructing replicas of old 'good' buildings or by covering/obliterating more recent 'bad' ones. Their desire not to forget or excuse the recent past was expressed in a call to preserve those buildings that make present-day Germans uncomfortable, precisely because they cause discomfort (see also our earlier remarks on the case of Auschwitz). Apart from the (rejected) proposal to retain the Reichstag building but leave it empty, the BBC programme featured, for example, a group who had uncovered in what is now an ordinary cellar the remains of a prison used by Nazi stormtroopers, and who were showing visitors around it.

We have chosen to examine this particular case (albeit briefly), because it illustrates two important points. One reflects the central argument or thesis of this book, concerning the importance of discourse itself in shaping the built environment and people's responses to it. The process of reconstructing Berlin has been remarkable in many ways, but one remarkable feature of it has been the sheer quantity of speech and writing which the process has generated. As Brian Hatton notes (1999: 76), a city whose pre-1989 form was the outcome of military and ideological conflict on a world scale is now being reshaped by other kinds of power: 'every monument and historical site is disputed all over again; not with bullets, but with words and Deutschmarks'. The words are important, as is illustrated dramatically by, for instance, the effect of the political keyword *transparency* on the design of new buildings, or the complex meanings woven around the issue of preservation. Reconstruction in Berlin continues, and the city that emerges will bear the marks of the semiotic system we have outlined here, or more exactly, the marks of the more varied discourses supported by that system. The particular meanings that were accorded during the debates of the 1990s to stone and glass, or planning and 'bricolage', may in time be modified or forgotten, but the city itself will preserve their traces.

The second reason why Berlin provides a useful case study is more specifically to do with the 'national question' in discourse about architecture as 'heritage'. Debates about Berlin give an unusually clear demonstration of what is at stake in this kind of discourse. The specific historical and political context in which debate arose made professionals and laypeople in Berlin particularly attentive to the narratives of nationhood underpinning the discussion, and the judgements implicit in those narratives. They were mindful of questions such as:

'what is being remembered and what forgotten?', 'Which values are being endorsed and which disparaged?' and 'Who is being attacked, explicitly or implicitly, and why?' In other places and different circumstances these questions may be less highly charged than in Berlin, but in our view they are no less relevant. Arguments about what to preserve in the name of 'the nation's heritage' and what to neglect, destroy or cover up are always also arguments about what version of the past will be carried forward as part of the ongoing, necessary process of imagining nationhood.

HERITAGE AND NATIONAL IDENTITY IN THE POST-COLONIAL WORLD

Cities and their buildings are, as we have seen, powerful instruments for the representation of national identity. As countries in Asia and Africa were achieving political independence from the colonizers after World War Two, they were all faced with the problem of how to establish their new, post-colonial identity. In this task urban planning, urban monuments and exhibitions, projects for housing renewal, and architecture all played a crucial representative role. And all of them were initiated, promoted, designed and built, and then managed, by texts. Here we consider one such case – that of twentieth century Indonesia. In doing this we are relying completely on Kusno's recent work (Kusno 2000).

The period has three phases. The first phase was that of the Dutch East Indies from 1920 to 1940, the period of so-called 'pacification'. During this time the Dutch attempted to implement their 'Ethical Policy' which sought to maintain the colonial order, and hold at bay anti-colonial movements based on ethnic and religious nationalism, through both modernization and the preservation of traditional values. This policy involved lively debate about appropriate architectural representation. On one side Kusno quotes Snuijff, a Dutch architectural engineer of the Public Works Department, who, in a 1914 government report whose underlying message is that bureaucrats should be replaced by technocrats in the management of the colony, writes that 'No national architecture exists at present . . . neither as regards size nor with a view to construction do the native buildings occupy a place of the slightest prominence in the architecture of the present time.' Larger buildings are said to be incapable of serving 'as a sample of local architecture . . . not to mention the fact that already then their structures were mere ruins' (Snuijff: 1–2). On the other side were politicians and architects who wanted to create an 'Indies architecture' to represent an 'Indies society' – a synthesis of Dutch and Indonesian characteristics. Two architects in particular promoted this aim – Henri Pont and Thomas Karsten. In 1920 (or possibly 1914, according to Jessup 1985) the latter wrote an article in a journal about the first Indies Architecture Exhibition in which he promoted the idea of a new integrative architecture: 'The absolute, inevitable, insoluble duality, lies in the essence of the colony: the tradition, degree of development and aims between dominating European and dominated indigenous life . . . A successful architecture must express a unity of the spiritual and material needs' (as cited in Jessup: 138). In this context 'spiritual' meant the traditional local culture, 'material' the supremacy of European technology and organization. Pont writes in a similar vein in 1924 in a journal published by the Java Institute, an Orientalist cultural organization: 'The invading people ultimately have an eye for the culture of the conquered and may prove receptive to it . . . Then no clash, no demonstration of supremacy is necessary, and the peoples draw together . . . [if there is] a living architectural tradition, a new mighty architecture can arise, heterogeneous and not pure in style' (Pont 1923: 113). This vision of a syncretic style, as Kusno illustrates, bore practical fruit in such projects as the People's Theatre at Semarang and the Yogyakarta Sonobuoyo Museum. Pont, according to Sudjarat (1991: 171–2), became convinced that such 'Javanese architecture is adaptable to present day purposes and is well suited with the Javanese way of life. Although this architecture does not yet fulfil modern hygienic, economic and construction requirements, through significant modification some limited adjustments can be made'. Pont put these ideas into practice in his 1920 design for the Bandung Technical College, where he incorporated the steep, hipped 'minangkabau' roof and traditional materials with Western Arts and Crafts details and forms.

This dream of a harmonious, integrated, power relationship and culture, after three hundred years of domination and supremacy, could not of course succeed; but it did leave behind a political and material system which presented its own contradictions when independence eventually arrived.

The second phase starts with the establishment of independence in 1950, and the 1957 'Guided Democracy' policy of the first president, Sukarno, and ends with his displacement in 1965. Sukarno strove to represent the new state's 'nation building' drive by a concept of the 'modern' which both embodied traditional Javanese values and culture and, at the same time, embraced an international modernism which denied the difference between Indonesia and the rest of the world. In 1962, in a speech on the transformation of Djakarta, he said:

> Build up Djakarta as beautifully as possible, build it as spectacularly as possible, so
> that this city, which has borne the centre of the struggle of the Indonesian people, will
> be an inspiration and beacon to the whole of struggling mankind and to all emerging
> forces. If Egypt was able to construct Cairo as its capital, Italy its Rome, France its Paris
> and Brazil its Brasilia, then Indonesia must also proudly present Djakarta as the portal
> of the country. (Sukarno 1962)

The four ancient cultures each created a modern city, without loss of the traditional heritage. Not only would Indonesia do the same, but it would present a model to the developing world of how to reconcile tradition and heritage with modernity.

Immediately after hosting the fourth Asian Games in 1962, in the year of hosting the First Games of the New Emerging Forces in 1963 and in the midst of a huge building programme of commercial tower blocks, urban motorways, and various grand parks and monuments, Sukarno promoted his ideas in a speech to the Indonesian Parliament:

> Projects such as the Asian Games, the National Monument, independence Mosque, the Jakarta By-pass, and so on, are examples of 'Nation-Building' and 'Character Building' . . . of the whole Indonesian people striving to recover our national identity. Who is not aware that every people in the world is always striving to enhance its greatness and lofty ideals? Do you remember that a great leader of a foreign country told me that monuments are an absolute necessity to develop a people's spirit, as necessary as pants for somebody naked, pants and not a tie? Look at New York and Moscow, look at any state capital east and west it makes no matter, and you always find the centres of nations' greatness in the form of buildings, material buildings to be proud of. (Leclerc 1993: 52)

There are several features of this text: the striking elimination of the Iron Curtain, the compression of the world into a homogeneous modernization project, of which Indonesia can be seen as the centre, and the absolute centrality of buildings in this process. Again (in a remark quoted by Cindy Adams) 'I have erected a brick-and-glass apartment building, a clover-leaf bridge, and our super-highway, the Djakarta Pass . . . I consider money for material symbols well spent' (Abeyasekere 1987: 210). In a speech on the occasion of the anniversary of Jakarta's 435 years of existence the nation is held to be great 'not just because of its skyscrapers . . . [but great] even in the little houses of the workers of Jakarta' (Abeyasekere: 168).

The third phase stretches from the establishment of Suharto's regime in 1965 to its final demise in the riots of 1998. This was the 'New Order', which emphasized stability, (capitalist) economic expansion and defence of traditional cultural values. And, as before, the architecture of the New Order was a key instrument in its implementation. Initiated in 1975, a 'Beautiful Indonesia in Miniature Park' was established outside Jakarta; in it the art and culture of the various indigenous regions of the state were represented by twenty-seven replica 'authentic' houses, which were said to form, around a lake, a traditional village. These houses were supposed to serve as points of reference for future housing. Mrs Suharto, in a speech during the opening of the park, saw in their representation '[houses] . . . which are found in our country from one end to the other, and which constitute the heritage of our invaluable culture' a way of preventing 'the possible extermination [of this heritage] as a result of the demand for the development of modern society' (*Indonesia Magazine* 1975: 32, 28–9).

The progress from tradition, through transition, to modern was materially represented in three zones, labelled as such, in the Institute of Technology at Bandung. The first had Pont's original syncretic forms; the second reinterpreted these traditional external forms behind which modern functional demands were satisfied; and the third used unashamedly postmodern, high-tech forms, which celebrated science and technology as the way forward. In the new 1990s University of Indonesia the three formal languages were combined into a single 'modern national style' of multi-storey layered roofs, peaked pyramids and open colonnades. Kusno shows how throughout the 1980s and 1990s national congresses of Indonesian architects struggled with notions of 'traditional', 'Indonesian', 'cultural identity' and 'Indonesian tradition'. The language was contentious, and reflects both a recognition of the inauthenticity of what was being promoted and practised, and the genuine struggle to express a national, indeed an Asian, identity. This was expressed by the Filippino architect Locsin in his 1981 address to the first Asian Congress of Architects: 'Western technology has introduced greater efficiency in production, but it has also led to the destruction of the environment, the pollution of the air and water and the depression of natural resources . . . The confrontation with Western culture has impelled us to delve into our Asian identity lest we lose that which is most precious. I venture to ask whether the present thrust towards modernisation is complemented by a reaching back to the past, to rediscover one's history and to reaffirm the value of tradition' (*Philippines Quarterly of Culture and Society* 1984: 12, 275).

In Germany the problem was to construct a 'democratic' national identity after a period of totalitarianism. Architectural forms and materials were held to play crucial roles in this. In Indonesia national identity had to be constructed following a period of colonial and neo-colonial domination by Western powers. Here too forms, materials and decorative details were charged with meaning. So for Germany the past was and remains a problem, requiring both obliteration and representation. But for Indonesia the past is more of a resource though, as always, it is a specific version that is rejected or drawn upon; this is most clearly seen when there is a change in regime.

Chapter 7: Images

READING AND LOOKING – A PERPLEXING DOUBLE ACT

Most texts about buildings contain images alongside linguistic elements to different degrees of complexity. The images may be models, films, videos, drawings, photographs, diagrams or symbols. These constitute another way, besides language, of representing buildings.

This chapter tries to show the crucial role of images in both the public's and the professionals' evaluation of buildings. When the images are combined with language we have a complex text, often with contradictions and obscurities. Our book, on the natural language about architecture, adds one to a very limited number. Studies of drawings and other visual representations are equally few. But studies of the two combined, which is typical of the majority of architectural texts, are almost non-existent. So there is a lot of work to do before we begin to understand the potency of such texts in the production of the built environment, and this chapter can only set out some suggestive lines of enquiry.

The skill in creating images, whether using pencil, camera or computer, has always been at the core of architectural education. For most professional or educational purposes the images are as crucial as the written text, which 'place' them. Of course, an apparently textless image is still meaningful provided that some earlier text (such as a description) has been read; this would be an example of the intertextual 'hybrid' we have already discussed in Chapter 4. It is difficult to imagine how one could enter a competition, present design ideas to a client, obtain planning approval for a scheme, assess student performance or use the media to sell or criticize a project without recourse to visual representations. Though of course it would be equally difficult to do these things without recourse to words. The effect and power of images and words is critically dependent on how they are used alongside each other.

In the 1998 international competition for Scotland's new Parliament building in Edinburgh, one of the five finalists (who, in the event, was the chosen winning architect) submitted on the required six display boards texts which had a rich and complex mixture of language and image. We have already commented in Chapter 4 on one aspect of the competition brief – its textual contradictions; later in this chapter we will look at the actual entries in more detail, especially in the combined use of text and images. In the winner's submission we find these cryptic phrases: 'The people sit in the land. The Parliament is a fragment of a large gathering situation . . . [it] is a form in people's mind, it is a mental place . . . [it] should belong to a broader thought.' Because these phrases were written in a mixture of capitals and lower case, in various colours, scattered over the surface of the boards, interwoven with coloured sketches (of such places as a 'gathering field') they became an integral part of the text in which they framed and which punctures the images. No one, including members of the jury, could have looked at or assessed the images without the words unavoidably occupying some, if not most, of their attention. It is therefore interesting and important to try to answer the questions: to what extent does the interaction of language and image affect the perception and evaluation – the reading – of such a text? To what extent did this language influence the jury in its assessment of this design, and hence ultimately shape the material reality of Scotland's capital?

The literature about images, in the fields of art, psychology, philosophy and cultural studies is immense. But here we are concerned less with images *per se*, but with architectural texts where image and language work together as multi-modal texts. A number of key questions arise from this interaction; we will use these questions as a framework for analysing our material, though we cannot always answer them.

First, had the relationship between language and image changed in the late twentieth century? It is possible that in earlier cultures which were more 'literate', that is, more dominated by the conventions of a specific form of literacy, namely print literacy, each, even when used together, preserved its own proper interpretative domain. The text was read either as an introduction to the image to *be* seen, or as an explanation of what had just *been* seen. And this separation in time was paralleled by a separation is space – broad gaps or margins, or, in museums, a large space between an object and its label. And each had it own conventions of representation. If today, under the influence of advertising, television, and new media – especially on the Internet – culture has become more visual than literate, or become 'multiliterate' in the sense of Cope and Kalantzis (2000), then the *appearance* of the text, text *as* image, may have become crucial. Therefore the way it is compositionally integrated with the image, the choice of typeface, colour, the shape and positioning of blocks of text and so on, may be important ways of transmitting meaning, perhaps with a corresponding decrease in the significance of what the text actually says. This would explain not only how the semantic chaos in some architectural texts such as the Scottish Parliament competition drawings is tolerated, but also the need for new graphic techniques for combining words with images. These include montage, juxtaposition, and the interlacing of the text into the projections of the building seen from multiple viewpoints. Computer graphics have opened up spectacular possibilities for all these.

Second, bearing in mind the first question, are these images read as illustrations of the linguistic text, or is the text a commentary on the images? Or does this question, with these two alternatives, indicate too simple a view; is it rather that neither language nor image preserve the properties they might have in isolation but both, in their very juxtaposition, change into something new?

Third, does the interaction, or the order of priority between them, depend on the reader? Does a lay person and a professional accord them different relative value? Does it depend on the purpose and genre of the text – for instance, a competition display like that for the Scottish Parliament, a technical text intended to guide a builder, or Prince Charles's polemical and popularizing text *A Vision of Britain*?

Fourth, do words and images converge towards similar meanings (including covert, ideological ones), or diverge? If the latter, which meaning is likely to prevail? And if one is seen as transient and the other as stable, is the latter likely to prevail? For instance, in the Scottish Parliament competition drawings the winning architect had already declared that the design was merely illustrative of his general approach but was not be taken as the final design concept. That was to remain open to continuous revision. The text, however, was his once-for-all creation – unlikely to be rewritten. Is it not probable, therefore, that the text would be, and was, the prevailing influence over the jury?

Fifth, if the actual method of representation of images of buildings – choice of scale, use of colour and shadows, and types of projection, for instance – can affect not only what is seen but its critical evaluation, and if the ways of presenting the text are equally numerous, is it not possible that some combinations might be more powerful in forming critical judgement than the inherent qualities of the building design? Does that question even make sense – *are* there inherent properties, free of representational influence? This is an analogous question to that which has long puzzled philosophers – *are* there wordless concepts or ideas?

We resist the recent polemical trend towards blurring the distinction between text and buildings (as, for instance, exemplified by Taylor (*Assemblage*, 5, 1990)), or images of buildings. Equally we resist one distinction that is often made between word and image, the implication that somehow non-verbal representations, images, are 'truer', more transparent, than verbal ones. 'Pictures or models cannot lie.' Of course this debate about words and images is ancient. It started as an argument about the relative merits of literature and painting, an undertaking in which painters (Leonardo da Vinci), philosophers (Edmond Burke and G.E. Lessing), poets (John Dryden) and art historians (Ernst Gombrich and Erwin Panofsky) have all taken part. W.J.T. Mitchell (1986: 43) reformulates it as the 'dialectic of word and image . . . a constant in the fabric of signs that a culture weaves around itself', the struggle between them being a 'struggle for territory'. The image 'is the sign that pretends not to be a sign, masquerading as (or, for the believer, actually achieving) natural immediacy and presence. The word is the "other", the artificial, arbitrary production of human will that disrupts natural presence by introducing unnatural elements into the world – time, consciousness, history and the alienating intervention of symbolic mediation.' But, he continues, 'the modern pictorial image, like the ancient notion of "likeness", is at last revealed to be linguistic in its inner workings'. Consciousness of 'this sign that pretends not to be a sign', when we are thinking about architectural discourse, and especially in discussing images of buildings, is important as a defence against misplaced faith in the veracity of drawings.

A recent participant in this debate is Adrian Forty (Forty 2000), who cites conventional claims made by certain architects, exemplified in his quotation from Scarpa to the effect that 'drawing is the architect's only medium'. Forty argues that language is central to every stage, from conception, through drawing, building, and experiencing, and not merely, as is conventionally assumed, in the final step, the description of the experience. In particular he distinguishes between the power of language as a precise system of differences (on the semiotic principle that signifiers such as 'heavy' or 'complex' only make sense in contrast to their opposites – 'light' or 'simple') whereas a drawing invokes only itself and has no opposites. At the same time, Forty maintains, language's ability to deal with ambiguity and metaphor, compared to drawing's finite precision (either a line is there or it is not) makes the former a richer and more powerful instrument of representation (18). He also argues a point which we think is significant – that drawings, unlike language, are not experienced sequentially but all at once, in a *gestalt* mode where everything is seen at once.

THE ARCHITECTURAL IMAGE IN HISTORY AND TODAY

In Chapter 2 we have referred to Vitruvius and the post-Vitruvian treatises. These not only devoted substantial space to discussions of drawing and perspective, but the latter were interlaced with illustrations – of, for instance, the Classical orders, plans, constructional details and machinery. Vitruvius requires an architect to have '. . . a knowledge of drawings so that he can readily make sketches to show the appearance of the work which he proposes' (Morgan: 6). Alberti (Rykwert *et al.* 1988: Book 2) sees the labour and cost of producing a building as such a risky undertaking that he always recommends the 'time-honoured custom, practised by the best builders, of preparing not only drawings and sketches but also models of wood or any other material'. The implication here is that drawings, whilst not essential, are desirable.

The drawing practices of twentieth century architects – Alvar Aalto, Le Corbusier, Frank Lloyd Wright or Carlo Scarpa, for instance – have been carefully recorded and analysed, and they themselves have tried to explain how their design intentions were developed through drawing; Michael Graves (1981) finds

'. . . the tension of lines on paper . . . has an insistence of its own that describes possibilities which perhaps could not be imagined in thought alone' – or in words, he might have added (cited by Fraser and Henmi 1994: 163).

Evans (1997) has argued for the enormous generative power of drawings in architecture. Painters and sculptors, whilst they do use preliminary studies in the form of sketches and maquettes, rarely bring the creative act to an end in such studies; their real attention and most sustained effort being on the final object itself. For architects this is not the case. Whilst they too use preliminary sketches and models, they then focus, with the greatest concentration and attention to every detail, on drawings and complete their work in that form.

We accept this argument that drawings are no longer means but ends – objects in their own right. Their translation into concrete, built form is a specialist task for technical, building and construction experts. Not surprisingly drawings now carry great prestige and often commercial value. Not surprisingly, too, students and practitioners have developed a rich repertoire of imaginative and seductive drawing techniques, recently further enhanced through computer graphics and virtual reality representations.

Fraser and Henmi (1994) see drawings, with the editing, simplification and differential emphasis processes through which they have passed, as 'modes of seeing':

> . . . a drawing itself has the effect of shaping perception. It acts as a filter for a mode of seeing . . . When one has seen the plan of a building, the experience of walking through it is altered by its memory. Drawings create their own recall, establishing a conceptual framework of a place, predating and prefiguring perceptions . . . having experienced the drawing first, one views a building relative to its representation. (161–2)

So architectural drawings are, first, implicated in the very process of creation. Second, they are a representation, after the creative act, of the envisioned object and therefore a means of communication both to the designer, reflectively, and to anyone else. But reading drawings is itself a skill, which has to be acquired. And because there is such a variety of drawing techniques and styles this skill is not easy to acquire and therefore drawings are often incomprehensible or misunderstood, either because decoding them is inherently difficult, or because they have been made deliberately mystifying.

Much of what we are saying applies most obviously to high prestige images, whether drawings, photographs, three-dimensional models (and photographs of these) or computer generated perspectives. Less obviously, but with equal force, it applies to more mundane images such as technical and constructional drawings, diagrams, site plans and maps. The difference between the rich pictorial representations by architects such as Boullée and Ledoux and technical drawings or diagrams is not one of degree but of kind. Savignat (1980) traces the evolution of artistic and technical architectural drawings to two diverging trends. The former, as they became more artistic and elaborate, marked a loss of control by architects over the functional, practical programme of buildings, which began to be assumed by scientists, intellectuals and politicians whose functional demands were spelled out in written briefs, using natural language; the architects' artistic drawings became a *habillage* (= a dressing up), whilst their technical drawings served the practices of builders and craftsmen who needed drawings to work with concrete materials. Alberti already foresaw this division between intellectual, artistic production, and manual, material production – conception and realization – when he defined architecture in his Prologue and first Book (Rykwert *et al.* 1988) as consisting of 'lineaments and structure' – meaning abstract design and material construction.

HOW IMAGES WORK

In his pioneering book *Iconology – Image, Text, Ideology* (1986), Mitchell elaborates on Nelson Goodman's theory of images (1976). Goodman distinguishes between 'differentiation' and 'density' in images and his distinction may help us in considering the difference between pictorial, artistic and imaginative architectural representations on the one hand and technical, practical drawings and diagrams on the other. The simplest example is in the contrast between a graduated and an ungraduated thermometer:

> With a graduated thermometer every position of the mercury is given a determinate reading: either the mercury has reached a certain point on the scale, or it is read as being closest to that point. A position between any two points on the scale does not count as a character in the system; we round it off to the closest determinate reading. In an ungraduated thermometer, on the other hand no unique, determinate reading is possible at any point on the thermometer: everything is relational and approximate, and every point on the ungraduated scale (an infinite number, obviously), counts as a character in the system. Every tiny difference in the level of the mercury counts as a different indication of the temperature, but none of these differences can be assigned a unique, determinate reading. There is no possibility of finite differentiation of the 'articulation' of a single reading. (Mitchell: 67)

Mitchell applies this distinction to distinguish between a picture and a text. The former '. . . is read like and ungraduated thermometer; every mark, every modification, every curve or swelling of a line, every modification of texture or colour is loaded with semantic potential . . . It might be called a "super-dense" or what Goodman calls a "replete" symbol, in that relatively more properties of the symbol are taken into account' (67). Normally the thickness or colour of a mercury column is of no significance, but would be highly significant in a graphic symbol. '. . . no mark may be isolated as a unique reference . . . Its meaning depends rather on its relations with all the other marks in a dense, continuous field . . . A differentiated symbolic system, by contrast, is not dense and continuous, but works by gaps and discontinuities. The most familiar example of such a system is the alphabet which works (somewhat imperfectly) on the assumption that every character is distinguishable from every other [syntactic differentiation] . . .' (67–8). It does not matter who writes or types the letters, or what their detailed form is, their meaning remains constant.

We might well consider this distinction to be relevant to distinguish between a full colour perspective, or a fully coloured set of plans, sections, and elevations, and a set of fully dimensioned line drawings, including constructional details, produced for the building contractor. In the former we have something like Goodman's dense system, in which every specific detail of drawing and colouring is of immense significance in the reading of the object being represented. If there is writing on the drawing its placing, size, location and lettering style (as in the Scottish Parliament competition submissions considered below) are, equally, of significance. In the latter, provided there is no ambiguity, it matters not at all what the line thicknesses, colours of lines and style of lettering are. Any writing, notes or dimensions have only to be legible – their form or style are of no relevance – the information they carry is the same, no matter what the representational technique.

Not only is there a wide range of image genres, but within each there is a huge range of actual techniques. Objects can be represented in orthographic projection of plan, section and elevation, and increased depth can be given by the use of shadows. It can be a two-dimensional representation of three dimensions, by using the variety of possible metric projections of which isometric and axonometric are the most important, or perspective, with single, double or multiple vanishing points. Images can be linear or consist of solid surfaces. They can be black and white, or in colour. Lines can be of any thickness, freehand or instrument-produced. The scale of drawings can be varied and, of course, there is no limit to the actual finished size. Where some kind of realism is desired, human figures, animals, trees, plants, and natural or urban scenery can be incorporated, sometimes by importing existing objects through montage.

These possible techniques yield a vast combinatorial repertoire, even for the making of images themselves. But when images are combined with words the repertoire of possible texts increases even further. Words and images can be in any proportion to each other. They can be composed on a sheet of paper or on a computer screen so that one or other dominates; they can carry meanings which are closely related (effectively using two modes of representation for the same idea or object) or ones which are quite different but nevertheless related so as to form a single text.

With both images and words there is a relationship between a mental image, or idea, and its representation. The question as to the degree to which a mental image or idea actually exists until it can be made concrete in image or language has been a subject of much philosophical speculation. For images, Barthes (1977: 29), drawing on the work of Bruner and Piaget, suggests that:

> if . . . there is no perception without immediate categorisation, then the photograph [authors' note: an example of an image] is verbalised in the very moment it is perceived; the image – grasped immediately . . . by language itself – in actual fact has no denoted state, is immersed for its very social existence in at least an initial layer of connotation, that of the categories of language. (cited by Prinz 1991: 20)

Barthes (1987) comments specifically on architectural drawings; not only do they carry 'first order meaning' – information about walls, doors, windows, rooms, etc. – but 'second order', ideological, meaning both about the building and the designer (cited by Fraser and Henmi: 173).

But meaning occurs at the interface of the object – the text – and the subject – the reader or viewer. The object has its formal and structural properties, the subject his or her personal, social and cultural history, sex, race and class. The position of the reading subject, their subjectivity, is something which designers try to take into account in generating such complex texts, even if only unconsciously. Competition entrants imagine the position of members of the jury; students of their tutors and examiners; journalists of their special readership; and exhibition organizers of the expected visitors.

There is little of practical help to try to anticipate how viewers will respond to such texts. The key work about image-making and image-reading is in the fields of art scholarship, the creation of optical illusions and caricature, the meaning of 'seeing and knowing' (Gombrich 1960), children's image-making and reading (e.g. Malchiodi 1998; Thomas and Silk 1980), map making (e.g. Muehrcke and Muehrcke 1998; Scott 1986), perceptual psychology (e.g. Gibson 1950; Feldman c 1994), and more recently in information theory (Marr 1982). From such sources one might find, in the idea of signal to noise ratio for instance, clues about what essential parts of a building to represent in a drawing, and what details might, with advantage, be omitted. But it is easy to be seduced by the fascinating speculations and experiments of art historians, philosophers and perceptual psychologists, and to forget that hardly any empirical work exists on the ways images of buildings and towns actually work; how we see them and respond to them. In particular we know hardly anything about how our responses *vary* with different kinds of text using different kinds of image. Even the limited work that has been done, for instance about the degree to which responses to photographs or videos of buildings are similar to those to the real buildings represented (Hershberger and Cass, in Nasar 1988), takes as a starting point a narrow perceptual perspective which excludes questions about buildings as experienced social or historical objects.

If the same set of design proposals, responding to a given building brief, are represented by, say, freehand sketches, coloured orthographic scale drawings, computer-generated perspectives, wooden models, photographs of the models, or a dynamic virtual reality 'walk' through the project, how do our understanding and evaluation – that is our cognitive and affective responses – change? And how do our decisions – for instance, rank ordering – change if we are presented as clients, competition judges or teachers with such a range of representations? It would appear that much of the built environment may come about as a result of judgements based on representations which the designers have chosen either by chance or whim or as a deliberate act of persuasion or camouflage.

SOME CASES

Introductory comments

To see how text and image work in combination, we will look at three cases. The first is a book about architecture which is well known in Britain; the second is a prestigious French architectural journal; and the third is a prescriptive text, a competition brief, where our interest is its relation to the submissions by designers who use such combinations. In one sense this represents a progression from the traditional use of illustrated texts for a lay readership, to a text addressed to a professional readership, and finally to a more complex text created *by* professionals but addressed *to* both professionals and a lay public.

Case 1 – Prince Charles's 'A Vision of Britain'

Background to the case

In 1984 Charles Prince of Wales addressed the Royal Institute of British Architects at their Gala Evening at London's Hampton Court Palace on the occasion of the 150th anniversary of its foundation. In the course of his speech he referred to the recently announced winning design for the extension to London's National Gallery as 'a monstrous carbuncle on the face of a much-loved and elegant friend'. The comment caused a furore, both in the profession and in the popular media. The former launched an all out campaign to discredit him, whilst the latter was split, some of it supportive, some hostile. Almost certainly the speech was the cause of the rejection of the design and with that came accusations of anti-democratic political interference from someone said, by his enemies, to be constitutionally barred from expressing a view. He was labelled by one side as a nostalgic reactionary, by the other as a visionary who merely expressed a deep-seated popular revulsion against the aridity of modernism and the confusions of postmodernity. The debate continues.

Whatever the merits of his case, there is wide agreement that this and his subsequent interventions opened up architecture as a topic of popular debate in the media – and not only in Britain – in a spectacular and lasting way. It was not only that the subject became popular, but the whole landscape of the discourse changed, with a shift towards the feelings of the person in the street. Charles followed with another speech, this time to the Corporation of the City of London in 1987, where he took the opportunity to condemn the range of proposals for high rise buildings in the historic Paternoster Square, both for the way they would ruin the skyline around St Paul's, and the desecration they would cause at street level. The planners, architects and greedy commercial developers all came in for a hammering.

After several further interventions in debates surrounding major proposals, Charles eventually went on air in 1988 with a BBC television programme entitled *A Vision of Britain*. This was followed by the publication of his book, under the same title and with the subtitle *A personal view of architecture*, in the following year (HRH The Prince of Wales 1989). This case study concerns that book.

The book

Two things are immediately striking. First, the shape and lavishness of the book, which seem to presuppose a certain kind of reader, and a certain place for reading it. It is in 'landscape' format, which, when open, is wider than a seat on a train, plane or bus. It is between cloth covered hard covers carrying, on the front, the gold embossed feathers of the Prince of Wales. Its paper is heavy and glossy. The reproductions, in both colour and monochrome, are of the highest quality. The white space and margins are generous. And it uses sophisticated graphic techniques, such as a double page coloured reproduction of Canaletto's painting of the Thames in London, on which is superimposed a semi-transparent photographic print of the same view at the time of writing.

The second striking feature is the ratio of images to words; not one of the one hundred and fifty-six pages is without images. Sometimes these are full or nearly full page, and frequently there are several to the page. About two-thirds of the total space is taken up by images which include drawings and paintings, water-colours (by Charles), monochrome and colour photographs of rural and urban scenery, buildings and their details, and people (mainly of Charles by himself or with architects and members of community organizations). In other words this is a picture book with commentary, rather than a text illustrated by images. Following our earlier discussion of the priority and sequence of reading between text and image, this makes it improbable that most readers systematically read this from cover to cover. It is more probable that the process would be driven by the images, perhaps not read strictly in the page sequence, and so that chunks of text function as captions, whether they are or not. The flow of this process is also likely to be fragmented, the narrative being constructed by the reader's choice of image sequence rather than by the author.

Two questions then are 'What is the function of such a (horizontal) picture book?'; *where* is it intended to be read – on the familiar coffee table, in libraries, or on tables in scholars' studies? Everything about the book – its shape, cost (£16.95 in 1989) and lavish presentation subverts its overt intention of being a people's architectural manifesto.

The written text

In order to understand the role of the images in supporting the text, we need to say a little about the underlying message of the latter, though it is not our intention here either to embark on a critical debate, or to carry out a detailed textual analysis, fascinating and important as both these would be. Rather we are interested in the way words and images function together.

The text is constructed around a series of binary oppositions, one good, one bad, which are, in the book's central section, embedded in ten 'principles' or 'ground rules' which can themselves be reformulated in binary form as:

1. *Sense of place versus global anonymity*. Buildings should respect the character of the open country or the cityscape in which they are set, and draw on a 'heritage of regional styles' and materials, which are said to have been 'eaten away by [this] creeping cancer'. Large volumes should be broken down so as not to dominate in mass, and to give a 'gentler skyline and enhance the picturesque quality of the landscape'. Above all 'we must protect the land'.
2. *Hierarchy versus uniformity*. Buildings should be in a range of sizes and forms, which express differences in 'public importance' and 'social organization'. Within a single building its component parts should make clear varying functions; for instance, entrances should not disappear within an anonymous, mechanical grid, and functionally important elements, like the council chamber of a town hall, should be marked by higher ceilings, more elaborate window details and more lofty entrances, instead of being hidden by 'the dogma of modernism [which] ensures a deadening uniformity'.
3. *Human scale versus gargantuism*. The argument is not only for respect for the human scale but also for the varied and intimate scale of small buildings thus distinguishing between (large) 'emblems of faith, enlightenment or government' and 'our intimate lives'. There is an argument against the coagulation of small urban sites into the megasites needed for viable commercial development.
4. *Harmony versus discord*. ('Sing with the choir and not against it.') Buildings are said now to be 'boastful', working in competition with, or against, the existing fabric instead of blending with it. 'Outlandish modern design(s)' and buildings designed on 'abstract principles' following 'transient international architectural fashions' are 'jarring'.
5. *Enclosure versus unstructured openness*. The key references are squares, almshouses, inns of court, university quadrangles, often with sculpture, fountains or gardens in them, and large enclosed public space such as the

interior of St Paul's Cathedral. The sense of enclosure and security is said to be destroyed by too many openings and, in housing estates, by 'strewn clusters of separate houses set at jagged angles along windswept planners' routes'.

6. *Identifiable local materials versus anonymous mass produced products.* The good examples are stone, brick, flint, cob and thatch – each identified with particular areas of Britain and 'in danger of being eroded'. The bad ones are reconstituted stone, machine-made bricks, concrete, plastic cladding and aluminium. These latter have created 'an overall mediocrity: a kind architectural soap opera'.

7. *Decorative detail versus bland plainness.* Architecture needs the enrichment of decorative details, the products of 'hand, brain and eye'. Buildings with 'no hint of decoration give neither pleasure or delight'. The 'gropings of some critics towards the imposition of "meaning" on what they call post-modern architecture has been fairly unfruitful'. It is decoration which can fill 'this vacuum'.

8. *Art versus architecture.* The traditional link between these 'common disciplines' has been broken, and 'artists and architects might as well be educated on different planets'. The recipe is a return to shared life drawing and a study of nature, and the integration of painting and sculpture as 'an organic and integral part of all great new buildings'. The National Theatre and the, as yet unbuilt, British Library in London, are both dull in comparison with the Whitehall Banqueting House or the Leicester Square Warner Cinema.

9. *Orderly streetscape versus commercial chaos.* Shop fronts, street lights and traffic signs are often the 'commercial junk trailed by the car and commerce'; plastic lettering, fluorescent and high intensity orange sodium lighting, and ugly advertising are 'demoralizing'. On the other hand incandescent street lighting can retain the 'magic quality of great cities'.

10. *People versus professionals.* 'Planning and architecture are much too important to be left to the professionals.' The 'fashionable theories . . . have spawned deformed monsters . . . Frankenstein monsters, devoid of character, alien and largely unloved, except by the professors who have been concocting these horrors in their laboratories'. The descendants of the heroic figures of modernism 'still retain prestige, and a kind of glamour, among their peers: they set the style, control the curriculum, and have commanding positions in the Royal Institute of British Architects, the Royal Fine Arts Commission, and the Royal Academy. It is they who keep a tight grip on architectural education and who are the heroes of a largely sycophantic architectural press, and the focus of much uncritical attention from the media . . .' Against these Charles ranges the views of the community and residents and 'determined conservation groups who drove back the juggernaut of the 60s [sic] planning, not the professionals'.

In summary, then, Charles makes a concerted attack on professionals, academics and developers. In a populist appeal he wants power to be transferred to grass roots communities. He does nevertheless have praise for, and illustrate in high quality photographs, a select group of modern, and even one postmodern, buildings. Royalty are models to be followed: the Queen Mother (to whom the book is dedicated), and a bevy of royal ancestors from the nineteenth and twentieth centuries – the Prince Regent, Prince Albert, George V and Edward VIII – all of whom promoted architectural and housing projects, are the heroes. There are two main categories of built precedents held up, and illustrated, for imitation or inspiration. First, heroic examples, icons of state, class and church power: the Taj Mahal, the Houses of Parliament, Greenwich Hospital, Notre Dame, Paris, The Circus, Bath, Brighton Pavilion, Cheltenham, and his own 'homes' of Kensington Palace in London and his country house Highgrove in Gloucestershire. Second, small, vernacular buildings, market places and towns, almshouses, and Georgian town terraces.

The images

But, above all, Charles himself emerges as the real hero. The whole text is in the first person, the first word is 'I', preceded by the first picture-in-the-text – a portrait of himself, smiling, debonair and with a red buttonhole. The closing image on the last page shows a woman grasping Charles's hand with both of hers, in an attitude of adoring supplication. There are numerous references, many illustrated, to his involvement with community groups and more radical community architects. Of the Charles images where he appears in conversation with another party – be it community leader, architect or tenant – in most (as in the final image), but not all, cases he is on the left, the other party on the right. In their analysis of images Kress and van Leeuwen (1996) argue that left-right positioning has symbolic meaning, the left usually denoting the Given, the right the New. The former is something the viewer already knows, a familiar point of departure, whilst the latter represents something problematic, contestable or something 'at issue'. If there is something in this, its origin (in the West) is related to left-right reading, and left-right page sequences in printed material. Kress and van Leeuwen themselves assign similar meanings to written English language structure, with 'wave-like movement from left to right (or rather, from "before" to "after", since in language we are dealing with temporarily integrated texts), and it is realized by intonation' (187–8). It can be argued that Charles's authority and position of power is the Given, whilst the conflicts, campaigns and design ideas of those he represents as his partners in the images, are the New.

There are in all some three hundred and seventy images. Of these, three in monochrome and fourteen in colour, show Charles alone, or in the company of architects, community groups and site building or demolition operatives; he also appears as a marginal figure in a few others, such as the Louvre Pyramid or on the central axis seated in front of the Taj Mahal. There are seven of his water-colours, including the frontispiece, one of which is juxtaposed with a photograph of him sketching at Balmoral. The caption to the frontispiece asks the reader to 'look carefully' to find the rest of his water-colours, though they are difficult to miss, especially as three of them are full page.

Of the good examples of buildings and townscapes, some forty-three are in monochrome and nearly two hundred in colour – a ratio of about 1:5. Of the bad examples some thirty-seven are in monochrome and sixty-six in colour – a ratio of less than 1:2. Thus colour is strongly favoured to demonstrate good qualities. Moreover there are about two and a half times as many 'good' images as 'bad' ones, so that images *per se* are seen as more powerful for positive visual promotion than for negative visual critique. All the buildings or urban scenes are described in words in the captions or the adjacent text – sometimes, as in the case of St Paul's in London, several times over – which powerfully identifies the intended audience as one with no prior knowledge of towns or buildings.

A favourite device is the use of similes, both in words and in images, for what are regarded as ugly built forms. Generally they are technological or pathologically biological, as in the case of the 'monstrous carbuncle', or the 'Frankenstein monsters'. Runcorn housing in Cheshire is like 'a grubby laundrette'; Quarry Hill flats in Leeds are 'fortress-like'; Birmingham's new central library is like an 'incinerator'; the National Theatre in London a 'bunker'; Mondial House on the Thames is an 'excrescence', like 'a word processor'.

The rule for image shape and location is generally the use of rectangles, placed within an ample frame of blank paper, aligned with the page edges. But frequently, bleeding-off on one or more edges is used. Only two images break this rule; both are reproductions (the only ones in the book) of other texts with images. In these cases the image is placed at an angle to the edge of the page. The first is the front of an 1851 copy of *The Builder* magazine, which shows the plan of a 'model house for the working man . . . a member of the class of manufacturing and mechanical operatives' – designed by Prince Albert, Queen Victoria's husband and Charles's great-great-great grandfather, exhibited at the 1851 Great Exhibition, and still, in built form, visible in South London's Kennington Park (Figure 10). The second is the cover of an early twentieth century promotional leaflet for Letchworth New Town entitled *Where shall I live* (sic) which describes 'model urban cottages'. These two images are in fact pictorial quotations, texts-within-a-text, and the slanting edge is the pictorial equivalent of quotation marks.

Another powerful graphic technique is to use faintly drawn images as a background to overprinted text or other images. Of the eight occasions on which this is used, one is of a contemporary proposal, by James Stirling, for a replacement for the Mappin and Webb building in the City of London, whose tower is ridiculed as a diving board. The remaining seven are admired exemplars (two of recent date) which teach various lessons. So these images represent a ghostly, hovering historic presence which, literally, underlie today's thinking and building.

It is clear from contemporary reviews and critiques of the accompanying TV programme that, for many readers and viewers, especially those hostile to Charles's thesis, the agony was that there were so many points to agree with, even allowing for the underlying élitism, sentimentality and nationalistic nostalgia. They include the railings against planners, developers and prima-donna architects, who combined in an unholy alliance to create meaningless skylines and urban chaos; the standing up for grassroots communities' voice and power; the denigration of crude materials, poor detailing and global, anonymous gigantism; and the attack on professional and academic hegemony. But, in the final analysis, the real issue went beyond these specifics; it was (and remains) how is the nature of architectural discourse itself (in which images play a key role) being defined or redefined here?

An important part of any discourse is silence – the things that are not said or represented. The most glaring in this book is the total absence of any building plans (with the exception of Prince Albert's model house) – as if the property of spatial arrangement and function, which cannot be adequately represented without plans, was of no significance in architecture. This is classic evidence of buildings being perceived only visually. Equally the resource implications of producing or running a building remain a silent issue, though an occasional hint is dropped that buildings *do* cost something. Thus despite the populist rhetoric, in both words and images, the idea of buildings as social objects is totally obliterated by the discourse of form – buildings as a kind of large public sculpture.

ure 10
GE FROM PRINCE CHARLES'S
OK A VISION OF BRITAIN
byright of, and permission
m, Trans-World Publishers
ubleday), Michael Peters
sociated Design
nsultants), Mary Evans
ture Library, and
Pictures, London
ansell Collection)

This view of architecture, which crosses boundaries of space and time, is shared by lay people and professionals, and is now shown to be classless since Charles seemed to share it with tenants on housing estates. It is so powerful that it is truly mythical. So whilst opening up the architectural debate to the population at large, Charles effectively ratifies the myth.

In this book the relationship between text and images is 'traditional' – that is, there is a clear differentiation between what is verbal text and what is image, and each works according to its own conventions. However, they are interdependent in producing the overall meaning. For instance, although the images are dominant in terms of how much space they take up and how prominent they are in that space (they also seem to have dictated the book's design as an object), it is the *text* which does the crucial job of making clear to the reader whether the building under discussion is positively or negatively evaluated. The visual coding (e.g. the distinction between colour and monochrome) echoes and reinforces the intended evaluation, but the precision of language is needed to enable us to interpret this code with certainty (this is a good example of Forty's point about the distinction between language and images).

Case 2 – An issue of 'Techniques et Architecture'

In the third case, which we will shortly discuss, architects were addressing both a professional jury and the lay public. In the first, Prince Charles was addressing a lay readership but, through them, attacking architects, planners and politicians. In this second case the text is specifically addressed to professional architects. *Techniques et Architecture* (T&A) is a long established glossy bi-monthly prestigious French journal (with brief English summaries) whose avowed purpose is, and has been, to explain the technical means – structures, materials, service systems and construction systems – through which some of the most innovative architectural designs are achieved. Its founding members are amongst the seminal figures of modern architecture: A. Perret, A. Hermant, Le Corbusier, R. le Ricolais and J. Prouvé. Though the European, and more specifically French, approach is clear, it is internationally recognized as a leader in its field. We chose the latest issue at the time of writing, Number 442 for April 1999, which happens to be dedicated to the theme of stone in modern architecture.

Whilst the Scottish Parliament material and Charles's book represent architecture-as-art, more specifically as large, public sculpture, this journal might be expected to represent architecture-as-technology. These are the two discourses, formally ratified over two centuries ago in the two institutions of French architectural education and practice – the *École des Beaux-Arts* and the *École Polytechnique* – discourses which have remained dominant to this day.

The issue has a dual structure. First, twenty-seven short illustrated articles around the theme of stone, the majority being specific case studies from France, Spain, Switzerland, Iceland, Israel, and the USA. One article concerns 'stereotomy'

– the technique of geometric projection required to draw the forms into which individual stones have to be cut. These occupy about three quarters of the journal. Second, a group of some ten loosely related texts concerning recent buildings, exhibitions, lighting, the technology of lifts, and urban design competitions, with, in addition, book reviews and product information.

The stone case studies have a similar format, of one to six pages of text-with-images per case, within the total of seventy-four pages:

- general and detailed description of the building in question
- exterior, interior and detailed photographs – in colour and black and white
- site and building plans, and sections
- constructional details.

Of the total of one hundred and ninety-four images, almost a half are in colour, mostly photographs of the exterior and interior of the building or models, and a few 3-D computer simulations. Of the one hundred and fourteen black and white images, eight are labelled and legible building plans, six are building plans so much reduced from the original drawings as to make the inscriptions illegible, and twelve are unlabelled plans. In addition there are four constructional details with legible inscriptions, one with numbered details but no key to the meaning of the numbers, four with over-reduced (illegible) inscriptions and three without inscriptions. Finally, there are twelve building sections of which two are unlabelled and the inscriptions on one are illegible.

The story of the other material in the remaining thirty-four pages is similar: almost half colour images; one labelled, legible plan, five plans with illegible inscriptions and four unlabelled ones; and one section. Two of the colour images are 3-D representations of lift systems.

For a journal dedicated to technology the choice of images shows an aston-ishingly cavalier attitude to identification of space, function, materials and con-structional details. The text is of little help in filling the vacuum, concentrating, as it does, on formal issues, landscape, and architectural biography. The article on stereotomy, in a curiously unself-conscious way, identifies that underlying problem of replacing reality by representation. It describes the history of the subject, start-ing with Philibert de l'Orme's 1567 treatise and reaching its greatest perfection two hundred years later in the engineering schools. The representations of complex curved surfaces, such as vaults, in two dimensions, made it possible to cut every stone exactly to size and shape. But by the end of eighteenth century such graphic skills began to be taught to architects as representational ends in themselves; difficult graphic exercises which imposed a drawing and geometric discipline. It was no longer a means to the end of making a material object.

The use of technology in this journal, as yet another vehicle for creating splendid visual images, not as a way of getting beneath the surface of visible forms, is a more generalized version of the stereotomy problem. So this is an old dilemma: how, against all the odds of design and representation having become dominated by graphic concerns focusing on form, can one refocus on construction and material detail? The journal appears to have lost the battle, and become barely distinguishable from the dozens of others which make no claim to being rooted in the technical discourse.

The seduction of the graphic representations used here, often computer-generated, has increased the gap between representation and material reality. This is the technical equivalent of the social situation we have mentioned throughout this book – the gap between visual forms, and their representation, and the social reality of the object represented.

Again there is strong differentiation here between the body text (i.e. text that is not part of an image, as opposed to label/caption text) and the illustrations. On inspection, however, they are not interdependent in quite the same way as the text and images in *A Vision of Britain*. They are thematically linked, but one does not reinforce or comment on the other, and in particular you do not need one in order to be able to understand the other. Even those images which belong to a 'technical' tradition stand in contrast to the body text which belongs to a rather different and less technical discourse, rich in imagery. For instance, a new thermal bath at Vals, in Switzerland, designed by Peter Zumthor, is described thus (the authors' translation):

> The entrance is not visible, it is even invisible from the buildings of the Vals baths. As one turns round the building, one could [even] jump in from the grassy roof which continues the mountain slope and from which one can see the bathers but not the entrance. When one does find it, in the adjacent hotel , via a long tunnel whose lighting is [deliberately?] a little vulgar, when one has left one's clothes in a little cabinet in the mahogany wall (the locker), by black curtains and wide leatherette seats – one penetrates into a chtonic space, a gneiss-enclosed environment, a cave of subdued light whose 'minerality' is welcoming.

In addition, the captions and labels are in many cases illegible, suggesting that the producers of *T&A* have *aestheticized* their drawings, diagrams and computer simulations – whether the reader can take a technically precise meaning from them appears to be less important than how they look. This is odd given that historically the technical discourse as a whole stands *in opposition to* the fine art discourse and suggests that *T&A* has capitulated to the 'hegemonic', formalist and aestheticized conception of what building design is about.

Case 3 – The Scottish Parliament

Background

As a result of the majority wish expressed in a referendum in 1997 the British Government enacted legislation to set up a Scottish Parliament, with substantial devolved powers, to sit in Scotland's capital, Edinburgh. An open worldwide invitation (one aspect of which we have already discussed in Chapter 4) was made to architects to design the new Scottish Parliament building on a site near the end of the Royal Mile, on Canongate, near Holyrood Palace. The invitation resulted in expressions of interest by some one hundred and thirty architects, of whom some seventy completed the pre-qualification questionnaire. Of these twelve were invited to make detailed presentations early in 1998 showing their past work and outlining their approach to the project, and finally a shortlist of five was drawn up. The designs they submitted were exhibited in a number of urban centres in Scotland in June 1998, and, within three days of the end this exhibition, the assessors selected the partnership of two firms – Enric Miralles, Benedetta Tagliabue with Robert Matthew, Johnson Marshall – as the winners.

As part of the process the Scottish Office drew up and published a 'Building User Brief' of some sixty-six pages (brief 1) in 1998. This was made available on the Internet to anyone interested. A second, more elaborate brief in two volumes totalling one hundred and thirty-one pages (brief 2) was published later that year and was used by the five shortlisted design teams. The difference between them was significant in volume rather than content. Brief 1 had four sections – Planning and functions; Space requirements and uses; Schedule of accommodation; and Building fabric. Brief 2 added to these – Services; Site; Budget; Master development programme; and Project administration. In addition it added six Appendices: two about an important listed building on the site, Queensberry House, which was to be incorporated into the project; one about the roles and activities of the Project Manager; one about the Design Team's responsibilities; another contained site and other essential drawings; and, finally one, an Interpretative Environmental Desk Study and Ground Investigation Report, which did not materialize for the first edition. So these formed the architects' instructions.

We are interested in the way the competitors responded to the briefs both in their designs and in the language of their submissions. But first we highlight some additional aspects of the brief, with which we were not concerned in our earlier discussion. We have consciously eschewed making architectural criticisms of the design submissions themselves; what interests us is their representation in the texts.

The briefs

In Chapter 4 we have already commented on one of the central themes, open government, and on the apparently contradictory emphasis on security.

There are also four subtexts in the briefs.

The first is that of national identity. There is specific mention of the 'Scottish people's authority (and) their aspirations as a nation'; 'a landmark building reflecting the aspirations of Scotland as a nation'; 'the first landmark, political building of the 21st Century . . . of which the Scottish people can be proud'.

The second is history. The chosen location is within both a UNESCO World Heritage Site and the Edinburgh Old Town Conservation Area. The scheme was to incorporate the seventeenth century Queensberry House, and one of the site boundaries, Canongate, is the 'historic regal processional route between the Castle and the Abbey and Palace of Holyroodhouse'.

The third subtext is modernity. The project must be 'modern'. The design 'must take account of the latest advances in technology . . . *IT* will play a prominent part in the management of information' – using electronic voting, television and broadcasting technologies, not to mention electronic surveillance.

Finally the fourth subtext is a deeply traditional definition of architecture as art – large public sculpture. In brief 1 the success of the project was defined in terms of 'design *and* use' (our emphasis). This implies that design (by implication form) is something separate from function and use, as is indeed confirmed in brief 2 which defines this something as art; it requires the building to be 'a piece of art in its own right . . . [which] should reflect the cultural dimensions of the country'.

With this range of requirements, some contradictory, some cryptic, some reinforcing the myth of architecture-as-art, and all in the form of sweeping generalizations, it is not surprising that the submission of the finalists, both as designs and even more so in their language, should have the same characteristics. Sometimes the words reproduce the wish-thinking of the brief almost verbatim.

A submission

Though the designs of all five finalists went on public exhibition, and we refer to some of their features, we focus our discussion on the six exhibition boards of the winners.

Apart from the obligatory single board describing and illustrating the work and personnel of the practices, the remaining five boards have a rich and informal mixture of language and image, colour, varied typography, with geometrically controlled and freehand drawings. This well matches the complexity and fragmentation of the design itself.

As indicated earlier, the architects based their entire scheme on the *land* of Scotland. It is worth repeating and expanding their articulation (on the boards) of this. 'The Parliament sits in the land . . . Scotland is a land . . . it is not a series of cities . . . The Parliament should be able to reflect the land which it represents.' 'The Parliament sits in the land because it belongs to the Scottish Land.' Indeed 'the building should be land . . . built out of land . . . to carve in the land the form of gathering people together . . . almost out of the rock'. Thus its form derives from 'a series of identifications between the building and the land, between citizens and the building'. It is this focus which will make the building 'fundamentally distinctive from other European Parliaments'. Here nature has become a metaphor for ageless tradition, permanence, strength, and growth. In keeping with this metaphor the dominant colours of both images and text are green and brown, and text is composed in blocks, lines and typefaces which relate organically to the images. Moreover buildings are seen, in themselves, as anthropomorphic living objects; along the Royal Mile 'one sees other buildings' – besides John Knox House – 'sticking their noses out to look at each other'. On Panel 3 a montage of landscape images and blocks of text are tied together by sweeping, freehand line sketches.

A number of other images are invoked. Some, such as the university campus and the monastery, are intended to create a place of 'rest . . . and meditation . . . an enclosed garden', and these descriptions are next to plans of enclosed courtyards. Another image, that of upside down boats 'offered by the land . . . [which] flout the landscape . . . [and are] a delicate presence in a place', occur not only in this language, but in images and in the design of the roofs. There is a quaint notion, rooted in ignorance of the industrial history of Scotland, that 'the idea of considering the Chambers as a kind of boat [which] insists on prefabrication' will be achieved by 'Scottish shipyards [who] will be more than happy to collaborate in such a task', rooted in an apparent belief that these shipyards still exist.

In keeping with these ambitions and metaphors the materials will be 'turf, stone, wood and glass'. Some of the other competitors interpreted the brief's aspirations to transparent government literally, by the use of glass; for one (Rafael Viñoly and Reiach Hall and Partners) this 'becomes an accessible icon, which represents the open nature of the new Scottish Government'. (We note in Chapter 4 the analogous debate about, and the use of, glass in the new dome over Berlin's Reichstag.) But to the winners this is too obvious; they propose a more introspective, solid, enclosed debating chamber, which should allow 'a clear atmosphere of concentration' on 'speeches and discussion', which 'makes glass and excessive transparency an inconvenient quality' – a statement that appears alongside an aerial view of a (wooden?) model of the proposed building, in which solid brown roof forms dominate.

Some designers used conventional metaphors. For instance, Rafael Viñoly and Reiach Hall and Partners proposed to put the debating chamber on a base of committee rooms, a formal allegory of 'underpinning the volume of the [debating] Chamber [to stress] the importance of the democratic interchange'. This strongly recalls Boullée's language in placing the prisons underneath the Palace of Justice as a 'metaphorical image of Vice overwhelmed by the weight of Justice' which we quoted in Chapter 2. Michael Wilford and Partners, with Bruno Happold, drew a 45° line radiating from their proposed tower which carries, apparently, an 'Internet connection to the whole world and expatriates throughout the world', a kind of radiating beam of latter day Scottish Enlightenment; and the upper part of their drum is crossed by two pedestrian bridges 'in the form of a Saltire' (the diagonal St Andrew's cross on Scotland's flag).

The winners' text, with its language of land, boats and natural materials such as turf, rocks and water ('pumped from the foundations'), whilst mystifying and obscure by itself, when combined with the rustic images into complex and memorable visual compositions, was more subtle and more powerful.

The key difference between the Miralles *et al.*'s and the other designs is in the fragmentation of the project, its low height, lack of monumentality, absence of an overriding formal language and, in the block plan, its fine grain and permeability. This was a self-conscious aim – yet the only place in the whole submission where language is used to state it is in the bottom margin of one panel, where, in the smallest of all the typefaces, we find this direct statement: 'It is not a big building, it is a series of different and almost independent ones.' The truth of this statement emerges not so much in the design, as in the fragmented images, the angular juxtapositions, the use of montage with jagged edges, and in the rich variations of visual techniques – line drawings, photography, conventional orthographic projection and abstract diagrams (Figure 11).

All the major themes of the brief are present in this, as indeed the other competitors', text: national identity, history and tradition, open government and access, modern technology, and art. The additional representation of the land and of sturdy rural virtues in the winning design carries an uncomfortable whiff of 1930s ideologies of national identity. Somehow this ancient land, and the simple virtues of those living on it, would have the amnesic effect of wiping out the memories of an often bitter, urban, socially complex history.

Frequently the vocabulary and phrases reproduce almost verbatim the brief's specifications. And just as those emphasized, as we have noted, that the security and surveillance measures must be unobtrusive, so this text maintains almost complete silence about these matters, with just an occasional indication of, or reference to, that issue. So an explicit statement in the brief is transformed in the text of the design into silence.

If there are such close parallels between both what is said and what is silent in the briefs and in the competitor's text, how does this fact influence what is designed and what is represented?

It is clear that there is an unarticulated assumption here, that forms 'speak'. That is, a belief in the power of forms as metaphors which embody and express complex historical and political ideals, ideas, concepts or narratives. This is no less than the theory of neo-Classical architects of the eighteenth century in *l'architecture parlante* – a theory which, as we show in Chapter 2, is alive and well today and being articulated by eminent architects such as Colin St John Wilson. When a prescriptive text such as a brief articulates objectives, the belief in forms as metaphors then works for the designer in one or both of two chronological sequences; there is no way of discovering which one actually occurs in a given case. In the first the designer first transforms the prescriptive text into his or her own real language, creates appropriate forms, and then presents a text which combines image and (transformed) words. In the second alternative the forms are created as immediate words-to-form translations of the brief in the designer's

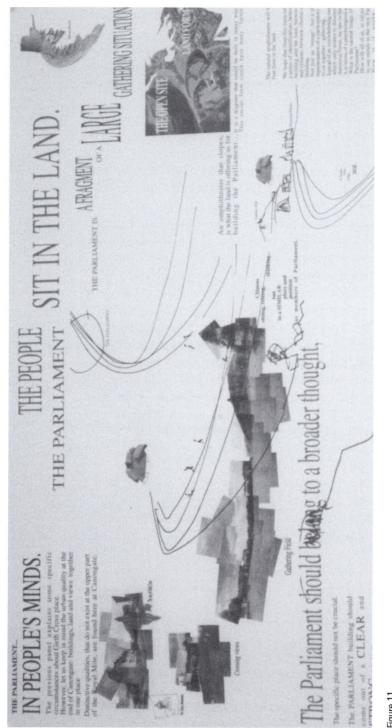

Figure 11
DRAWING BY ENRIC MIRALLES, BENEDETTA TAGLIABUE WITH ROBERT MATTHEW, JOHNSON MARSHALL, FOR THE SCOTTISH PARLIAMENT COMPETITION ENTRY

head, after which follow verbal elaborations and explanations, and both are then incorporated into the final text of the design proposal.

But clearly the *architecture parlante* belief applies here not only to the forms of the building, but to the forms of the text, though no designer acknowledges this. In other words the designers appear to realize that the *visual form* of the text, irrespective of its content, is capable of telling a story.

And just as we cannot be certain in which sequence the designer works, so we cannot be certain in which sequence, if any, the viewer reads. Is the image seen first, and then elaborated or explained by the words, or is the image an elaboration of words that have already been read? How much iteration, flitting to and fro, is there? If there *is* a sequence for the reader, the two operations follow each other closely in *time* – perhaps only separated by microseconds. Moreover such displays as Miralles *et al.*'s boards make every effort to integrate the language and image in *space*. So in the absence of very detailed empirical (perceptual and cognitive) experiments about this process, speculation about sequence or near-simultaneity in reading words and images is fruitless.

What is, however, evidently important, whatever the details of the psychological process, is that the meaning of forms cannot be uninfluenced by the language (and by the *forms* in which that text is presented), and, moreover, that both cannot but be powerfully influenced by the language of the brief.

This case exemplifies the new multimodality in that differentiation between text and image is relatively weak – they occupy the same space rather than different/adjacent spaces, and the text cannot be taken as merely a label for or comment on the images – while the images, conversely, are not straightforwardly illustrations of what is said in the text. Thematic juxtapositions are used, like rhetoric about land being embedded in a panel whose dominant colours are green and brown, but juxtaposition is a fairly 'loose' kind of connection which invites a considerable range of response on the part of the viewer rather than telling him or her explicitly how to make sense of the text overall. The result is a rather fragmentary discourse from which it is not easy to extract a clear meaning, and which is apparently produced to be judged in a fairly impressionistic way (i.e. the whole makes an impact greater than any of, or indeed the sum of, the fragments). This seems potentially quite significant in the context of a competition entry, where the intended viewers include the jury which decides who gets the commission.

We have tried to relate the sculptural properties of Miralles *et al.*'s design to the prescriptive text of the brief and to the text of competition entry itself. But, of course, many other aspects of the design are the outcomes of the brief: security, energy and environmental systems, and the range, types, function, adjacency and sizes of spaces. These are less mysterious transformations. In total, however, insofar as the formal, functional and spatial features of the building are formed by the brief, that competition text 'designed' this building.

A FINAL COMMENT

These case studies begin to suggest some answers to the questions we posed at the start of this chapter. For instance, it does appear that whilst new multimodal texts are emerging, like that for the Scottish Parliament, and new drawing conventions, like those of Zaha Hadid for the Cardiff Opera House, at the same time more traditional representational conventions seem to be alive and well. We still know too little about how any of these are read in practice, but clearly it would be too simple, even in the most 'traditional' case such as *A Vision of Britain*, to say that there is a straightforwardly hierarchical relationship whereby words just comment on images or images just illustrate words. All three cases show that in the production of meaning there is a division of labour between words and images, and that the resulting discourse is complex, with plenty of potential for generating ambiguities and contradictions. Whether these are 'liberating' (reducing the tyranny of the text-producer and freeing the creativity of the audience, as postmodernists might argue) or whether they are just confusing and mystifying, will presumably depend on the context in which texts are produced and interpreted. The text of two of the case studies (*A&T* and the Scottish Parliament) had the avowed purpose of informing (professionals regarding technical issues or the public about the intentions of shortlisted designers). In this context, it could be argued that the illegible images produced in one case, and the ambiguous ones in the other, are indeed mystifying rather than liberating. It seems that how they work is to mobilize our ingrained belief that a picture is worth a thousand words, or more specifically that architectural drawings are accurate and neutral representations of buildings; but since in fact the drawings actually provided are less than informative, putting them in is itself no more than a rhetorical gesture. The image signifies 'true and informative' just by being an image – but on inspection it does not contain the kind of information on which that signification was based in the first place. It appears that many texts which combine language with images are a form of persuasive discourse which persuades by masquerading as informative.

Afterword

Some Applications

This book, like all books, must stand or fall on its own merits, which will ultimately be judged by its readers. Since it is an academic book, we would expect most readers to base their judgements on whether they were intellectually engaged by it: whether the ideas were fresh and thought-provoking, whether the arguments were coherent and persuasive, and whether the text as a whole was interesting enough to justify the time and effort required to read it. However, we imagine many of our readers as belonging to (or preparing to enter) a specific professional milieu – as architects in training, or as practising architects, or as educators working with the practitioners of the future. These readers may legitimately ask a further question about our book: is it *useful*? Is it, in other words, relevant to the challenges and dilemmas faced by architects in the real world? What does it have to say about those challenges and dilemmas?

We should, of course, make clear that our main intention in writing this book was not to provide architects with a set of practical guidelines for using and interpreting language. As we have said, this is an academic book, designed primarily to explore ideas. If we had intended to produce a 'how-to' book we would have written it very differently. Nevertheless, we believe that our arguments in these pages do have potential implications for practitioners, and the purpose of this afterword is to draw readers' attention to some of these.

The most general and most important point we have argued here is that *language matters*. The linguistic classifications and labels for people, activities and objects that appear in a client's brief, for instance, will materially affect the way space is organized in the resulting design (a point we have illustrated in our discussions of buildings as different as a commercial office, a museum, a parliament house and a lunatic asylum). The words and metaphors used to evaluate buildings affect the way they are perceived and experienced. If we have succeeded in making this point, we think it implies that being conscious of the way language is commonly used in relation to buildings is not just an 'academic' (in the sense of 'pointless') exercise.

The word 'conscious' in the last sentence is important. As we pointed out in Chapter 1, architects in practice find themselves constantly dealing with texts, and indeed producing them. As Dana Cuff (1992) demonstrates in her study of practice, verbal encounters of various kinds are frequently the most important arenas where design decisions are made and design problems resolved – often not in the way the designers had initially envisaged as they sat at their drawing boards or computer screens. But whereas designers are normally intensely conscious of what they are doing at the aforementioned drawing boards and computer screens, they are usually far less conscious of what they are doing when they speak and write: they are just responding 'naturally' (that is, without conscious reflection) to the linguistic demands of the situation. Without disputing that their responses will be adequate in many or most cases, we think there are occasions when a more considered approach to language could benefit architect and client alike. For example, if the designers of the homoeopathic hospital discussed in Chapter 3 had consciously noticed and pointed out the mismatch between the 'holistic' discourse of the first part of the brief and the conventional medical discourse reproduced in the schedule of accommodation, this might have led to a productive discussion with the client, and possibly to a more appropriate arrangement and labelling of spaces in the subsequent design.

According to Dana Cuff, architects entering practice may find themselves challenged, confused and occasionally overwhelmed by the complexity of the interactions they are required to engage in. In the real world, as opposed to the design studios they spend so much of their time in as students, they discover that sheer 'talent', much emphasized in schools of architecture, is not always enough to ensure professional success: interpersonal and verbal skills are also crucial. Architects in practice have to learn to 'read' hidden meanings, working out, for example, which (or whose) contributions to discussion at a meeting are 'powerful' and which are unlikely to influence the ultimate outcome; or which parts of a text are 'written in stone' and which may be open to negotiation. These are essentially questions about the politics of institutions as they are expressed in institutional discourse, and arguably they are questions that could be addressed more systematically in the education and training of architects (just as, today, questions of finance and management are sometimes addressed explicitly). It would be possible, for instance, for the training of architects to include some attention to important text-types, such as briefs – who writes them, how they are structured, and what meanings may lurk under their apparently bland surfaces.

Studying examples of language about architecture would also put architects in a better position to make choices about their own writing later on, if circumstances and their own inclinations permitted. In writing, most of us use linguistic structures and forms which are matters of habit, shaped by the generic conventions of texts relevant to our work which, in turn, form part of the taken-for-granted linguistic practice of an academic or professional institution. In this practice there are often embedded, not always obviously, ideological assumptions which may not represent our own position and values. They have crept in from other sources and remain present, in a way analogous to the way viruses can, invisibly, infect all the files and supporting structures on a computer. Awareness of this process can help us to use language productively, not merely *re*productively, in ways which express more clearly where we stand and what we do or do not mean to communicate to our audience.

One way to become more conscious of the position and values embedded in our own texts is to ask readers to describe both the explicit and the implicit meanings of what has been written, looking closely at every level of the text (its overall structural organization, the grammar of particular sentences, the words which have been chosen, the metaphors that are used). Students and their teachers could enter into such dialogues, adopting alternating roles. This may sound like an 'academic' exercise (and indeed, at this point we are recommending it as such – as something that could be practised specifically in academic institutions), but it could also be adapted to be usable in the 'real world'. For instance, architects might occasionally find it helpful to engage in a similar kind of dialogue with clients or user groups, probing more explicitly than usual what they mean by particular words and phrases and what assumptions they have made about the meanings of the architects' own terminology. Though it may seem unrealistic because of the time it would take, a dialogue of this kind might in some cases justify the time expended upon it, if it prevented serious misunderstandings. Not uncommonly these appear only at a late stage in the design process, when it is discovered that someone has said or written something whose full implications were far from evident, either to themselves or to their audience.

When we make this suggestion, we are thinking in particular about the kind of project where the client is a public body and the architects it commissions are required or encouraged to engage in consultation with the ultimate users of the building (e.g. a clinic or a school). In this enterprise – whose democratic aims many practitioners are strongly committed to – language is an important issue. It is obviously an obstacle to effective democratic consultation if the parties involved use language with conflicting assumptions about its meaning, or if one party uses language in ways that are not fully intelligible to the other. In some cases, unintelligibility may be intentional and deliberate: far more often, though, it results from not reflecting consciously on the implications of one's habitual ways of using language.

More effective (and more equal) interaction between professionals and lay people is not, incidentally, just a matter of avoiding professional jargon. Jargon is the one linguistic problem that most practitioners in most professions (e.g. medicine and law as well as architecture and planning) are consciously aware of. But it is not only unfamiliar technical terms that can make an architectural text difficult for outsiders to interpret. For instance, it seems likely that the Scottish Office's public display of shortlisted designs for the Scottish Parliament (see Chapters 4 and 7) failed to elicit much useful comment from the public because the graphic features of the texts displayed were 'difficult' for the average untrained reader, and the texts were in some cases more allusive than informative. To someone familiar with the verbal and visual conventions entrants used, much could be inferred that was not directly communicated. But the public whose views were allegedly being sought did not have access to the relevant codes (indeed, we doubt that all members of the jury did either, since it included 'lay' as well as expert judges). Viewers were thus compelled to fall back on impressionistic judgements of the display boards – a proceeding more appropriate when deciding what colour to paint a wall than when evaluating designs for a large and significant piece of architecture which will permanently change its surrounding environment. If public consultation was an important aspect of this competition, it would have been possible – and arguably, desirable – for the Scottish Office to issue guidelines for designers on presenting their designs more 'readably' for a general audience. (In this connection, we repeat our observation that more research is needed to elucidate how people other than architects actually do read representations of buildings, especially the multimodal representations that are becoming increasingly common.)

That public consultation was incorporated in a project such as the Scottish Parliament competition at all is one manifestation of the now widely held view that the lay public has a role to play in architectural decision making, not only by providing information that designers can refer to in making their own decisions, but by actually giving opinions on designs. As we observed in Chapter 5, many experts on architecture (critics and curators as well as practising designers) have expressed the view that if the public were better informed and more articulate about architectural matters, the quality of the built environment could only improve. We agree (though we might not agree with all these experts about what would actually constitute 'improvement'!) And once again, we think that language is relevant here. If a wider section of the population is to engage in the intelligent criticism of buildings, they will need a critical language that speaks – intelligently and intelligibly – to their concerns. The language of popular judgement, with its 'monstrous carbuncles', 'wobbly bridges'[1] and 'erotic gherkins', is intelligible and occasionally amusing, but it does not support serious, extended discussion of the merits of the buildings most people routinely use.

In Chapter 5 we examined the language used in a range of 'expert' evaluative texts about buildings, and found it strongly oriented to the formal, the aesthetic, and increasingly, the promotional, where emphasis is placed on buildings (and celebrity designers) as commodities. As Adrian Forty (2000) argues, the language available to evaluate buildings in *social* terms is impoverished by comparison. We dispute Forty's view that this is so because language is inherently less well suited to making social distinctions than it is to making formal ones. Rather we think that the massive elaboration of formalist discourse is a historical and cultural phenomenon that serves particular (professional and academic) interests. Experts who wish to educate the public in relation to the built environment might make a start by reflecting on the limitations of their own evaluative terminologies, and making conscious efforts to develop a more 'social' discourse in which to speak and write critically about buildings.

In much of what we have said so far there has been an underlying assumption that architects and related professionals actively want to engage in dialogue and to communicate more effectively with their clients, the users of their buildings and the public at large (and also vice versa – that clients, for instance, view architects as partners in a dialogue, not subordinates employed to do whatever they are told). But of course architecture and planning are sometimes practised – and frequently debated – in situations of overt or latent conflict. Language in such situations may have an openly adversarial function. This is the case, for instance, where a controversial planning decision becomes the subject of a public inquiry. Parties with interests in the outcome invariably try to frame their oral and written contributions in ways that support their aims, and while some of their strategies may be obvious enough, important presuppositions or patterns may only be revealed by a 'deeper' critical analysis. Being able to analyse the techniques of verbal persuasion used in adversarial contexts is often a useful 'real world' skill.

Even where there is no overt conflict, discourse about buildings may have a hidden agenda which it is useful to be able to bring to light. In this book we have discussed, for instance, two cases – the Scottish Parliament and the 'glass torpedo' call centre – where high levels of surveillance and control were incorporated in designs whose surface appearance was intended to connote something very different (openness and 'transparency' in the Parliament case, informality and playfulness in the case of the call centre). These are (covertly) instances of 'conflict' in the sense that there are differing interests in play (the state's and the public's, or the employer's and the workers'), and the client proposes to use design as a way of playing down those differences. Architects will of course vary in their personal responses to cases of this kind. But however they choose to respond, the ability to read texts critically will at least help them to recognize what kind of agenda they are dealing with.

In this book we have tried to show that there is more to the language used to speak and write about architecture than is immediately obvious on the surface. In this afterword we have tried to suggest ways in which that insight might be applied to the conditions of the 'real world'. If in the teaching, learning and practice of architecture there develops a more conscious and habitual interest in what is beneath the surface of language, we will have achieved our aim.

Notes

Foreword

1 For readers who would like to know rather than guess: Chapters 1, 4 and 5 were written by Deborah Cameron; Chapters 2, 3 and 7 were written by Thomas Markus; both of us contributed sections to Chapter 6. Of course, we read and commented extensively on each other's chapters: every part of the book is ultimately the product of collaboration between us.

2 Though we do make reference to texts dealing with Indonesia and Japan, and written by insiders to these cultures, neither of us speaks Bahasa Indonesian or Japanese, so we have been obliged to reply on translations, and accordingly we do not attempt any detailed analysis of their discourse. The text dealing with Chinese architecture which we analyse in Chapter 5 is neither written in Chinese nor by a Chinese author, but rather represents a Western view of its subject.

Chapter 1: WHY LANGUAGE MATTERS

1 Linguists use the term 'natural language' to denote entities like 'Arabic', 'English', 'Haitian Creole', 'Japanese', and so on, distinguishing these from artificial languages such as those used in computer programming, or languages invented for specific (and often quite limited) purposes by individuals, of which the best known example is probably Emil Zamenhof's Esperanto (a more recent case is Klingon, the 'language' of a fictional alien planet in *Star Trek*. Klingon has become popular among humans, some of whom now learn and use it as a hobby). Put very simply, the main distinguishing characteristic of a 'natural' language is that it has native speakers – people who have acquired it in childhood without formal instruction.

2 This is not to make the claim that thought is entirely dependent on language, for it is clear that pre-linguistic children can think, as can adults who have been deprived of language. Linguists and cognitive scientists have studied a number of people in this unfortunate position. Some have been deaf individuals whose condition was either undiagnosed or disregarded until

adulthood; they could not hear spoken language and were not exposed to sign language. Others have been abandoned or severely abused children discovered after puberty.

3 The word 'text' here is neutral as to medium, i.e. a 'text' may consist of either spoken or written discourse.

4 Another recent, historically oriented volume on the subject of the architecture/language connection is Clarke and Crossley's edited collection *Architecture and Language* (2000).

5 Some theorists and practitioners have been attracted by a specific analogy between architectural 'grammar' and the generative syntax developed by the linguist Noam Chomsky, an early version of which was the source of the concepts 'deep structure', 'surface structure' and 'transformation'. A clear explanation of why linguists regard the use of Chomsky's terminology in relation to architecture as misguided is given by Keyser and O'Neil (1984) (thanks to Nigel Fabb for this reference).

6 For the purposes of the argument developed below, we will not consider the differences between Saussurean structuralism and Peircean semiotics; undoubtedly there are differences, but for our purposes here these are relatively unimportant. We use Saussure's work rather than Peirce's as our main reference point because of the significance of Saussure's thought for the development of modern linguistics.

7 Sceptics might point out here that red and green are not arbitrary unmotivated choices for traffic signals – they are maximally contrasting colours, for instance. It might also be pointed out that the relative placement of the signals (red above green) is part of the system. These are reasonable points, and what they illustrate is the principle that if a message is really important (e.g. 'stop or you'll crash'), and the recipient must grasp it instantly, you should make it as readable as possible by encoding the same information in several different forms. Information scientists call this 'redundancy'. Traffic signals are highly redundant: you can read them by colour, by placement and by sequence. This reduces the probability that colour-blind or inattentive drivers will come to grief. It will not, however, save a driver who simply does not understand what the contrast is meant to signify (stop/go); in this respect traffic lights are different from those road signs which are iconic (e.g. signs warning of a steep incline or sharp bend which use stylized pictorial representations of those features).

8 Eco contrasts architecture here with other art forms such as poetry; for some critical comments on this element of his argument, which is marked by the idealism we will argue below is a problematic feature of the Saussurean and semiotic traditions in general, see Markus (1993: 35–6).

9 Pragmatics is the more relevant of these disciplines for our purposes in this book (see further below). An accessible introduction to the subject is Jenny

Thomas's *Meaning in Interaction* (1995); another widely used textbook is Stephen Levinson's *Pragmatics* (1983).

10 For Foucault's own definition and discussion of 'discourse', see *The Archaeology of Knowledge and the Discourse on Language* (1972).

11 Note the use of a spatial metaphor here: just as architects may figure architecture linguistically, so linguists often figure language spatially or architecturally. Not all linguists subscribe to this particular metaphor, however. Another way of imagining the same thing might be to think of subsystems like phonology and syntax being files or directories of information, stored in different virtual locations on an imaginary disk and integrated with each other in the act of language production (the metaphor here is 'mind as computer').

12 The writer and the reader do not have to be, and typically are not, co-present in the same space and time. This has marked effects on the form of written as opposed to spoken language. For example, the former usually has to be more explicit than the latter to compensate for the lack of shared context and the absence of feedback. Another consequential difference is that speech, consisting of sound waves in the air, is inherently ephemeral and must be processed in real time (even if you record it, all you can do is repeat the same real-time processing on an infinite number of occasions). There are of course kinds of speech (e.g. on the telephone) which permit the parties to be widely separated in space, though temporal separation is rarer and the real-time processing constraint still applies.

13 Social and power relations may appear in briefs as preconditions which an architect cannot question; all s/he can do is explore different formal solutions to the same social equation. As Ellen Dunham-Jones notes, 'the competition system encourages young architects to challenge formal conventions, but not the programmatic or social dictates of the brief' (1997: 21, n. 8).

Chapter 2: BUILDINGS AND THEIR TEXTS: A BRIEF HISTORY

1 The text-types we consider in this chapter are, of course, types of *writing*. While architecture has no doubt been spoken about for as long as it has existed, the resulting discourse has left no record that we can use to construct a historical account.

2 Alberti's work was written in about 1450, but its first publication was 1485.

3 *Procès-verbaux de l'Académie royale*, I, 6, 4 February, 1672.

4 For details of these and other modern manifestos see Frampton, K. (1980) *Modern Architecture: a Critical History*, London: Thames and Hudson.

5 Even such rudimentary texts seem not to have been produced routinely; few examples have survived.

Chapter 3: CLASSIFICATION

1   One of us has developed this idea in Markus, Thomas A. (1987) 'Buildings as Classifying Devices', *Environment and Planning B: Planning and Design*, 14, 467–84.

Chapter 4: POWER

1   For instance, some call centres serving customers in the UK are located in the Republic of Ireland, and one of the present authors, Deborah Cameron, studied a call centre in London which was the clearing house for inquiries from businesses located all over western Europe. The only constraint here is language; centres have to be able to recruit workers who speak the language their customers use (hence Ireland or India rather than China or Chile for the English-speaking market, and Britain rather than, say, Italy, for the European business market, where many languages are spoken natively but English is the single most widely spoken second language).

2   This finding is supported by interviews carried out by Deborah Cameron in 1998–1999. Asked what were the good and bad things about working in a call centre, most of Cameron's twelve 'rank and file' interviewees cited as 'bad things' repetition ('I could do it in my sleep'), time and target pressure, and having to tolerate abuse from customers. Only one interviewee even mentioned the working environment, and this was under the heading of 'good things': compared to some industrial sites where the interviewee had worked in the past or would be able to find work, call centres were, he said, at least clean and relatively comfortable. (See Cameron 2000.)

3   Though the association may take on different meanings across cultures, it has been noted by feminists that there is in many cultural traditions a persistent tendency to project anxieties about purity and pollution disproportionately onto women. (Consider, for instance, the common and ancient belief that women who are post-partum or menstruating are 'unclean' and need to undergo purification rituals to make contact with them safe for men. Surviving examples in modern religions include the orthodox Jewish *mikvah* [ritual bath] and the Christian rite of 'churching'.) In that context, it is not obviously radical or subversive of patriarchal attitudes to choose a washbasin as a privileged symbol of women's central place within the household.

Chapter 5: VALUE

1   This content analysis was carried out on twenty-six weekly architecture features published in the *Independent* newspaper in 1996, i.e. half a year's output. The breakdown of buildings selected for evaluative discussion in this sample is as follows: historic monuments 4, museums and performance spaces 4, government buildings 2, churches 2, industrial buildings 1, commercial buildings 1, schools 1, military buildings 1. This list includes both

new buildings and old ones (some undergoing restoration or conversion, others threatened with demolition and one – an airforce base built round a series of concrete hangars – problematic because unwanted but impossible to demolish). As the numbers suggest, not every item in the sample featured a building or buildings as its main topic: some focused on a person, others on an issue.

2   An analogy may help to clarify the point. Feminists have pointed out that English possesses very large numbers of words referring to women as prostitutes, and a similarly elaborate repertoire of terms denoting the penis (see e.g. Cameron 1992). In these cases, we suggest, no one would argue that the lexical elaboration results from the propensity of 'language' to make fine distinctions. It is obvious that the terminologies have developed as they have in discourse – language in use – because of the sociocultural significance of prostitution/male genitals for users of English over a long period of time.

Chapter 6: HERITAGE

1   All three guides are available on the Internet.

2   The three publications are:

A *Auschwitz-Birkenau Museum and Reflection Centre Oświęcim, Poland*, Bulletin No. 1, August 1996.

B Kazimierz Smolen (1995) *State Museum in Oświęcim, Auschwitz Birkenau Guide* Book, Oświęcim.

C *The Bulletin(s) of the State Museum, Auschwitz-Birkenau and the Foundation for the Commemoration of the Victims of Auschwitz-Birkenau Extermination Camp*, Oświęcim.

3   For a full account of stone, and especially granite, production for Nazi architecture see Jaskot, Paul B. (1999) *The Architecture of Oppression: The SS, Forced Labor and the Nazi Monumental Building Economy*, London: Routledge.

AFTERWORD: SOME APPLICATIONS

1   The 'Wobbly Bridge' is a nickname given to Norman Foster's Millennium Bridge, a pedestrian bridge across the River Thames in London, after it had to be closed on the day it officially opened because of swaying which, in conditions of 'heavy traffic', caused some users to complain of nausea.

Bibliography

Abeyaskere, S. (1987) *Jakarta: a History*, Singapore: Oxford University Press

Alberti, Leon Battista (c 1450, 1485) *De Re Aedificatoria*, trans. Joseph Rykwert, Neil Leach and Robert Taverner (1988) *On the Art of Building*, Cambridge, MA: The MIT Press

An Act to Explain and Amend the Laws Relating to the Transportation, Imprisonment, and other Punishments, of Certain Offenders (1779) 19, Geo. 3, CAP. LXXIV, 1397 ff.

Anderson, Benedict (1983) *Imagined Communities: Reflections on the Origin and Spread of Nationalism*, London: Verso

Apollonio, U. (ed.) (1973) *Futurist Manifestos*, London: Thames and Hudson

Baly, P.P. (1852*) A Statement of the Proceedings . . . Baths and Washhouses for the Labouring Classes*, etc., London

Barnard, H. (1848) *School Architecture*, etc., New York: Barnes

Barthes, Roland (1977) *Image-Music-Text*, ed. and trans. Stephen Heath, New York: Hill and Wang

—— (1987) *Mythologies*, trans. Annette Lavers, New York: Hill and Wang

Bentham, Jeremy (1791a) *Panopticon; or the Inspection House*, London

—— (1791b) *Panopticon: Postscript*, London

Billig, Michael (1995) *Banal Nationalism*, London: Sage

Boullée, E.-L. (1780s) *Architecture , Essai sur l'Art*, trans. and ed. Helen Rosenau (1976) *Boullée & Visionary Architecture: including Boullée's 'Architecture, Essay on Art'*, London and New York: Academy Editions

Cameron, Deborah (1992) 'Naming of Parts: Gender, Culture, and Terms for the Penis among American College Students', *American Speech* 67(4): 367–82

—— (2000) *Good To Talk? Living and Working in a Communication Culture*, London: Sage Publications

Castells, Maurice (1977) *The Urban Question: a Marxist Approach*, trans. Alan Sheridan, London: Edward Arnold

Chadwick, E. (1842*) Report . . . on an Inquiry into the Sanitary Conditions of the Labouring Population of Great Britain*, London: HMSO

Clarke, Georgia and Crossley, Paul (eds) (2000) *Architecture and Language: Constructing Identity in European Architecture c 1000–c 1650*, Cambridge: Cambridge University Press

Committee on the State of Madhouses (1819) *Report*, etc., London

Cope, Bill and Kalantzis, Mary (eds) (2000) *Multiliteracies*, London: Routledge

Council on Education (1840) *Minutes of the Committee of Council on Education with Appendices and Plans of School-Houses, 1839–40*, London: William Clowes and Sons

Cuff, Dana (1992) *Architecture: the Story of Practice*, Cambridge, MA: The MIT Press

Derrida, Jacques (1986) 'Point de Folie – Maintenant l'Architecture: Bernard Tschumi: La Case Vide – La Villette 1985', *AA Files* 12, Summer 1986, 65–75

van Dijk, Teun (1987) *Communicating Racism,* London: Academic Press

Douglas, Mary (1966) *Purity and Danger: an Analysis of the Concepts of Pollution and Taboo*, London: Routledge and Kegan Paul

Dunham-Jones, Ellen (1997) 'Stars, Swatches and Sweets: Thoughts on Post-Fordist Production and the Star System in Architecture', *Thresholds* 15, Fall, 16–21

Durand, J.-N.-L. (1801) *Receuil et Parallèle des Édifices de tous Genres, Anciens et Modernes*, Paris

—— (1802–1809) *Précis de Leçons d'Architecture Données à l'École Polytechnique*, Paris

Durm, J. (ed.) (1880 *et seq.*) *Handbuch der Architektur*, 13 Vols, Darmstadt

van Eck, Caroline (1998) 'The structure of *dere Aedificatoria* reconsidered', *Journal of the Society of Architectural Historians* (USA), 57(3): 280–97

—— (1999) 'Enduring principles of architecture in Alberti's *On the art of building*: how did Alberti set out to formulate them?', *Journal of Architecture*, 4(2): 119–27

Eco, Umberto (1986) 'Function and sign: semiotics of architecture', in M. Gottdiener and Alexandros Lagopoulos (eds), *The City and the Sign: an Introduction to Urban Semiotics,* 55–86, New York: Columbia University Press

Egbert, Donald Drew (1980) *The Beaux-Arts Tradition in French Architecture: Illustrated by the Grands-Prix de Rome*, ed. David van Zanten, Princeton: Princeton University Press

Eldridge, John (ed.) (1995) *The Glasgow Media Group Reader*, Vol. I, London: Routledge

Ellen, Roy F. and Reason, David (eds) (1979) *Classifications in their Social Context*, London: Academic Press

Engels, F. ([1845] 1969) *The Condition of the Working Class in England*, London: Granada

Evans, Robin (1997) *Translations from Drawings to Building and Other Essays*, London: Architectural Association Publications

Fairclough, Norman (1992) *Discourse and Social Change*, Cambridge: Polity Press

—— (1995) *Media Discourse*, London: Edward Arnold

Feldman, David (c 1994) *Beyond Understanding in Cognitive Development*, 2nd edn, Norwood, NJ: Able Publishing Corporation

Filarate (c 1460) *Treatise on Architecture* (1965), trans. and with notes by R. Spencer, 2 Vols, Newhaven and London: Yale University Press

Forty, Adrian (2000) *Words and Buildings: a Vocabulary of Modern Architecture*, London: Thames and Hudson

Foucault, Michel (1963) *Naissance de la Clinique*, Paris: Presses Universitaires de France

—— (1972) *The Archaeology of Knowledge and the Discourse on Language*, New York: Pantheon

—— (1975) *Surveiller et Punir: Naissance de la Prison*, Paris: Gallimard

—— (1980) *Power/Knowledge: Selected Interviews and Other Writings, 1972–1977*, ed. C. Gordon, Brighton: Harvester

Franklin, Jill (1981) *The Gentleman's Country House and its Plan 1835–1914*, London: Routledge and Kegan Paul

Fraser, Iain and Henmi, Rod (1994) *Envisioning Architecture: an Analysis of Drawing*, New York: Van Nostrand Reinhold

Furttenbach, J. (1628) *Architectura Civilis,* etc., Ulm

Garnier, Tony (1917) *Une Cité Industrielle: Étude pour la Construction des Villes*, Paris

Gathercole, Peter and Lowenthal, David (eds) (1996) *The Politicising of the Past*, London: Unwin Hyman

Gibson, James J. (1960) *The Senses Considered as Perceptual Systems*, Boston: Houghton Mifflin

Glasgow: UK City of Architecture and Design 1999 (1999) *Glasgow Homoeopathic Hospital: Architecture Competition, Record of Entries*, Glasgow UK City of Architecture and Design 1999: Glasgow

Goldman, J. (ed.) (1720) *L.C. Sturm Anweisung allerhand Öffentliche Zucht und Liebes Gebäude*, etc., Augsburg

Gombrich, E.H. (1968) *Art and Illusion*, 3rd edn, London: Phaidon Press

Goodman, Nelson (1976) *Languages of Art*, Indianapolis: Hackett

Gottdiener, M. and Lagopoulos, A.Ph. (eds) (1986) *The City and the Sign: an Introduction to Urban Semiotics,* New York: Columbia University Press

Grajewski, Tadeusz (1993) 'The SAS Head Office – Spatial Configuration and Interaction Patterns', *Arkitekturforskning* 2: 63–74

Guadet, J. (1902–1904) *Éléments et Théorie de l'Architecture: Cours à l'École Nationale et Speciale des Beaux-Arts*, 4 Vols Paris: Librairie de la Construction Moderne

de Haan, Hilde and Haagsma, Ids (1988) *Architects in Competition: International Architectural Competitions of the Last 200 Years*, London: Thames and Hudson

Harper, Roger H. (1983) *Victorian Architectural Competitions: an Index to British and Irish Architectural Competitions in The Builder; 1843–1900*, London: Mansell Publishing Limited

Harris, Sandra (1984) 'Questions as a Mode of Control in a Magistrate's Court', *International Journal of the Sociology of Language* 49: 5–27

Harvey, David (1973) *Social Justice and the City*, London: Edward Arnold

Hatton, Brian (1999) 'Berlin 1999: Phantoms and Formulae', in *Vertigo: the Strange New World of the Contemporary City*, ed. Rowan Moore. London: Laurence King Publishing: 74–89

Hayden, Dolores (1976) *Seven American Utopias: the Architecture of Communitarian Socialism 1790–1975*, Cambridge, MA: The MIT Press

Hershberger, Robert G. and Cass, Robert C. (1988) 'Predicting User Responses to Buildings', in Jack L. Nasar (ed.) *Environmental Aesthetics: Theory, Research and Applications*, Cambridge: Cambridge University Press

Hewison, Robert (1987) *The Heritage Industry: Britain in a Climate of Decline*, London: Methuen

Hillier, Bill (1996) *Space is the Machine*, Cambridge: Cambridge University Press

Hillier, Bill and Hanson, Julienne (1984) *The Social Logic of Space*, Cambridge: Cambridge University Press

Howard, John (1777, 1784) *The State of the Prisons in England and Wales*, 1st and 3rd edns, Warrington

Jencks, Charles (1977) *The Language of Post-Modern Architecture,* London: Academy Editions

Jessup, H. (1985) 'Dutch architectural visions of the Indonesian tradition', *Muquarnas* 3, 138–61

Karsten, T. (1920) 'Bij de eerste Indiese Architectuur Tentoonstelling' (On the occasion of the first Indies Architecture Exhibition), *De Taak* 3, 33, 12 March

Keyser, Samuel and O'Neil, Wayne (1984) 'Architectural Linguistics', *Spazio e Socitá/Space and Society*, 26 June, n.p.

Kleine, Holger (1999) 'Theatre of Democracy: Reinventing Berlin's Reichstag', *Architecture Today* 98: 48–59

Kress, Gunther and van Leeuwen, Theo (1996) *Reading Images: the Grammar of Visual Design*, London: Routledge

Kusno, Abidin (2000) *Behind the Postcolonial: Architecture, Urban Space and Political Cultures in Indonesia*, London: Routledge

Leclerc, J. (1993) 'Mirrors and the Lighthouse: a Search for Meaning in the Monuments and Great Works of Sukarno's Jakarta, 1960–1966', in Nas, P. (ed.) *Urban Symbolism*, Leiden: E.J. Brill

Le Corbusier (1923) *Vers une Architecture*, Paris: Éditions Crés

—— (1935) *La Ville Radieuse*, Boulogne: Éditions de l'Architecture d'Aujourd'hui

Ledoux, C.N. (1804) l'Architecture Considerée sous le Rapport de l'Art, des Moeurs et de Législation, Paris, Vol. I, reprinted Alfons Uhl (1981), Nordlingen: Uhl

Lefebvre, Henri (1974) *La Production de l'Éspace*, Paris: Anthropos; trans. Donald Nicholson-Smith (1991) *The Production of Space*, Oxford: Blackwell

Levinson, Stephen (1983) *Pragmatics*, Cambridge: Cambridge University Press.

Lowenthal, David (1996) *The Heritage Crusade and the Spoils of History*, London: Viking

McCormac, Richard (1995) 'Don't knock it till you've seen it', *Independent Section Two*, 11 September, 8–9

Malchiodi, Cathy A. (1998) *Understanding Children's Drawings*, London: Jessica Kingsley

Markus, Thomas A. (1994) *Buildings and Power: Freedom and Control in the Origin of Modern Building Types*, London: Routledge

—— (1999) 'Is there a Built Form for Non-patriarchal Utopias?', paper presented at Conference *Embodies Utopias: Gender, Social Change and the Built Environment*, Center for Gender Studies, Chicago University, 16–18 April 1999, to be published (2001) as: Amy Bingham, Lise Shapiro Sanders and Rebecca Zorach (eds) *Embodied Utopias*, London: Routledge

Marr, David (1982) *Vision: a Computational Investigation into the Human Representation and Processing of Visual Information*, San Francisco: W.H. Freeman and Company

Middleton, Robin (1978) AD Profiles 'The Beaux Arts', Introduction, *Architectural Design* 48, 11, 1–89

Ministry of Education (1949–1963) *Building Bulletins*, London: HMSO

Ministry of Health (1949) *Housing Manual*, London: HMSO

Ministry of Health and Ministry of Works (1944) *Housing Manual*, London: HMSO

Mitchell, W.J.T. (1986) *Iconology: Image, Text, Ideology*, Chicago and London: The University of Chicago Press

Modleski, Tania (1991) *Feminism without Women: Culture and Criticism in a 'Postfeminist' Age*, New York: Routledge

Moore, Rowan (1999) 'Vertigo: the Strange World of the Contemporary City', in *Vertigo: the Strange World of the Contemporary City*, ed. Rowan Moore, London: Laurence King, 9–59

Muehrcke, Phillip C. and Muehrcke, Juliana (1998) *Map Use: Reading, Analysis, and Interpretation*, Madison, WIS.: J. P. Publications

Mumford, Lewis (1961) *The City in History: its Transformations and its Prospects*, New York: Harcourt Brace and World, Inc.

Onions, John (1988) *Bearers of Meaning: the Classical Orders in Antiquity, the Middle Ages and the Renaissance*, Cambridge: Cambridge University Press

Orwell, George ([1937] 1962) *The Road to Wigan Pier*, London: Penguin Books

Papworth, J.W. and Papworth, W. (1853) *Museums, Libraries and Picture Galleries*, etc., London

Pont, Henri Maclaine (1923) 'Javaansche Architectuur', *DJAWA* 3

Poor Law Commissioners (1834 *et seq.*) *First* [and subsequent] *Report(s)*, London

Preziosi, Donald (1979) *The Semiotics of the Built Environment: an Introduction to Architectonic Analysis*, Bloomington: Indiana University Press

Prince of Wales, HRH The (1989) *A Vision of Britain: a Personal View of Architecture*, London: Doubleday

Prinz, Jessica (1991) *Art Discourses/Discourses in Art*, New Brunswick, NJ: Rutgers University Press

Quatremère de Quincy, M. (1823) *Essai sur le Nature, le But et les Moyens de l'Imitation dans les Beaux Arts*, Paris: Treuttel et Würtz

——— (1832) *Dictionnaire Historique d'Architecture*, 2 Vols, Paris: Librairie d'Adrien le Clere

Ritzer, George (1996) *The McDonaldization of Society: an Investigation into the Changing Character of Contemporary Life,* revised edn, Thousand Oaks, CA: Pine Forge Press

Robson, E.R. (1874) *School Architecture*, etc., London

Rose, Nikolas (1990) *Governing the Soul: the Shaping of the Private Self*, London: Routledge

Rudofsky, Bernard (1965) *Architecture without Architects*, New York: Museum of Modern Art

Rykwert, Joseph (1972) *On Adam's House in Paradise: the Idea of the Primitive Hut in Architectural History*, New York: The Museum of Modern Art

della Santa, L. (1816) *Della Construzione e del Regolamento di una Pubblica Universale Biblioteca*, etc., Florence

Saussure, Ferdinand de ([1916] 1974) *A Course in General Linguistics*, trans. Wade Baskin, London: Fontana

Savignat, J.-M. (1980) *Dessin et Architecture du Moyen-Age au XVIIIe Siècle*, Paris: École Nationale Supérieure des Beaux-Arts

Scott, David H.T. (1986) *Mental Imagery and the Process of Visualisation in Map Reading*, London: London School of Economics and Political Science, Graduate School of Geography, New Series No. 16

Scottish Home and Health Department (1973) *Health Centre Guide*, Edinburgh: HMSO

Select Committee on Gaols (1819) *Report*, etc., London

Sennett, Richard (1998) *The Corrosion of Character: the Personal Consequences of Work in the New Capitalism*, New York: W.W. Norton

Sewell, G. and Wilkinson, B. (1992) 'Someone to watch over me: surveillance, discipline and the just-in-time labour process', *Sociology* 26(2): 271–89

Snuijff, S. (1914) 'Architecture in Netherlands East India', Netherlands East Indian San Francisco Committee, Department of Agriculture, Industry and Commerce, No. 11, Semarang-Soerabaja-Den Haag: Van Dorp and Co.

Stark, W. (1807) *Remarks on Public Hospitals for the Cure of Mental Derangement*, etc., Edinburgh

St John Wilson, Colin (1992) *Architectural Reflections: Studies in the Philosophy and Practice of Architecture*, Oxford: Butterworth Architecture

Sturm, L.C. (1720) *Vollständige Anweisung . . . Spitäler vor Alte and Kranke*, etc., Augsburg

Sudjarat, I. (1991) 'A study of Indonesian architectural history', PhD Dissertation, University of Sidney

Sukarno (1962) 'Transformation of Djakarta Raya', in *Indonesia 1962*, Department of Foreign Affairs, Republic of Indonesia

Summerson, John (1963) *The Classical Language of Architecture*, London: Thames and Hudson

Suzuki, Akira (1999) 'Gifu Housing, Japan: Reversed Planning through Gender', in *Vertigo: the Strange World of the Contemporary City,* ed. Rowan Moore, London: Laurence King Publishing: 128–41

Thomas, Glyn V. and Silk, Angele M.J. (1989) *An Introduction to the Psychology of Children's Drawings*, New York: Harvester and Wheatsheaf

Thomas, Jenny (1995) *Meaning in Interaction: an Introduction to Linguistic Pragmatics*, London: Longman

Tostrup, Elizabeth (1996) *Architecture and Rhetoric: Text and Design in Architectural Competitions, Oslo, 1939–90*, Oslo: Oslo School of Architecture

—— (1999) *Architecture and Rhetoric: Text and Design in Architectural Competitions, 1939–1997*, London: Andreas Papadakis Publisher, New Architecture Group Ltd

Viollet-le-Duc, E. (1863) *Entretiens sur l'Architecture*, Vol. I, Paris

Vitruvius, Pollo (1960) *The Ten Books on Architecture* (*De Architectura, Libri Decem*), trans. Morris Hickey Morgan, New York: Dover Publications Ltd

[Walters, Tudor] (1918) *Report of the Committee . . . Provision of Dwellings for the Working Classes*, etc., Local Government Boards for England, Wales, and Scotland, London: HMSO

West Glasgow Hospitals University NHS Trust, Glasgow Homoeopathic Hospital (1999) *Glasgow Homoeopathic Hospital: Architectural Competition, Outline Brief*, Glasgow: West Glasgow Hospitals University NHS Trust, Glasgow Homoeopathic Hospital

Index